The Performances of Sacred Places

The Performances of Sacred Places

Crossing, Breathing, Resisting

EDITED BY

Silvia Battista

Bristol, UK / Chicago, USA

First published in the UK in 2021 by
Intellect, The Mill, Parnall Road, Fishponds, Bristol, BS16 3JG, UK

First published in the USA in 2021 by
Intellect, The University of Chicago Press, 1427 E. 60th Street,
Chicago, IL 60637, USA

A catalogue record for this book is available from
the British Library.

Copy editor: Newgen KnowledgeWorks
Cover designer: Aleksandra Szumlas
Cover image credit: Silvia Battista. *Attending Trees* (2013), London.
Production manager: Laura Christopher
Typesetting: Newgen KnowledgeWorks

Print ISBN 978-1-78938-387-4
ePDF ISBN 978-1-78938-388-1
ePUB ISBN 978-1-78938-389-8

Printed and bound by Severn

To find out about all our publications, please visit
www.intellectbooks.com
There you can subscribe to our e-newsletter,
browse or download our current catalogue,
and buy any titles that are in print.

This is a peer-reviewed publication.

Contents

Acknowledgements

The idea of this book stemmed from the conference *Sacred Places: Performances, Politics and Ecologies* organized in 2017 by the research group Cartographies of Belonging of Liverpool Hope University, in partnership with the group Performance Religion and Spiritualities of the International Federation for Theatre Studies (IFTR). I am therefore extremely grateful not only to all the people who supported the organization of the event, but also to all the participants who made these two days special, 'sacred' and inspirational in many different ways. These include all the undergraduate students who volunteered and Liverpool Hope University as a whole, which not only offered the facilities for the conference to take place, but also provided the continuous support that led eventually to the publication of the book.

I would like to thank my colleagues Dr Annalaura Alifuoco, Dr Kris Darby, Professor Simon Piasecki and Dr Rachel Sweeney for their collaboration and suggestions.

Last but not least, I would like to thank all the contributors to the volume, who made me think about sacred places in ways that I could not have envisaged before.

The Performances of Sacred Places: An Introduction

Silvia Battista

> *Yet every time we look around ourselves and see things, mysterious in their uniqueness and wonderful in their difference, majestic just in their 'being there', and any time that we look at them and somehow fall in love with them [...] we open the world to a radical 'elsewhere' [that] is both within and without.*
>
> (Campagna 2018: 49)

Clarifying biases

An horizon stands, in modern hermeneutics, for what is possible to see from the position of a specific observer. That is, not only a location in space but also a position in the cultural and historical apprehension of the world. If the observer is aware of the limitations of their position, then their perspective can consequently be expanded through dialogue with those situated at different angles of incidence in relation to the same object.

Therefore, I would like to start this introduction by sharing with the reader a story of infatuation with sacred places. The story is aimed at revealing the horizon that led to the processes and choices behind this edited volume, and disclosing the biases which haunt this critical endeavour.

Although coming from an atheist family, around the age of 23, I developed the 'compulsive' habit of visiting churches in the centre of Rome in Italy, the city where I was born and raised. I started making my daily visits to these holy places especially during summer time, around noon, when the heat was unbearable and the sunlight dazzling; when tourists found refuge in hotels and restaurants; and the traffic, with its noise and pollution, was at its peak. At this time of the day even popular churches such as La Chiesa di Sant' Ignazio, la Basilica di Santa Maria Maggiore and Santa Maria in Trastevere were invariably empty, apart from two or three silent presences praying their worries away in contemplative murmurings. I used to love entering those places from the conditions described and immersing myself in an utterly opposite environment – an outrightly contrasting context from that outside. Indeed, as soon as the doors closed behind me, I was immediately cut off from the ordinary scene of the city with its typical Roman, summery, chaotic, urban, hallucinatory landscape. I was immersed in a silent and dark space: an unexpected Artaudian, visceral theatrical apparatus.[1]

Try to envision how the heated skin of summer feels when touched by the air of a cool environment, and how the eyes experience the time needed for visibility to return when acclimatizing to the passage from the sunlight to the shades of the church's interior. Visualize the emergence of the flickering candlelights, slowly revealing the convoluted, suffering naked bodies depicted in the various paintings and frescos adorning the walls together with the enigmatic, bleeding figure on the crucifix. Contemplate the beams of light that from the outside traverse the stained glass of the windows and activate the glimmering gold of the Byzantine mosaics shimmering before the eyes; the human semi-silent figures whispering their prayers; the confessional wooden box with its tricks of visibilities and invisibilities; and among all of this, my body traversing the space slowly like a Butoh dancer, walking and defusing gravity.

These ordinary and at the same time extraordinary events were the intersecting and intoxicating activating performances that affected my senses and transformed my perception of spatial relationship to these places. These silent pilgrimages of mine, although not a believer, were led by an enchanting apparatus of macro and micro agents/actants[2] that profoundly touched me. Indeed, they transported and transformed my perception to the point of offering me unexpected, nourishing, spiritual experiences that proved to be seminal to my future research interests. The theatricality of these charged spaces, wherein all kinds of unpredictable micro performances could potentially occur, are still strongly impressed in my consciousness, informing not only the questions behind this publication, but also the biases that a scholarly contribution necessarily brings with it. Indeed, although there are purely theoretical instances across the various contributions that this volume brings together, there is also an unconditional experiential approach that characterizes the perspective from which the editorial work has been carried out.

Introducing questions and contexts

While the aforementioned churches are spaces established as sacred by a specific, religious creed – in this case Catholicism – the questions around what makes them, in and of themselves, sacred for a non-believer is still a relevant one. In addition, sacred places can also be locations that are not institutionalized as such, but become special through intentional acts of separation, effects of contrast or through spontaneous collective processes of identification with a specific place that in time is confirmed as special. Therefore, what is a sacred place? Is a place inherently sacred or does it become sacred? Is it a paradigm, a real location, an imaginary place, a projected condition, a charged setting, an enhanced perception? What kind of practices and processes allow the emergence of a sacred place in human perception? And what is its function in contemporary societies?

How we approach these questions, contexts and processes is not a straightforward exercise. On the contrary the different perspectives presented in this volume demonstrate that the sacred, far from being a stable, universal condition, is actually a complex, variable affair. For example, each of the chapters presented in this volume defines and explores the notion of sacred place differently: it might be theorized as atmosphere; as a container of affective traces; as inner, uncharted landscapes; as a land to be crossed and sensually engaged with; as a repository of specific traditions; as a contested hub of crossing cultural practices; or as the locus of political resistance. This means not only that the phenomenon of sacred places is a complex and multilayered field for analysis, but also that it is a condition that moves and shifts according to contexts and functions. For example, although a sacred place might be established as means for the maintenance of status quo, the same location might operate as the catalyst for profound individual and collective transformations; as the container or holder of cathartic experiences; as an invitation for human and non-human dialogical encounters; for inner and outer journeys; or even as a tragic repository of traumatic experiences, depending on the perspective to which we give voice.

Consequently, the notion of sacred places constitutes in itself a paradigm under which established religious settings go hand in hand with other situational conditions that, by escaping the given boundaries of religious theologies, overflow the mundane into the religious and vice versa: the sacred into the profane. It is a composite conceptual and factual environment that induces specific, but also multiple, affective human responses.

Hence, this volume's objective is to reflect on and respond to this unstable territory of investigation without reducing its complexity to one single perspective. For instance, some standpoints that our contributors engage with include the increasing relevance that sacred places occupy in present local and global geopolitics; their role in processes of conflict and peacekeeping; in relation to therapeutic and healing processes; ecological and environmental discourses; and in regard to forms of resistance against the ongoing human exploitation of natural resources.

To conclude, despite the relevance of these topics in contemporaneity and the privileged viewpoint that sacred places afford, this is a thematic context that is largely ignored by studies outside the fields of theology and religious studies. Thus, this publication engages with this scholarly gap specifically from the perspective of performance studies, so as to acknowledge and compensate for the lack of critical engagement with the role that performances and their materialities play in the production and activation of such contexts.

Performance studies

Performance studies is a multidisciplinary methodological perspective that emerged in the 1970s out of the dialogue between theatre studies scholar Richard Schechner and anthropologist Victor Turner. They were both interested in the sophistication of the language of theatre and its potential application to other human endeavours and also in the working of the bodies involved, their materialities and performances. By engaging with the language of theatre, performance studies explores human actions beyond the perimeters of what is considered canonically to be theatre and stresses the importance of investigating the practices and actions through which things are generally conducted and processes activated.

In the context of this volume, the paradigm propounded is of performance as the starting point for the analysis of the means through which places become sacred; of the activities through which they are maintained or contested as such; and of the processes through which places are capable of affecting the psychophysical conditions of human consciousness, potentially activating transformations in individual and collective perceptions.

In this regard, the religious studies scholar Anna Taves in the book *Religious Experience Reconsidered: A Building-Block Approach to the Study of Religion and Other Special Things* argues that

> we need to turn our attention to the processes whereby people sometime ascribe the special characteristics to things that we (scholars) associate with terms such as 'religious', 'magical', 'mystical', 'spiritual', etcetera.
>
> (2009: 8)

In doing so we must focus our attention on the interaction between psychobiological, social and cultural-linguistic material and performative processes in relation to carefully specified types of experiences, sometimes considered religious (Taves 2009: 8). This approach recognizes the value, function and role that practices have in the constitution of special places, and foregrounds their developments in culture, especially in their materialities and performances. Therefore, this is a scholarly effort that instead of focusing on what has been institutionalized as sacred, and therefore revolves around fixed, established apprehensions of sacred locations, interrogates the processes through which sites become ascribed with special, sacred qualities, recognizing the unstable and mercurial nature of such attributes.

Contextualizing the sacred

Etymologically, *sacer*, from which the term 'sacred' is derived, means an area that stands apart. The Hebrew term *k-d-sh*, which is usually translated as 'holy', is based on the idea of separation; and the Latin word *templum* is derived from the Greek *templos*, of which the root *tem* means 'to cut out' (Tuan 2009: 16). According to the geographer Yi-Fu Tuan, the activity of differentiating the undifferentiated space through the establishment of sacred places is an operation analogous to the geographer's cartographic activity of mapping a territory (1977: 5). Both are attempts at confining nature within demarcated boundaries, creating potential possibilities of intimacy and protection within an undifferentiated territory.

The analogy with geography and the activity of mapping a territory is useful to introduce the theme of this volume as it highlights the relations between the grid and the territory, the meanings and values exerted by the former onto the latter and therefore the relationship between perceived and lived space. The activity of map-making is indeed always a matter of interpretation, and the methodologies applied determine the way the territory is perceived and navigated. What becomes apparent when reflecting on the relationship between the map and the land is that cartography is a contentious activity where the borders between the physical and the mental, the real and the imaginary, the present and the absent are not permanently determined. This question is even more relevant when referring to sacred locations. Here the reciprocal porosity and permeability of these dichotomies become especially evident when looking at the practices employed to create special places where outer and inner landscapes, although divided by practices of separation, are paradoxically, often pandemically, interconnected through the spiritual practices that are performed there. It is indeed when and where the conceived and lived spaces theorized by Henri Lefebre coincide, or when the relationship between ontologies and practices lose their binary, hierarchical and chronological order, that is possible to revisit the paradoxical nature of their reciprocal influence.

For example, David Wiles's analysis of the theatrical space endorses a dualistic model by offering clear distinctions between Christian and pagan religious traditions and approaches to sacred places. In the book *A Short History of Western*

Performance Space, Wiles (2003) highlights the ways in which religious ontologies are used to inform the modalities, processes and practices through which sacred places have been historically recognized and constituted as such. He argues that Christianity originally understood sacredness as an inherent and unique quality of the human soul, whereas paganism viewed sacredness as an inherent quality of specific locations. According to the former, sacredness was believed to be a product of human agency in its capacity to create, through separation, special places for the divine to dwell. On the contrary, within paganism, humanity recognized, distinguished and protected places in which inherent sacredness and distinctiveness have been previously recognized (Wiles 2003: 38).

Wiles's historical account provides a model of analysis whereby processes of agentic allocation of spaces and embodied processes of recognition clearly emerge in distinction. For instance, the modalities of operations of constitution and recognition reveal different ontological understandings of reality and interpretations of what human agency can do and how it can do it in relation to the environment. However, the question around the modalities through which the environment and its agencies determine recognition is largely ignored.

Although this model offers a useful grid for differentiating between religious belief systems and their approaches to sacred locations, this volume aims to leave aside these charted landscapes in order to venture into the more nuanced territories of contemporary art processes, performances, rituals and other practices which blur the safety of binary thinking. Hence, questions of ownership, control and power, inclusion and exclusion, human and non-human agencies come to the surface, sometime overlapping each other, producing sacred places that are each time differently occupied, open, sometime closed, public, private, intimate, hidden, fluid, internal, external, animated or all at the same time, depending on the practices established and the gaze through which they are perceived.

If we accept paradox as a possible framework of interpretation, a potential hypothesis emerges that, in spite of separation, sacred places might also constitute extreme instances of cross-pollination, dense focal points of encounter between opposites that might give rise to both healing processes and conflictual conditions. In support of this thesis the theologian Rudolf Otto describes the numinous – a term close to the sacred – in paradoxical terms. He employs the Latin *mysterium tremendum* and *mysterium fascinans* to characterize the numinous experience as a feeling-response bringing and holding together contrasting inner responses such as terror and ecstasy (Otto 1958: 14–38).

In addition to this, the sacred is often associated with the holy. Both the numinous and the holy as re-visited by Otto are helpful in disentangling the sacred from the moralities of religious creeds and binary thinking and reveal more complex renderings. For example, the term 'holy' is, according to Otto, 'a category of interpretation and valuation peculiar to the sphere of religion' (1958: 5); nevertheless it has been applied by transference to the sphere of ethics. In Otto's view, this is an interpretative misunderstanding of the meaning of 'holy', which originally 'in Latin and Greek, in Semitic and other ancient languages, denotes first and foremost *only* overplus' of meaning (1958: 5, original emphasis). This overplus of meaning is always and inevitably situated somewhere beyond the rational and moral interpretation of the 'completely good' and the completely bad, often reciprocally associated with the idea of divine (*numen*) and the devil.

To substantiate this thesis further the scholar Melissa Raphael, by reclaiming a sense of the numinous that is different from the fixed, often dogmatic schematization and moralization offered by religious creeds, proposes a feminist interpretation (1997a: 8). This is a possible lens that finds fertile ground in Otto's conception of paradox and its complex and unsettling configurations of meaning-making (Raphael 1997b: 34). In doing so Raphael problematizes interpretations tending to corral and orders the numinous within defined codes of behaviour informed by the text, the *logos* and its controlling, patriarchal, authoritative force, proposing instead an intuitive and feminine approach to the numinous grounded in embodied experiences (1997a: 8–10).

This is also a proposition that problematizes the anthropological tradition based on structuralist principles – that by ignoring the perspective of the body and its experiences have always favoured dualistic interpretative perspectives (Mason 2019: 124).

On the contrary, this is a contextual methodology that recognizes the dynamic nature of reality and its plasticity under the influence of practices, materialities and languages, the latter understood as a material configurator in itself.[3]

At this point of the argument it is crucial to engage with the notion of performativity as all the texts included in this collection engage directly or indirectly with it. This is a critical analytical tool that considers activation as a dynamic force worthy of attention – a reciprocally influential trigger between the perceiver and the perceived in their capacity to activate each other in processes that produce changes or, conversely, maintain existing systems of value. Indeed, sacred places are themselves animated zones fit to actuate possibilities, desires and at the same time tensions. The renowned 'Zone' depicted in the film *Stalker* (1979) by Andrey Tarkovsky is an example of an area of boundless power; a deep receptacle for human desires that is activated by projected yearnings. It is also a real location where 'nature' and 'culture' contaminate each other to such an extent that a numinous sense of otherness hovers around it to instigate human protection, restriction, control and prohibition.

Understanding performativity

The term 'performative' both as a noun and an adjective is often loosely used 'to indicate something that is "like a performance" without actually being a performance in the orthodox or formal sense of the word' (Schechner 2010: 123). Originally employed by the linguistic philosopher J. L. Austin to argue the performative nature of certain verbal utterances (in contradistinction to the constative[4]), it has developed into a very useful concept in performance studies, sociology, gender and queer studies, to mention a few.

In Austin's words, to utter performative sentences 'is not to *describe* [...] [but] it is to do' (1955: 6, original emphasis). For example, the sentence 'I name this ship the *Queen Elizabeth* – as uttered when smashing the bottle against the stem' (5) is one typical example of a performative utterance.

Most performative utterances enact promises, or stipulate contracts and agreements between two or more individuals, and there is a sense of appropriateness and ritualized behaviour linked to their success within the context that they take place (Austin 1955: 13). This is given by the truthfulness of the premises within which they are uttered that confirms their 'happy' or 'unhappy' endings (Austin 1955: 14). These sentences, for instance, the wedding declaration of agreeing to take a person as your spouse, must be uttered following a specific script that validates the action and accordingly brings about a 'happy ending'. Within this notion of a 'happy ending' Austin does not refer to the future development of the marriage, in other words whether the couple will live happily together, but rather to the legal value and status shift that is produced by a specific script performed by specific actors within a specific system (Austin 1955: 14).

The concept of an underlining theatrical script enacted in daily life, outside the context of theatre, has proved to be a powerful metaphor not only to Austin but to a variety of postmodern and post-structuralist theorists interested in bringing forward the idea of culturally constructed identities. Indeed, performativity is a term that represents a model of investigation

> covering a whole panoply of possibilities opened up by a world [...] [where] increasingly, social, political, economic, personal, and artistic realities take on the qualities of performance.
>
> (Schechner 2010: 123)

According to scholar Karen Barad, performativity challenges the linguistic faith in the power of words to represent pre-existing things and proposes that words are performative in the sense that they do things because they are part of the world with which they engage (2007: 133). Furthermore, she 'provides an understanding of *how* discursive practices matter', contributing to the idea that not only our perception of things as they are, but also our descriptions of them, are specific material configurations of reality (Barad 2007: 136, original emphasis). In other words thinking, observing and theorizing are all 'practices of engagement with, and as part of, the world in which we have our being' (Barad 2007: 133). This entails questioning discursive practices that give to language and culture their agency but consider matter to be fixed and unimportant in the world's becoming, arguing therefore that matter, in its complexity, is an active participant (Barad 2007: 132, 136).

Barad's hypothesis is not an isolated research undertaking as other scholars engage with similar issues. For example, the political theorist Jane Bennett argues something similar when she talks about the 'vitality' of matter and things (2010: viii). Bennett's philosophical account calls for a theory 'of action and responsibility that crosses the human-non human divide', opening the idea of human agency to a complexity of other non-human things (Bennett 2010: 23, 24). She envisions a concept of agency 'distributed across an ontologically heterogeneous field [...] the confederate agency of many striving macro- and microactants'.[5] They include a variety of factors such as personal 'memories, intentions, contentions, intestinal bacteria, eyeglasses, and blood sugar', as well as many other actants such as the air in the room, the noises, the things used such as plastic computer keyboards, the weather, the clothes worn, the food eaten (Bennett 2010: 23).

Anna Furse in the essay 'Being Touched' encourages an engagement with the body to 'shift, or at least modulate power relations [...], hierarchies of power, ego, strength, gender and other roles', historically inherited and stored in our bodies (2011: 54). This may also entail the project of reconsidering what the body is, where its boundaries are set and how its material configurations are interpreted. The body, therefore, in its broader material manifestations, becomes the starting point through which to invent and discover a new ecology of relations for the self and the 'other(s)'. In this regard Jane Bennett emphasizes how the cultural assumption of

> an intrinsically inanimate matter may be one of the impediments to the emergence of more ecological and more materially sustainable modes of production and consumption [both within and outside our bodies].
>
> (2010: ix)

Bennett's idea of our bodies as assemblages of life forms and forces, and Barad's theory of agential realism, brought to my attention the fact that, as the Buddhist scholar Alan Wallace (2012) argues, introspective traditions such as Buddhism consider ontological relativism to be the fundamental nature of reality and that 'perceptual objects [and their dividedness] exist only relative to the means by which they are perceived or measured'. The state of *samādhi* is referred to as the state of being self-immersed in the field of indifferentiation where gender, class and nationality lose their meaning and where material distinctiveness dissolves (Wallace 2012) in performativity and multiplicity. This is the state of self-immersement in the proliferation and intricate dance of human and non-human contingencies and conglomerations.

The religious studies scholar Mircea Eliade locates the question of the sacred in perception, describing it as a shift, a movement in consciousness that transmutes an ordinary element into what the theologian Rudolf Otto calls *numen praesens*, an object whose nature, transcending the known, breaks the boundaries of the conceivable and provokes, in the individual or collective encountering it, unique types of emotions (Eliade 1987: 10). These are processes that occur in the intersection between the object, in our case the space in question and the subject, the human entering the space, and in the relation and cycle of mutual influence between the two. However, from a new materialist perspective, the two are not two. Any space we enter is a complex system of forces, made by its size, smells, the materials that compose it, the light, the number of objects in it; in turn, the person entering is as multiple as the space. Think about the bacteria, the food we eat, the genetic code we carry within us, the material we wear, to mention only a few. This is a complex intersection of micro and macro agents, a complex apparatus where the two – the self and the space – turn into the many.

Furthermore, as philosopher Federico Campagna argues in his book *Technic and Magic: The Reconstruction of Reality* sacred places are located 'at the level of the imaginal world (*mundus imaginalis*), where things become forces and ideas become models for our existence in the world' (2018: 9). These are sacred apparatuses where 'the ineffable condition of existence' reveals itself to perception and by disrupting the given maps they allow the territory to touch the senses transforming the cartographer into a traveller, the observer into an explorer (Campagna 2018: 122). At this point the sacred is a quality that indicates a possibility for departure from the known to encounter another experience of being in the world. It becomes a coordinate from which to navigate the world following a different cognitive power or force that is embodied and imaginative and where 'space becomes a function of desire, because it is only the external aspect of an internal state' (Corbin 1964: 1–16).

Protection, mythology, control, material intra-activities and configurations, cultural apparatuses and performances are all actualities of sacred areas that render them active in their performative capacities to mobilize complex dynamics of reciprocal influence between human and non-human environments, subjects and objects, and eventually to confuse their relationships or radicalize their division.

Within this multilayered territory of investigation, this volume positions performance as the guiding thread that connects all the different perspectives offered in this book, which, as a whole, represents a balanced alternation of purely theoretical investigations and practices-as-research analytical accounts.

Summarizing sections and chapters

The book is divided into three parts that evidence the three approaches that are generally engaged with, through which sacred places are defined, actualized and activated. They are: 'Crossing', 'Breathing' and 'Resisting'.

The part 'Crossing' includes the work of Louise Ann Wilson, Kris Darby and Simon Piasecki. Crossing is an activity that is associated with traversing a landscape, but also with drawing a cross on a map in order to find the way through an unknown geography and pin down points of reference. It might stand as metaphor for the process through which we cross boundaries and thresholds to find a path in the mist of life, to overcome difficulties and make it to the other side of the various storms which confront all human lives.

Louise Ann Wilson, in the chapter 'A Place That Stands Apart: Emplacing, Re-Imaging and Transforming Life-Events through Walking-Performance in Rural Landscapes', shares her deeply touching practice-research where performance, scenography, walking and landscapes are woven together into individual and collective healing narratives. The text narrates pilgrimages/performances aimed at confronting and transforming personal traumatic experiences. Stemming from her own traumatic personal experience, the author's research is narrated through her impressive body of performances, walks and theatrical pieces that she craftly entangles with the non-human in ways which are embodied, experiential and transformative. By re-evaluating the early romantic texts of Dorothy Wordsworth on creative and physical approaches to landscape and walking as therapeutic means, she stands for a feminine sublime. She carefully emphasizes, however, that a feminine sublime is not a matter of gender but about sensitivities and abilities to cross the threshold dividing us from the environment in order to be immersed into the materialities that make us both within and without. Contrary to the masculine, romantic sublime theorized by Edmund Burke (1990), Wilson argues that the feminine sublime calls for immersion, for the experience of touching and being touched, of losing oneself into a landscape where detachment and hierarchical anthropomorphic positions do not find fertile ground.

Kris Darby, in the chapter 'Bordering the Sacred: The Labyrinth as Non-Site', invites the reader to cross the threshold of the labyrinth to explore the different facets of these fascinating structures in their many representations in both sacral traditions, contemporary versions and usages. Darby reveals that the walking of a labyrinth is an activity that operates on both metaphorical and physical levels, but always requires the crossing of the threshold where the labyrinth starts. Some examples can be physically crossed with the entire body and walked in and out of; however others are so small that the path can only be followed by the micro movements of the eyes. Walking is here the leading activity which activates the experiences of labyrinths. Nonetheless walking emerges interestingly in unexpected forms, in other conditions and practices that might happen through means of operation such as imagination or by a finger leading the mover through the shape of a small labyrinth into the micro/macro walks of the interior. All these examples are journeys of the inner dimension in their ability to shape and be shaped by circumstances and activities. The reader is finally introduced to the fascinating debate on whether the question of the historical authenticity of a labyrinth affects the journey of the walker and therefore to the question of whether there is an inherent power that a location acquires through the collective and repeated activity of having been walked through for centuries.

The art of crossing territories and landscapes in order to overcome grief, sorrow and loss is also a central preoccupation of Simon Piasecki in the chapter 'In Peril and Pilgrimage: Exploring the Experience of Suffering in Journeys Endured'. Here Piasecki looks at the practice of walking in the spiritual tradition of pilgrimages understood and experienced as mourning technologies. He argues that it is through walking and movement that both physical and metaphorical transformations occur. From Mount Kailas in Tibet to the walking that comes close to the practice of reading along the lines of the chapter, moving from side to side until you are transported into the intricate fabric of the author's journey, transformation occurs through endurance. The innovative aspect of this accurate analysis of the performances of pilgrimages is that the sacred place of arrival is substituted with the journey itself; in other words it is not about arriving, but rather about journeying. It is here that Piasecki leads the reader in the understanding and appreciation of the journey itself as a processual point of arrival that is nomadic rather than fixed. The encounter with pain that the crossing of long distances always produces is counteracted by the emergence of endurance as the means through which the thresholds of pain are crossed to produce in human consciousness renewed perceptions of the world and oneself.

The section 'Breathing' includes texts by Ilaria Salonna, Annalaura Alifuoco and Silvia Battista. Breathing is the basic cyclical condition of human life; it expands and contracts bodies, puts them in relation and confounds their apparent solid perimeters. It determines whether a human body is alive or dead and, in this sense, resolves the boundaries between life and death. Breathing is therefore foundational to life, the principal constituent activity of spiritual practices and of many forms of trainings in theatre and performance.

Ilaria Salonna, in the chapter 'Acting Atmospheres: The Theatre Laboratory and the Numinous', explores breathing as both an acting technique and a metaphor for feeling and creating the necessary atmosphere for the condition of a shared performance to emerge. In the tradition of the theatre masters of the twentieth century, where the practice of acting is deeply rooted in the paradigm of research, training is a way to life. It is an existential discovery of the many layers that human consciousness can hold. Research is adamant and occurs in what was conceived as 'the laboratory', the sacred place of the acting alchemists where transformation occurs and acting eventually is enabled. Salonna grounds her approach in her experience of training with Anatoly Vassiliev and centres her analysis around the theoretical thinking offered by scholars engaged with new phenomenology. This is a framework that offers her the necessary vocabulary for articulating a detailed analysis of the processes through which verbal utterances alternate with pauses as essential requisites for actor training.

Annalaura Alifuoco, in the chapter 'Holding Out: The Sacred Space of Suspense and Sustainable Ethics', offers an insightful exploration of the work of historical performance artist Nigel Rolfe. Here breathing stands as the metaphorical movement of perceptual expansion of the performer, who paradoxically reduces his acts to stillness and silence. By reanimating Rolfe's work Alifuoco conducts a journey into his ability to pause and employ the act of pausing as a creative and especially epistemological tool. Knowledge surfaces as the central point of Alifuoco's analysis as she argues for a sense of epistemological emergence that actually takes place through extreme forms of solitude, stillness and silence rather than through external forms of acquisition. Here, in this context, knowledge comes to the surface of consciousness through processes of deconstruction of the known through extreme acts of endurance. This is a knowledge that cannot be acquired, and it is never the direct result of an act of will. The author emphasizes this by arguing that knowledge comes through profound shifts in embodiment which the disciplined practitioner endures in his act of penance until a different sense of self emerges; a self that is dislocated, displaced and therefore able to see from a different angle.

A radical invitation to venture into the emblematic, infusive and pervading qualities of breath is provided by the inner processes of visualizations that Silvia Battista explores in the chapter 'The Introspective Theatre of *Spirits Read Foucault*: The Digital Space, the Inner Gaze and a Sacred Landscape'. The aim is to emulate the nomadic property of breath that is both body and spirit (Irigaray 2002: viii) and to confuse the line dividing the internal and the external to a point where the former acquires a form of objectivity in its own right and the possibility of observation is obtained in invisibility. This is a theatre that can be viewed only by what the philosopher Colin McGinn (2004) calls 'mindsight', which Battista conceives as introspective theatre. By offering evidences from the practice-research project

Spirits Read Foucault that includes ethnographic and analytical autoethnographic methods she reclaims the spatiality opened by active imagination as sacred. Her experiments with introspective spectatorship and performance defy the old Greek etymological definition of theatre as *theatron*, rooted in the ideas of visibility as a faculty directed towards the exterior. Instead Battista proposes a condition of theatre that is led by the unbound breathing – unknown, unpredictable and sacred. This spatial dimension recalls a sense of theatre that can be found in the Arabic word *masrah*, which interprets theatre as a place for dreaming, contemplation, wondering. Connecting to a culture that positioned the ontology of imagination in what we understand as the 'real', Battista proposes to her audience a participation in theatre that journeys through the threshold of visibilities to explore the interior as an unknown space of constant renewal and numinosity.

The section 'Resisting' contains the chapters by Lisa Lewis, Ruth L. Smith and Joshua Edelman. The act of resisting recalls acts of oppositions, the determination to stand against something else, but also the commitment to be firm in one place and not give in. It might entail two physical forces withstanding each other or more subtle forms of collective and cultural efforts. It talks of political and social struggles.

The notion of sacred places as sites of tension is insightfully explored by Lisa Lewis in the chapter 'Performing on the Tightrope: Sacred Place, Embodied Knowledge and the Conflicted History of Colonial Modernity in the Welsh and Khasi Relationship'. Here the act of resisting unravels both practices of closure and processes of dialogue and exchange in contexts where the legacy of transcultural exchange and colonial relationships is fully present. The hub of the analysis is the contrasting approaches to what a sacred place is and how it is lived. From the 'natural' environment of the Khasi people to the religious buildings of the Welsh, the conflicted history of colonialism persists. Lewis proposes performance in her practice-as-research project as both a method – ethnographic tool – and event where the heritage of colonialism can be examined and lived through embodiment. The contribution is a sophisticated project that with great sensitivity moves the coordinates of the given in order to work 'against the grain' of conventions and established norms. The objective is therefore clearly the activation, through the performance of possibilities to a common sharing condition that, nonetheless, would not reduce the complexity of these historical and transcultural relationships.

In the fascinating study offered by Ruth Smith in the chapter 'Performing Memorials as Intervening Grounds' resistance relates to the refusal of artists to offer monuments that provide resolutions after the tragic war losses as assurance for brighter futures. The memorials that Smith rigorously examines and reflects on are architectures and interventions that are meant to register injustice, suffering, agitation and disappearance. It is a matter of recognition, but also of doubting

14

the worth of sacrifices that often justify in time the horror of unnecessary deaths. Some of the memorials analysed here are micro punctuations in the grounds of cities that point out that something occurred there that should not be forgotten and most of all it should have never happened. They are the physical signposts of fractured collective memories, sacred places where the realities of history reveal themselves. For example, the author mentions the *Stolpersteine* project in Berlin where stones in the ground identify the street addresses where Nazis rounded up Jews and others. Each of these stones is sacred, a micro memorial that by penetrating into the fabric of the daily city life of Berlin requests attention and criticality to resist the ongoing commodification of history.

Joshua Edelman, in the chapter 'Sacred Space and Occupation as Protest: Jonathan Z. Smith and Occupy Wall Street', is preoccupied with the question of methodology when examining the relationship between sacred places and forms of resistance. By identifying in the religious studies scholar Jonathan Smith the appropriate lens of analysis for his chosen case study, he reclaims the role that rituals play in activating the sacrality of locations. The 2011 Occupy Wall Street movement is the main object of examination, an example that has attracted considerable scholarly attention. However, the originality of Edelman's narrative is in the methodological attention to the enduring sense of sacred that according to the author we retain in our post-secular societies. This is a particularly interesting approach when applied to strategies of resistance such as the occupation of public spaces. In a compelling manner, Edelman specifies that most of the political claims that the Occupy Wall Street movement demanded, rather than being limited to verbal claims, were actually lived in experiential modalities of alternative social orders that were performed within the micro society formed around the occupied camp. It is therefore the occupation itself unfolding in ordinary time that made, through repetition, that location special.

NOTES

1. According to Foucault, an apparatus is essentially strategic in manipulating the relations of forces within a specific system.
2. Here I am referring to Bruno Latour's understanding of the term.
3. Here I refer to Karen Barad's theory of agential realism.
4. Austin employs the adjective 'constative' to refer to those sentences that are used to describe and constate things as true or false.
5. An actant is viewed as an 'intervener'. It is a term that aims to question the unique position that human agency has acquired within what we call 'western' culture and to acknowledge a pluralities of agencies – human and non-human – intersecting within given environments.

REFERENCES

Austin, John Langshaw (1955), *How to Do Things with Words: The William James Lectures Delivered at Harvard University in 1955*, Oxford: Oxford University Press.

Barad, Karen (2007), *Meeting the Universe Halfway: Quantum Physics and the Entanglement of Matter and Meaning*, Durham: Duke University Press.

Bennett, Jane (2010), *Vibrant Matter: A Political Ecology of Things*, London: Duke University Press.

Burke, Edmund (1990), *A Philosophical Inquiry into the Origin of Our Ideas of the Sublime and Beautiful and Other Pre-Revolutionary Writings*, ed. D. Womersley, London: Oxford University Press.

Campagna, Federico (2018), *Technic and Magic: The Reconstruction of Reality*, London: Bloomsbury.

Corbin, Henri (1964), 'Mundus imaginalis, or the imaginary and the imaginal', *Cahiers Internationaux de Symbolisme*, 6, pp. 3–26.

Eliade, Mircea (1987), *The Sacred and the Profane: The Nature of Religion*, London: Harcourt.

Foucault, Michel (1980), *Power/Knowledge: Selected Interviews and Other Writings 1972/1977*, ed. C. Gordon, trans. C. Gordon, L. Marshall, J. Mepham and K. Soper, New York: Pantheon Books.

Furse, Anna (2011), 'Being touched', in J. Matthews and D. Torevell (eds), *A Life of Ethics and Performance*, Cambridge: Cambridge Scholars Publishing, pp. 45–68.

Gooch, Todd A. (2000), *The Numinous and Modernity: An Interpretation of Rudolf Otto's Philosophy of Religion*, New York: Gruyter.

Irigaray, Luce (2002), *Between East and West: From Singularity to Community*, New York: Columbia University Press.

Mason, David (2019), 'Ritual transformation and transmission', in R. Kemp and B. McConachie (eds), *The Routledge Companion to Theatre, Performance and Cognitive Science*, London: Routledge, 124–34.

McGinn, Colin (2004), *Mindsight: Image, Dream, Meaning*, London: Harvard University Press.

Otto, Rudolf (1958), *The Idea of the Holy: An Inquiry into the Non-Rational Factor in the Idea of the Divine and Its Relation to the Rational*, Oxford: Oxford University Press.

Raphael, Melissa (1997a), *Rudolf Otto and the Concept of Holiness*, Oxford: Clarendon Press.

Raphael, Melissa (1997b), *Thealogy and Embodiment: The Post-Patriarchal Reconstruction of Female Sacrality*, Sheffield: Sheffield Academic Press.

Schechner, Richard (2010), *Performance Studies: An Introduction*, New York: Routledge.

Taves, Ann (2009), *Religious Experience Reconsidered: A Building-Block Approach to the Study of Religion and Other Special Things*, Princeton: Princeton University Press.

Tuan, Yi-Fu (1977), *Space and Place: The Perspective of Experience*, London: University of Minnesota Press.

Tuan, Yi-Fu (2009), *Religion from Place to Placelessness*, Chicago: Center for American Places at Columbia College Chicago.

Wallace, Alan B. (2012), 'Restoring meaning to the universe', in *Buddhists and Scientists Explore the Nature of Consciousness and Its Role in Nature*, The Contemplative Consciousness Network, Regents College, London, 20 June.

Wiles, David (2003), *A Short History of Western Performance Space*, Cambridge: Cambridge University Press.

PART 1

CROSSING

cross (v.)
c.1200, 'make the sign of a cross as an act of devotion', from **cross** (n.) and in part from French *croiser*. Sense of 'to go across, pass from side to side of, pass over' is from c.1400; that of 'to cancel by drawing a line over or crossed lines over' is from mid-fifteenth century.

(etymonline.com)

1

A Place That Stands Apart:
Emplacing, Re-Imaging and Transforming
Life-Events through Walking-Performance
in Rural Landscapes

Louise Ann Wilson

Introduction

I am an artist and scenographer who creates socially engaged and applied scenography in the form of site-specific walking-performances in rural, often mountainous, landscapes. In this chapter I explore how, in my practice, a rural landscape becomes a 'site of transformation' – a 'sacred' place that 'stands apart' – where 'missing', challenging or marginal life-events, for which traditional rites of passage or ceremonies do not exist, are emplaced, re-imaged and transformed, even in the smallest of ways (*OED Online* 2015).

The term 'scenography' translates as 'drawing *in* or *with* the scene' – in my practice I draw walking-performances into and out of a specifically chosen landscape in a way that seeks to enable participants – individuals, groups and communities – to face, acknowledge and find alternative perspectives on a specific life-event subject matter (Palmer 2011: 52). I have made work that has addressed terminal illness, death and bereavement, biological childlessness and the effects of ageing.

In order to explore how my practice seeks to create 'sites of transformation' I provide an exploration and analysis of three walking-performances created in rural landscapes to address a specific life-event experience. *Fissure* (2011) was a three-day-long walking-performance created in response to the death, aged 29, of my sister due to brain tumour, and the grief caused by her loss. The performance took the form of a pilgrimage across the Yorkshire Dales in which 80 participants descended beneath and ascended Ingleborough Fell. *The*

Gathering/Yr Helfa (2014) was a large-scale, site-specific walking-performance that revealed the seasonal and reproductive cycles of the ewes of Hafod y Llan Farm, an upland sheep farm on Mount Snowdon in Snowdonia, Wales. These cycles became a metaphor for human in/fertility and biological and non-biological motherhood. *Warnscale: A Land Mark Walk Reflecting on In/Fertility and Childlessness* (2015–ongoing, through a published walking-guide/art-book) – is a self-guided walking-performance specific to the Warnscale Fells near Buttermere in the Lake District, Cumbria, aimed at women who are biologically childless by circumstance.

Creating these walking-performances saw me develop and apply seven 'scenographic' principles. These principles offer practical and theoretical methodologies – a model – for creating walking-performance in rural landscapes that seek to enable transformative outcomes. They are informed by theories and aesthetics relating to landscape and an in-depth study of Dorothy Wordsworth's (1771–1855) creative and physical approach to, and therapeutic use of, landscape and walking that can be found in her *Grasmere Journals* (1800–03).[1]

Dorothy Wordsworth's therapeutic and creative approach to and use of landscape and walking practices suggests a 'mode' of engaging with 'a site' that enabled her to *notice* the 'common-place' and see afresh 'everyday' objects, people and experiences (including her own) that were ordinarily overlooked or on the edges of social and cultural discourses. This 'mode', which seemed to be closely allied with my own artistic approaches, aims and concerns, can, I suggest, be understood through the theoretical concept of the feminine 'material' sublime and offers a counterpoint to the masculine 'transcendent' sublime, which was dominant in the Early Romantic period in which Dorothy Wordsworth was writing.

Un-framed, un-composed and limitless, the transcendent sublime was considered to be beyond reach and comprehension, and a transcendent sublime landscape represented an un-graspable physical 'object' that created a psychological state of terror or else a metaphysical or spiritual experience that lay beyond the physical matter of the everyday. With the feminine 'material' sublime transformation is achieved by becoming immersed, and finding wonderment, in the material of the everyday, the physical landscape, environmental forces and the human and non-human body – and working with these elements, not as a place from which to escape or disappear but to 'reappear'. To be clear: the concept of the feminine 'material' sublime is not about the female gender but about a sensibility that manifests as a way of engaging with, walking or dwelling in *and* observing the landscape and environmental forces – human and non-human.

Fissure

I created *Fissure* because I needed but could not find meaningful or adequate social rituals around death and mourning, particularly for someone whose death is at a young age. Making and performing this work made me aware of, and established my belief in, the transformative potential of my practice.

During the three-day-long performance participants made a journey by train and then on foot across the landscape, covering a 40-mile route that circumnavigated, descended beneath and ascended the mountain of Ingleborough. Their physical journey through the landscape also took participants on a symbolic journey through a metaphorical landscape of illness, death and grief. As they progressed participants experienced a series of interventions and installations which were emplaced and performed in the landscape and which combined dance, music, sung poetry and earth and neuroscience. A local choir, an ensemble of hand bell ringers, a band of church bell ringers, a company of professional singers and female dancers – who represent my sister and me – a team of cavers, a geologist, a neuro-physicist and my sister's neurosurgeon and neuro-oncologist performed these interventions.[2]

In planning the route of *Fissure* I looked for locations that visually and symbolically reflected the underlying subject matter. Each location choice was informed underpinned by neuro-scientific knowledge of the brain – its function and dysfunction, conversations with my sister's surgeon and oncologists, the devastating physical and emotional effects of a brain tumour, personal memories of my sister's illness and her death, and the aftermath of grief it caused. These locations included fissured scars and fault lines in rocks, the glints and grykes of a limestone pavement, blasted quarries, massive erratics split in half, steep ascents, cairns, the places where a river descends below ground and the places where it resurged, and a subterranean cave system.

The liturgical shape of the Easter Trideum, which moves from light to darkness before returning to light and resurrection, also informed the route, structure and form of the performance, which I divided into six distinct phases. For example, on Day One, Phase 1: 'Flying High, Death Enters Life' was staged to echo a Last Supper scene which foretold of the death and resurrection that was to come. On Day Two, Phase 5: 'Death & The Underworld', participants entered the darkness of Endcombe Tunnel inside which the solitary figure of death – played by one of the singers – waits and sings 'death arrives and takes away / her breath, her breath, her breath' (Burns for *Fissure* 2011).[3] On the other side of the tunnel, the bell of St James's Church could be heard tolling 29 times, my sister's age when she died. Following the

FIGURE 1.1: *Fissure* by Louise Ann Wilson (2011), Robin Procter's Scar, Yorkshire. Choreographer: Nigel Stewart. Performer: Jennifer Essex. Photographer: Bethany Clarke/Artevents,

course of a river as it ran underground, participants then entered the subterranean depths of Ingleborough Cave (Figure 1.2) which echoed with singing while the dancers disappeared, beyond reach, into the darkness: 'to a place where there is only rock and water [...] where you cannot follow' (Burns for *Fissure* 2011).[4]

On Day Three, at dawn, participants gathered for Phase 6: 'Resurgence/ Resurrection'. Candles were lit, hand-bells rung and the poem 'After the Long Night' sung:

> After the long night
> the beginnings of dawn
> after the cave-dark
> the daylight
> after the underworld
> fresh air and sky

after the silence
the ringing of bells
after the heavy weight of grief
the lightness of her.[5]

Then, on foot, participants began an ascent of Ingleborough Fell. As they walked the dancers reappeared from below ground. Resurging with the river they were 'resurrected' from the cave-dark tomb and from death, to join the ascending walkers (Figure 1.3).

Feedback from participants who took part in *Fissure* reveals that, when walking the 'physical' landscape, they were also walking an 'interior' landscape of memory and imagination. This internal walking process – through deeply personal and often painful pathways of experience – enabled them, it seemed, to make new internal pathways of meaning that took them to 'places' that one participant said she 'never thought possible', adding:

FIGURE 1.2: *Fissure* by Louise Ann Wilson (2011), Ingleborough Cave, Yorkshire. Choreographer: Nigel Stewart. Performer: Sonya Perreten. Photographer: Bethany Clarke/Artevents, all rights reserved.

FIGURE 1.3: *Fissure* by Louise Ann Wilson (2011), participants ascending Ingleborough Fell, Yorkshire. Photographer: Bethany Clarke/Artevents, all rights reserved.

Fissure has haunted me. As we walked across this place, I found myself shaken by its vastness and velocity. [...] My sense of scale of the landscape completely shifted when I began to learn more about the mapping and function, or rather dysfunction, of the brain. This was punctuated by bells, song, wind, cries, conversation, exchange, memories. [...] And loss. How loss can seep into every part of you and the landscape. [...] How walking through this 'place' can lead you somewhere, ever so different from where you began [...] arriving somewhere you never thought possible.

(*Fissure* participant 2011)

The way that *Fissure* enabled this participant to be 'led' somewhere 'ever so different' from where they 'began' demonstrated, I suggest, how the performance functioned as a means by which they could emplace, re-image and transform the effects of death, illness and bereavement. Furthermore, the cross-disciplinary, image-led, multisensory scenography of *Fissure* gave different ways to connect to and seemed particularly well suited to articulating a painful life-event, for which words alone are inadequate. This merging of landscape, performance and participant parallels, I suggest, how individuals undertaking a pilgrimage or rite of passage 'may find themselves "in the zone" or "in the flow" experiencing a merging of action and awareness' where 'life is expanded and full of meaning [...] we are in a different dimension of human experience' (Turner 2012: 35, 50).

Echoing a pilgrimage, the durational and immersive structure of *Fissure*, the challenge and effort of the physical act of walking the terrain and the effects of weather all formed a crucial part of the experience and provided their own layers of metaphor. After the performance, one participant remarked on the extended physical effort that the performance required:

> I loved the way the piece tested my body's limits and on that climb on day three I could not help wondering what it must be like to be so ill that your body is tested to the limit and to the end.
>
> (*Fissure* participant 2011)

The 12-mile train journey from Settle station to Ribblehead station with which the performance began brought together 80 individual participants who had travelled from both within and outside the United Kingdom. Most of the participants did not know each other, where they would be travelling to or what they would experience en route. Later, one participant remarked, 'No one knew what to expect but all had surrendered, for three days, to the all of it. So what we had in common that May afternoon was being there' (*Fissure* Participant: 2011). Participants did however know the underlying subject matter of the production. Later it became clear that many had chosen to participate because of past, present or future experiences of terminal illness or death and grief, as this response reveals:

> I [...] have been excitedly attempting to describe to my friends something you really had to be there for ... I know we all brought our own experiences of love and grief – for me my ex-partner died of cancer a year ago; it would have been her birthday last weekend and I couldn't have imagined a better way to celebrate that anniversary.
>
> (*Fissure* participant 2011)

Another participant remarked how 'this hike in the Yorkshire Dales became a pilgrimage through death and bereavement' (*Fissure* participant 2011).

The participatory nature of *Fissure* and the 'strong sense of companionship, solidarity and bonding' that developed among participants as it progressed compare to processes of 'communitas' – a term used to describe the 'sense of sharing and intimacy that develops among persons who experience liminality as a group' – that can occur during a pilgrimage (*Dictionary Online* 2020). For example, during the three-day progress of *Fissure* the participants came together as a supportive social group where moments of silence and of conversation were underscored by a shared orientation towards the subject matter. They moved from being strangers, to passengers, to participants, to pilgrims, each making a personal journey through the performance separately but together. Later one wrote 'community was being developed through the walking' (*Fissure* participant 2011). Another commented on 'the sustaining atmosphere and the development of being in a group', and someone else spoke of how 'unexpected and particularly enjoyable [were] the number of interesting and inspiring conversations [they] had with fellow participants' (*Fissure* participant 2011).

On Day Three and in the final 'act' of *Fissure*, each participant was given a 'gift' to take home – a box containing a fragile pink-white shell – a symbol of the 'Karst' limestone landscape through which they had walked. The gift was a 'souvenir' – the acquiring of which is typically associated with the pilgrimage – that might help them 're-construct their sacred journey in the imagination' and act as a memory prompt (Coleman and Elsner 1995: 6).

Feedback revealed that journeys home gave participants time to reflect before returning to their 'normal' life. Many left 'changed' with a different perspective on life and death and fresh ways of seeing and experiencing inner and outer landscapes echoing, I suggest, how pilgrims return home and 'view' themselves, their communities and their everyday environment afresh, a process described by Victor Turner as going to a 'far place to understand a familiar place better' (Coleman and Elsner 1995: 206).[6]

The Gathering/Yr Helfa

The Gathering/Yr Helfa (*The Gathering*) was evolved over a four-year period of observational study of Hafod y Llan Farm that included in-depth 'primary/site' research into the farm, the shepherds at work and the landscape alongside 'secondary/subject' research into the ewes and the flock with a focus on their annual and reproductive cycles (Figure 1.4). In the performance these cycles became a metaphor for human fertility and infertility, biological and non-biological motherhood and other pathways to, and types of, mothering and parenting.

Performed by the shepherds of Hafod y Llan Farm, their dogs and a flock of ewes, a company of professional performers, the Deiniolen Brass Band and the children of Beddgelert Primary School *The Gathering* led a group of two hundred participants on a six-kilometre route into the mountain. Then, along with two hundred ewes, they were gathered 'off the mountain' and into the farm centre (Figure 1.5). As they walked, a series of ever-changing 'scenes' that combined visual installations, choreographed movement, poetry, sound, film music with 'real' farming activities unfolded and moved around them.[7]

28

FIGURE 1.4: *The Gathering* by Louise Ann Wilson (2014), 'Primary/Site' (Landscape/Earth Science) Research and 'Subject' (Fertility/Social Science) Research at Hafod y Llan Farm, Snowdon. Photographer: Louise Ann Wilson.

FIGURE 1.5: *The Gathering* by Louise Ann Wilson (2014), Roger Hughes gathering two hundred ewes off Snowdon into Hafod y Llan Farm. Photographer: Louise Ann Wilson.

Inspired by the landscape and inhabitants of Hafod y Llan Farm – past and present – these scenes were 'drawn out of' the site and then, using shepherds, performers, animals and materials (wool, slate, brass), 'drawn back into' the site at specific locations chosen for their visually striking or symbolic features, topography or history.

For example, as she ascended the red-carpeted track the figure of the 'Tramway-Walker' drew attention to the scars left by quarrying and the brass band drew the ear and eye to abandoned copper mines and forgotten industries (Figure 1.6). These scenes were not explicit but open to interpretation and accumulated meaning over the four-hour duration of the performance and in relation to each other.

Drawing on and then subverting the Early Romantic landscape-trope of the solitary figure I placed a female figure – 'The Woman' – in a series of visual and poetic scenes at carefully selected places in the landscape in order to explore different aspects of the reproductive and fertility cycle – human and non-human (Figure 1.7).

For example, at Hafod y Uchaf, a derelict shepherd's cottage, 'The Woman' filled the rooms with rolled up fleeces of wool until they overflowed with: fertility?

FIGURE 1.6: *The Gathering* by Louise Ann Wilson (2014), 'Tramway Walker' ascending the 'Tramway Incline' installation, Clogwyn, Hafod y Llan Farm, Snowdon, Wales. Performer: Kate Lawrence. Photographer: Joel Chester Fildes/National Theatre Wales.

FIGURE 1.7: *The Gathering* by Louise Ann Wilson (2014), 'The Woman' in the Hafod y Uchaf, Cwm Llan Slate Quarry, Afon y Llan and Tŷ Hafod y Llan (the 'Old Farm House') installations, Hafod y Llan Farm, Snowdon, Wales. Choreographer: Nigel Stewart. Performer: Ffion Dafis. Photographer: Lizzie Coombes.

desire for a child? pregnancy? Each fleece represented: an ovum? an embryo? a foetus? At Cwm Llan slate quarry, where sharp-edged shards of slate were heaped, 'The Woman' stands, dwarfed by the mountainous landscape and distant peak of Snowdon, which echo with the sound of shepherds whistling and calling to their dogs. Around her flocked the 'empty' not pregnant ewes who have been returned to the mountain 'without foetus / bearing their nothing like a stone' (Clarke for *The Gathering* 2014: n.pag.).[8] At the Afon y Llan waterfalls, barefooted, 'The Woman' stood stranded on a rock in the middle of the churning water as around her fleeces unravelled into the river, spilling like: a miscarriage? a stillbirth? a suicide? grief? In Le Tŷ Hafod y Llan (the 'Old Farm House'), lived in by generations of shepherds and their families, 'The Woman' stood among mounds of discarded fleeces, her 'black' coat echoing the black mark given to the empty ewes. Like them 'She must leave the mountain, / the end of her line, / the last cord cut' (Clarke for *The Gathering* 2014: n.pag.).[9] One participant described how *The Gathering* 'showed me my own pain head-on but disguised as the ewe's fate!!!' (*The Gathering* participant 2014: n.pag.).

FIGURE 1.8: *The Gathering* by Louise Ann Wilson (2014), 'Nativity/Resurrection' installation in the Lambing Barn, Hafod y Llan Farm, Snowdon, Wales. Photographer: Lizzie Coombes.

My focus was not just on broken cycles but also on cycles of repair such as the adoption of lambs by surrogate ewes – thus reflecting other pathways to non-biological mothering. For example, in the 'Lambing Barn' I created an alternative 'Nativity' scene. A film projected onto a triptych of empty woolsacks shows a shepherd skinning the fleece off a dead lamb before dressing a live lamb in the fleece and suckling it to a grieving mother-ewe who adopts it as her own (Figure 1.8).

Having created a large-scale performance that dealt indirectly with the subject of biological childlessness I wanted to make a work that dealt directly with this 'missing' and marginal life-event subject matter, and its effects, head on. *Warnscale* was the result.

Warnscale: A Land Mark Walk Reflecting on In/Fertility and Childlessness

Making *Warnscale: A Land Mark Walk Reflecting on In/Fertility and Childlessness* (*Warnscale*) involved a development in my performance-making methodology which saw me add a third tier of research so that I could integrate the landscape and science research with research with people effected by the underlying subject matter of biological childlessness (Figure 1.9).[10]

When working on *The Gathering* I was struck by the way in which the shepherds used the word 'empty' to describe a ewe that had not become pregnant and who was then sprayed with a black mark and 'turned up' the mountain. Working with the image of 'emptiness' for the location of *Warnscale*, I looked for an empty room on a mountain, 'a place traditionally associated with revelation, transition or inspiration' (Usher 2012: 70). The semi-remote mountainous location of Warnscale Head Bothy could provide participants with a 'space' and 'time' separate from their everyday routines that might have the 'capacity to reveal a world and self beyond our knowing' (Usher 2012: 12).

Having found the location, I wanted to understand the impact of the site on the people for whom the work was intended, and so I under took a series of mapping-walks in the area around Warnscale Head Bothy with women dealing with infertility and the effects of biological childlessness. I undertook these mapping-walks in order to investigate the ways in which features of the landscape reflected their concerns and how they responded to those features. During each walk I invited participants to notice landscape features and forces and think about them as

FIGURE 1.9: *Warnscale* by Louise Ann Wilson (2015), mapping-walk participants on-site in the Warnscale Fells, Buttermere, Cumbria. Photographer: Louise Ann Wilson.

metaphors for their personal experiences of biological childlessness. After the walk, I asked each participant to draw a map, using any notation they wished – words, drawings, symbols – that highlighted places or moments of significance and meaning. The transformational and metaphorical efficacy of the landscape emerged from these encounters (Figure 1.10).

The mapping-walk process I developed when creating *Warnscale* proved to be a major development in my performance-making methodology. It added a third tier of research with people affected by the underlying subject matter of biological childlessness that I then integrated with landscape/site and the science research. This third tier would now become of central importance to the work – and its transformational outcomes.

The words, feelings, images and conversations the mapping-walks produced also led to the development of a new (for me) performance form – a walking-guide/art-book (the book). Anyone, whether walking alone, with a partner, friend or in a group, can use the book to assemble or construct meaning and create their own self-guided walking-performance. The book is divided into thirteen sections, each based around a specific location or 'station'.[11] It is designed to lead walkers through the landscape and contains multiple-layered, non-prescriptive and metaphorical imagery, maps, texts and actions that provide ways to reflect upon and respond to the landscape in the context of their own specific experiences. Wanda Georgiades of the CARE Fertility Group described the significance of the book as follows:

> I have just opened your beautiful book – it is stunning. I have never seen the subject of infertility demonstrated in such a moving and graphic way. [...] We focus so much on achieving 'success' having that much wanted child, beating the odds to become parents through IVF. We probably don't acknowledge adequately the number of patients who will not have a baby this way – ever. *Warnscale* shows in a graphic form how different people cope with the loss of the baby they may never have, the grief for something that will never be.
>
> (Georgiades 2015)

The book also makes it possible for participants to revisit the performance – the site of transformation – physically or imaginatively, whenever they choose. For one participant the fact it can be 'done again and again' not only gave it a 'lasting legacy' but was for her a factor in it working as a 'unique' sort of repeatable 'ritual' that can be undertaken as a 'physical' 'act of doing' to 'mark an important life-event' (*Warnscale* mapping-walking participant, RGi).[12] Another participant described how she would 'go back to [the book and] dip in and out of sections [...] the book is a very beautiful reminder of the walk, but also feels like a deeper resource for thinking about land, children, belonging' (JH).

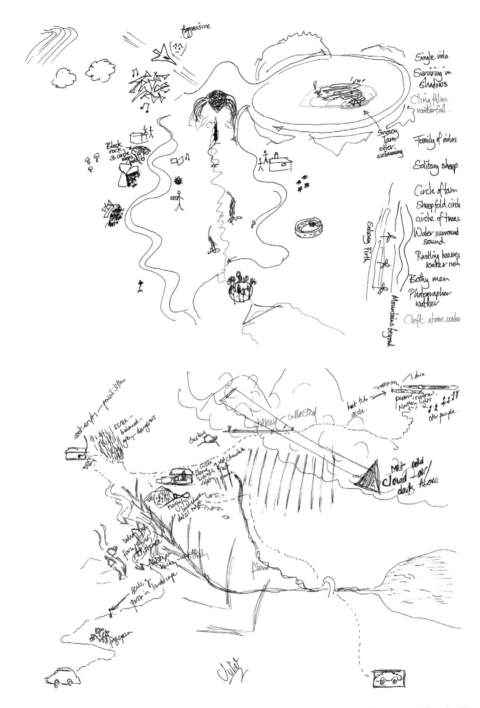

FIGURE 1.10: *Warnscale* by Louise Ann Wilson (2015), mapping-walk maps – Tier 3: 'Tertiary/Social' (Life-Event/Participant) Research.

FIGURE 1.11: *Warnscale* by Louise Ann Wilson (2015), launch-walk participants on-site in the Warnscale Fells, Buttermere, Cumbria. Photographer: Lizzie Coombes.

The book has become an artefact that might help participants reconstruct and remember the landscapes of the performance for themselves, a memory trigger that can be used away from the performance site and can enable participants to remember and revisit it in their minds over time. They can take different meanings from the book as their perspective and life circumstances change. In addition, the book can be used as a tool for them to 'walk' another person (partner, parent, friend) through the performance, even when away from the site, thus sharing their experiences. In this way it opens up conversations that might otherwise not have happened. A number of responses reflected this. For example:

> I return to the book, to remind myself of an issue that still feels unresolved to me, and hope very much to return to the walk soon. It is definitely something I will share with others in the same position as and when it arises.
>
> (RGi)

When asked if they could imagine undertaking *Warnscale* in the future either by themselves or with friends, partners, family members or a group, a number said that they already had revisited and re-walked the performance. One participant replied:

Absolutely. I would particularly like to do the whole walk on my own and with my partner, to share the time, the journey and reflection and the unique beauty of this particular place and experience.

(AD)

Another said she could 'imagine taking others on the walk and using the book to introduce both the ideas and concepts behind the book and the notion of using walking as a form of reflection was powerful' (RGi). Someone else cited the book itself as something that 'has helped me feel able to speak about the walk and its importance to me with greater confidence', adding that she has 'gifted a book to my ex-husband and plan to walk with him. I want to share the walk with him and give us a chance to reflect on our shared loss' (ZA). The same participant 'plans to revisit the walk annually' and sometimes with her Gateway Women 'mentorship group' (ZA).[13] This echoes another participant's remark that *Warnscale* offers 'a place where we "belong", in some way, a place that is ours to return to and celebrate/grieve/be' (NK). Another wrote that she would:

love to do the walk again – either alone, or with close friends who are also childless, or with another group of childless women. Although it might feel difficult, I think I would also like to do it with my sister, who has two children, in order to share some of this with her and think about our places in the family.

(RGi)

Combined, these reflections on *Warnscale* reveal, I suggest, how the work has given participants a material location for their experiences, their grief and their hopes. One participant saw the walking-performance as 'a "unique" response to the subject matter', adding:

There are plenty of blogs, forums, articles, etc. out there – this was an embodied experience [...] this was different. Having the courage to do the walk was, I guess, part of my own healing journey, and I have no idea how long that journey will be – maybe the rest of my life, who knows.

(RGi)

Seven 'scenographic' principles for creating walking-performances in rural landscapes

While making *Fissure*, *The Gathering* and *Warnscale* I interrogated my creative processes in order to develop a systematic – practical and theoretical – understanding and account of my practice. From this interrogation I identified seven 'sceno-graphic' principles – a model – which, using aspects of *Warnscale* to provide examples, I will now outline.

Principle 1: 'Being located' – site, subject and participant specificity

'Views from Somewhere': Combining specificity of site, biological and social science, and people affected by a life-event. 'Situated-knowledges' and trans-disciplinary exchange (Haraway 1988: 581, 590).

Dorothy Wordsworth's *Grasmere Journals* were part creative writing, part diary, part documentation and part field-study. She studied the skilled knowledge and working lives of local people such as shepherds 'salving sheep' or labourers working in the fields (Wordsworth 1991: 87). The way I captured 'raw' material in sketchbooks, notebooks, photographs, film and sound recordings compares to the way that Dorothy Wordsworth used her journals as a tool to provide an account of her experiences in landscape.

Fissure and *The Gathering* saw me develop two tiers of research into the land-scape/site and the biological and social science of the underlying subject. Creating *Warnscale*, I undertook the primary research into the landscape around Warnscale Head Bothy and the secondary research in fertility clinics and with sociologists. In addition, I added the third tier of participant-related research by collaborating with the women affected by biological childlessness through the mapping-walk

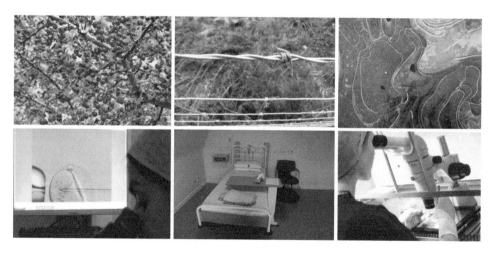

FIGURE 1.12: *Warnscale* by Louise Ann Wilson (2015), Tier 1: Primary/Site (Landscape/Earth Science) Research on-site in the Warnscale Fells, Buttermere, Cumbria; and Tier 2: Secondary/Subject (Fertility/Social Science) Research in fertility clinics. Photographer: Louise Ann Wilson.

process. Combined, all three tiers ensured each walking-performance provides and enables 'views from somewhere' that are located in, and specific to, the site and the underlying life-event subject as well as the people the work is made with *and* for.

Principle 2: 'Staying with the trouble' – auto/biography

First-Person Points of View: Facing and giving-voice to life-event experiences that sit on the edges of mainstream dialogues and discourses. A place to reappear. This principle is informed by Donna Haraway's concept of 'staying with the trouble' (Haraway 2016: 1).

My practice is rooted in autobiography – mine as well as that of the participants it involves. It faces and gives a voice to life-events that sit outside, or on the edges of, mainstream dialogues and discourses and often remain unacknowledged. Similarly, Dorothy Wordsworth used her writing to voice and record her own lived experiences. She also witnessed, observed and wrote down the words and conversation of other women she met when walking the fells: hill-guides, vagrants, beggars and widows – women whose experiences, like her own, were ordinarily overlooked or undervalued.

This logging process quite literally gave these women a voice. Similarly, *Warnscale* gives-a-voice to those dealing with the little discussed and isolating experience of biological childlessness. It does this through the use of words, images and actions in a series of carefully chosen locations that offer participants ways to acknowledge and express the effects of their experience. For example, Station 3 – 'Warnscale Head Bothy (riven)', is a place where feelings of isolation are acknowledged: 'in this interior place of shelter you are invited to consider your walk (physical and emotional) to this place [...] in the journal provided, write an entry relating to your experience of biological childlessness' (Wilson 2015: Station 3). At Station 6 – 'Innominate Tarn (heaf)', 'a place of missing identity', the possibility of belonging is suggested through the use of the word 'heaf' reflecting the process by which sheep become attached to and hold an embodied knowledge of the land they inhabit (6). Here, participants are invited to 're-imagine mothering in a way that includes everyone who gives love and comfort to others' (6).

Principle 3: Materials of the site and landscape and environmental forces as metaphor (for self)

Harnessing and Using Features and Processes: Physical, topographical, geological, historical, human, non-human, botanical, meteorological, seasonal and planetary.

Dorothy Wordsworth's *Grasmere Journal* accounts of 'nature' struggling to survive are, I suggest, metaphors for herself. Often she identifies, and perhaps identified with, solitary flowers, such as the columbine she described: 'growing upon the Rocks [...] a solitary plant – [...] a slender creature, a female seeking retirement & growing freest & most graceful where it is most alone' (Wordsworth 1991: 103).

In *Warnscale*, at Station 12 – 'Solitary Violas (*solitary*)', participants are invited to notice the violas 'struggling but surviving in cradles in rocks' (2015: 12). However, one solitary viola, and then another, begins to make a family. A participant in New Zealand when receiving a copy of the *Warnscale* book for a friend wrote to say:

> There is also something in the solidarity of this process of getting the book, which is valuable in itself, bringing her close to those who have also trod this devastating path – surprised by a solidarity. Women who would have made wonderful mothers, contributing to the world but faced now with the sadness of knowing this is not to be.
>
> (SA)

Dorothy Wordsworth's journals also show an acute awareness of the fragility of life and the overwhelming forces of 'nature' and how these can cause 'random acts of destruction' (Pipkin 1998: 599). She described trees being uprooted and thrown over in a storm, hungry skeleton-like deer and starving children. She acknowledged the physical and emotional effects on people's faces and bodies of time passing, illness, poverty and loss.

In *Warnscale*, at Station 2 – 'Wooden Bridge (*transition*)', images of water running off the fell are layered with reflections on 'time' and fertility 'running out' while at Station 10 – 'Cairns and Waterfalls (*land mark*)' participants are invited to 'acknowledge their powerlessness to control the forces of nature within and around' (2015: 2, 10). Station 13 – 'Dying Wood (*regeneration*)' works with processes of destruction and repair. Participants are invited to 'look for signs of renewal *and* live the life unimagined [...] on the other side of nothing [...] of resurrection' (2015: 13). One participant said:

> The barrenness of the landscape and beauty and timelessness helped me recognize that my grieving and pain would pass in time. I have already begun to flourish.
>
> (ZB)

Principle 4: Composing and moving through constantly changing scenes and topographies

Hybridization of the 'Real' with the 'Imagined': Dwelling-in a landscape.

In her *Grasmere Journals* Dorothy Wordsworth's vivid use of language is scenographic in it use of sound, light, colour and image to evoke 'a scene' and create a sense of depth, distance, scale, time passing and season changing:

> The small Birds are singing – Lambs bleating, Cuckow calling – The Thrush sings by Fits, Thomas Ashburner's axe is going quietly (without passion) in the orchard – Hens are cackling, Flies are humming, the women talking together at their doors – Plumb & pear trees are in blossom, apple trees greenish – the opposite woods green, the crows are cawing. We have heard Ravens. The Ash Trees are in blossom, Birds flying all about us. The stitchwort is coming out, there is one budding Lychnis. The primroses are passing their prime. Celandine violets & wood sorrel for ever more – little geranium & pansies in the wall.
>
> (Wordsworth 1991: 96–97)

Warnscale, in contrast to *Fissure* and *The Gathering*, is small and intimate in scale and involves no artistic interventions in the landscape. Instead, the landscape and its ever-changing seasons and weather are both 'scene' and performer *and* the participants, through walking, listening and noticing the landscape in the context of the underlying subject matter, are themselves performers and part of the 'scene'. This allows participants to compose their own performance and make meaning that is personal to them. One wrote how she thinks the book:

> strikes a powerful balance between presenting information and ideas and allowing space for the reader to make their own connections. The way it is organized means there is both a freedom and a guiding structure.
>
> (RGi)

Principle 5: Walking beyond knowledge and beating new tracks

Walking as scenography: Therapeutic, solitary, side-by-side, companionable walking and surrogate walking.

41

In the context of her time Dorothy Wordsworth's walking challenged social norms. She would quite literally beat new tracks to find a new route or path, a waterfall, a specific plant or a viewing place that offered an alternative scene or perspective.

Warnscale invites participants to walk beyond their 'knowledge' and imagine different life paths and alternative perspectives. The effort and duration of the walk become metaphors for the arduousness of IVF and the uncertainty of biological childlessness. At Station 7 – 'Haystacks Summit (geld)' participants are invited to 'consider the arduous physical and emotional effort it has taken to reach this place (literally and metaphorically), and the cycles we might be trapped in' (Wilson 2015: 7).

Sometimes Dorothy Wordsworth walked in order to talk with friends. *Warnscale* also uses walking and talking as a creative, therapeutic, conversational and performative tool. It allows for 'communitas' through its application of companionable or side-by-side walking, sharing and talking in the landscape with others. For one participant:

> *Warnscale* made the cold abstract hard fact of not having biological children into something lived, real, a ritual almost that did have some spiritual significance for me, which is hard to articulate (perhaps the connection with others, perhaps the being in nature). The walk showed me that I'm not alone, and it was good to be able to both literally and metaphorically 'walk the same path' alongside others. Also, the walk opened up a space between myself and my husband – I was able to talk about the experience with him.
>
> (RGi)

She added that the 'public nature of the performance starts to combat some of the shame around childlessness. It is important to give childless women a voice – they are shamed into hiding themselves and staying silent' (RGi).

Principle 6: Close-up looking and alternative/shifting perspectives

Finding different points of view and new ways of looking, feeling and thinking – literal and metaphorical.

Dorothy Wordsworth's close observational study was underpinned by botanical knowledge. At times she must have walked slowly and deliberately, perhaps crouching to seek out flowers or to get a closer look. She also literally changed her physical viewpoint by lying down to look at or listen to trees, light, birds, water and sheep from an alternative perspective.

Warnscale also invites similar multisensory modes of walking and dwelling that give participants a variety of ways in which to physically and imaginatively enter the landscape and literally and metaphorically seek out new ways of 'looking' and viewing that may lead to new ways of thinking about childlessness. For example, at Station 5 – 'Black Beck Tarn (*wait*)', I used Dorothy Wordsworth's words to encourage participants to take time and become absorbed in the landscape by listening to it and watching the play of light and wind on the tarn:

> We amused ourselves for a long time in watching the breezes some as if they came from the bottom of the lake spread in a circle, brushing along the surface of the water, & growing more delicate [...] till they died away – others spread out like a peacocks tail, & some went right forward this way & that in all directions. The lake was still where these breezes were not. But they made it all alive.
>
> (1991: 60–61)

Participants are then invited to 'step into the water and feel the sensation of it, listen to the rhythm of its movement, climb the rocky outcrop, lie on top of it and change their perspective' (Wilson 2015: Station 5).

Principle 7: 'Moments of being' – wonderment and defamiliarization

Aliveness-to and observational looking-at the material of the everyday. Making it visible. This principle is informed by Virginia Woolf's concept of 'moment of being' (Woolf 1978: 81).

The 'transformative' capacity of Dorothy Wordsworth's approach to landscape comes, I suggest, from her aliveness to her environment and the way she could 'see' and 'find' the feminine 'material' sublime – a form of 'wonderment' – in the human and non-human material of the everyday. The sun glittering on the wool of a sheep, the light moving over water, the movement of the planets or a favourite birch tree 'yielding yielding to the gusty wind with all its tender twigs, the sun shone upon it & it glanced in the wind like a flying sunshiny shower' (Wordsworth 1991: 40).

This 'wonderment' serves to defamiliarize and 'refigure' the familiar in such a way that can lead to re-imaging and transformation. It is a process, I suggest, that parallels Virginia Woolf's 'moments of being' where 'sudden shocks' rupture 'the cotton wool of daily life' – a state Woolf describes as 'non-being' – and bring acute awareness to the familiar and the common place: the grey-green creases of bark on a tree, a puddle on a path, the lined face of an old woman or moonlight on water (1978: 81–87).

Warnscale defamiliarizes and brings 'moment of being' to the everyday by drawing attention to things that are overlooked, ordinarily invisible to the naked eye or rarely seen in close up (Woolf 1978: 81). The book juxtaposes images of human oocytes, sperm and embryos, the womb lining (endometrium) 'thickening' then 'emptying' and micro fauna of a tarn. Binoculars bring the distant landscape closer, and participants are invited to use the geology lens that comes with the book to look at the detail of volcanic rock, lichen and sori on the underside of a fern leaf (Figure 1.13).

In the book, photographs and images make-visible these life forms and processes. This making-visible led one participant to 'notice the creativity and growth in the smallest details and most "barren" areas' (RG). Another said:

> I loved engaging with the environment both microscopically and through the lens. It connected me to the here and now. Created a different perspective to the typical one.
>
> (ZA)

FIGURE 1.13: *Warnscale* by Louise Ann Wilson (2015), launch-walk participant using geology eyeglass during *Warnscale*, Warnscale Fells, Buttermere, Cumbria. Photographer: Lizzie Coombes.

The responses from *Fissure*, *The Gathering* and *Warnscale* participants demonstrate, I suggest, how a feminine 'material' sublime approach to the creation of rural walking-performance enables the landscape to become a site of transformation. Furthermore, I believe that my methodology, embedded in the seven 'scenographic' principles I have presented in this chapter, offers a model for future work.

NOTES

1. The work of her Dorothy Wordsworth's female contemporaries, including Ann Radcliffe (1764–1823) and Charlotte Smith (1749–1806), also informed these principles.
2. *Fissure* was created by Louise Ann Wilson, written by Elizabeth Burns, composed by Jocelyn Pook and choreographed by Nigel Stewart. It was made in collaboration with Michael Brada (neuro-oncologist), Andrew McEvoy (neurosurgeon), Chris Clark (neuro-physicist), Mike Kelly (geologist) and Colin Newlands (conservationist).
3. Extract from *Her Birth, Her Breath, Her Birth*, written by Elizabeth Burns for *Fissure*.
4. Extract from *Take This Thread*, written by Elizabeth Burns for *Fissure*.
5. Extract from *After the Long Night*, written by Elizabeth Burns for *Fissure*.
6. See Victor Turner's 'Death and the Dead in Pilgrimage Process' (1992: 35).
7. For *The Gathering*, Gillian Clarke, National Poet for Wales (2008–16), wrote landscape poems and a twelve-month poem cycle, and Louise Ann Wilson, who created and designed the performance, wrote other farming texts based on conversations with the shepherds. Nigel Stewart choreographed movement material based on the shepherds' activities.
8. Extract from *Scan*, written by Gillian Clarke for *The Gathering*.
9. Extract from *Scan*, written by Gillian Clarke for *The Gathering*.
10. I created *Warnscale* with thirteen 'mapping-walk participants' and a team of advisors, including: Joyce Harper, Institute for Women's Health, UCL; Celia Roberts, College of Arts and Social Sciences, Australian National University (formerly Department of Sociology, Lancaster University, UK); Jody Day, Gateway Women; Wanda Georgiades and the CARE Fertility Group; the embryology team, The Centre for Reproductive & Genetic Health, London.
11. My use of the word 'station' relates to Stations of the Cross, a process of pilgrimage found in Christian liturgical practice during Lent, which moves between fourteen stations.
12. From here on, responses from *Warnscale* mapping-walk participants will be identified by their initials.
13. Gateway Women is an online forum 'united by and beyond childlessness'. See https://gateway-women.com. Accessed 16 December 2020.

REFERENCES

Coleman, Simon and Elsner, John (1995), *Pilgrimage Past and Present: Sacred Travel and Sacred Space in the World Religions*, London: British Museum Press.

Dictionary Online (2020), https://www.dictionary.com. Accessed 16 September 2020.

Haraway, Donna J. (1988), 'Situated knowledges: The science question in feminism and the privilege of partial perspective', *Feminist Studies*, 14, pp. 575–99.

Haraway, Donna J. (2016), *Staying with the Trouble: Making Kin in the Chthulucene*, Durham, NC: Duke University Press.

OED Online (2015), Oxford: Oxford University Press, http://www.oed.com.ezproxy.lancs.ac.uk/view/Entry/169556?redirectedFrom=sacred+place#eid123876704. Accessed 1 June 2016.

Palmer, Scott (2011), 'Space', in J. Pitches and S. Popat (eds), *Performance Perspectives: A Critical Introduction*, Basingstoke: Palgrave Macmillan, pp. 52–87.

Pipkin, John G. (1998), 'The material sublime of women Romantic poets', *Studies in English Literature, 1500–1900*, 38, pp. 597–619.

Turner, Edith (2012), *Communitas: The Anthropology of Collective Joy*, New York: Palgrave Macmillan.

Turner, Victor (1992), *Blazing the Trail: Way Marks in the Exploration of Symbols*, Tucson: University of Arizona Press.

Usher, Graham B. (2012), *Places of Enchantment: Meeting God in Landscapes*, London: Society for Promoting Christian Knowledge.

Wilson, Louise Ann (2011), *Fissure*, Ingleborough Fells, Yorkshire Dales, Yorkshire, England: Art Events with Louise Ann Wilson Company Limited.

Wilson, Louise Ann (2014), *The Gathering/Yr Helfa*, Hafod y Llan Farm, Gwynedd, Snowdonia, Wales: National Theatre Wales with Migrations and Louise Ann Wilson Company Limited.

Wilson, Louise Ann (2015), *Warnscale: A Land Mark Walk Reflecting on In/Fertility and Childlessness*, Leeds: Louise Ann Wilson Company Limited.

Woolf, Virginia (1978), 'Sketch of the past', in J. Schulkind (ed.), *Moments of Being: Autobiographical Writings*, London: Triad/Panther, pp. 71–159.

Wordsworth, Dorothy ([1800–03] 1991), *The Grasmere and Alfoxden Journals*, ed. P. Woof, Oxford: Oxford University Press.

2

Bordering the Sacred:
The Labyrinth as Non-Site

Kris Darby

Introduction: Entering the labyrinth

In the summer of 2014 I entered the Chartres labyrinth (Figure 2.1). Although the centre is a few metres away from me, I know that it will take me some time to get there. By its very nature, a labyrinth offers a direct route to its centre, but not the most direct. It is this characteristic which has been retained throughout its myriad of iterations, in which an initially perceived short amble becomes a journey that, literally and figuratively, borders on the sacred. The leap into metaphor is therefore not too difficult, the journey being 'the master trope of modern drama' after all (Chaudhuri 1997: 53). This particular labyrinth within a Roman Catholic cathedral in the northern French city of Chartres has become symbolic of a labyrinth 'renaissance', which has reasserted the spiritual significance of these mysterious patterns (Köhler-Ryan 2013: 87). However, the modern labyrinth movement's association with New Age religious practices and the growing number of replications of labyrinths such as Chartres have made this pattern a contested territory. In her chapter 'The Beginning That Is Already an End: Finding the Significance of Labyrinthine Travel', Renée Köhler-Ryan (2013) focuses on a perceived hijacking of the medieval Christian labyrinth of Chartres, suggesting that the copying of it has led to a loss of understanding of its original usage. She argues for 'setting the labyrinth back in its place' by highlighting its imbrication within the building of the Chartres Cathedral (Köhler-Ryan 2013: 101). Köhler-Ryan's argument is a provocative and quite convincing one, highlighting how the church building relates 'both to the microcosm of the individual and to the macrocosm of God's universe' (Wiles 2003: 44). She asserts that the Chartres labyrinth was conceived for a specific spatio-religious context and that its abstraction from this undermines its medieval purpose as a 'substitute pilgrimage directed specifically toward

Jerusalem' (Köhler-Ryan 2013: 95). This runs counter to the modern labyrinth movement's desire to rediscover 'a certain innate mechanism' that precedes the Christian narrative applied to it (Bloos and O'Connor 2002: 224).

As a scholar of theatre and performance, for me, Köhler-Ryan's concern bears an uncanny resemblance to some of the critical discussions regarding site-specific performance, echoing sculptor Richard Serra's often quoted dictum: 'to move the work is to destroy the work' (1994: 194). An argument could be made for the framing of the Chartres labyrinth as a site-specific performance; however, what complicates this is that the site that it is 'specific' to is over two thousand miles away. This chapter will therefore instead assert that the medieval labyrinth functions as a 'non-site', facilitating an imaginary pilgrimage to sacred place(s) (Smithson [1968] 1996). Beginning with an introduction to the fundamental tenets of the non-site, this chapter will contextualize the labyrinth, highlighting its ability to displace the sacred through various means. Particular attention will be given to the medieval church variant and how the origin of the modern labyrinth movement centres around the resiting of the non-sited labyrinth. My own experiences

FIGURE 2.1: The Chartres labyrinth (2014). Black and white photograph. Author's own.

of walking two different versions of the Chartres labyrinth will close this chapter, highlighting how the same pattern fosters two different journey narratives.

The double path

The 'non-site' was coined by land artist Robert Smithson as an umbrella term for a series of artworks which broadly consisted of materials gathered from his walks to the outskirts of New Jersey. The trigger for these works stems from the artist's desire to find 'new sites outside of the white walls of the gallery or museum' (Toner and Smithson [1970] 1996: 234), which existed at the edge of places. He brought back photographs, which, when exhibited with a negative map of the location, became *The Monuments of Passaic* (1967). In later works, the non-sites took the form of documents and mineral samples from the site, housed within geometrically shaped containers which 'functions as an index of their position on the site' (Linder 1999: 11). The site and the contextual information accompanying it are essentially pulled apart from each other, in which the observer cannot exist with either in the same place. They are therefore encouraged to engage in an imaginary journey between the two, in which the 'site appears in *the promise* of its occupation by the Non-Site' (Kaye 2000: 99, original emphasis). Smithson termed this journey a 'non-trip', reflecting the wandering of the mind and the immovability of the body (1996: 364). Yet such a journey is invariably two-way, due to the object's subtraction from its original site creating uncertainty, which requires the observer to 'return' to the non-site for orientation. Both non-site and site are locked in an unresolved dialectical relationship, in which the 'site is mobile', existing somewhere else (Kaye 2000: 96). In order to comprehend this relationship, Smithson devised a table, presented here as Table 2.1.

The table implies that the non-trip prompted by the non-site is one of assemblage, in which an 'array of matter' is reconstituted into a 'series of points'. As a 'trip', this could be equated with the plotting of the points of a journey to the site itself, further conveyed by this perceived sense of distance between the 'centre' and the 'edge'. The site is what we perceive reflected within the non-sited mirror, yet each site can yield different versions of the same place it purports to direct us towards. The single-pathed labyrinth can take the walker to an almost infinite variety of destinations, indicative of the twin paradoxes of 'indeterminate (certainty)' and 'determinate (uncertainty)'. Although the physical trip into the labyrinth is clearly determined, its often ambiguous design necessitates quite an indeterminate non-trip. This aspect is what is of particular significance to this chapter, as throughout its history, the labyrinth's ambiguity has provided a point of entry for people to reappropriate or relocate sacred places and also a means by which an imagined sacred landscape can be projected and preserved.

Site	Non-Site
1. Open lines	Closed limits
2. A series of points	An array of matter
3. Outer coordinates	Inner coordinates
4. Subtraction	Addition
5. Indeterminate (certainty)	Determinate (uncertainty)
6. Scattered (information)	Contained (information)
7. Reflection	Mirror
8. Edge	Centre
9. Some place (physical)	No place (abstract)
10. Many	One

TABLE 2.1: Dialectic of site and non-site. Source: Smithson cited in Kaye (2000: 95).

The sacred path: Walking the labyrinth

Labyrinths of various forms are scattered throughout the world, ranging from small totems to larger architectural structures. Within civilizations isolated from each other, this archetypal image has been carved, drawn and built. It is a structure designed to lose oneself, but such loss is tempered by the aforementioned inevitability of a path that allows us to determine the degree by which we experience this loss. The literal path towards the centre does not need to be 'learnt', but the symbolic path that we may lose ourselves along is something that requires preparation in order for the physical and the spiritual to merge (Curry 2000: 6). This process of learning is hermeneutical in structure, as the walker slowly learns about themselves through a path shaped by others, becoming a movement between their 'own world on the one hand, and the world projected' (Zimmermann 2015: 67). Each step taken informs the walker's understanding of the larger path they are walking, which, literally in turn, gives weight to their subsequent steps. Grant R. Osbourne's (2006) model of the hermeneutical spiral goes some way towards capturing the 'gnostic sense' of discovery ascribed to the labyrinth (Curry 2000: 42), acknowledging a growth in understanding through a 'spiralling nearer and nearer to the text's intended meaning' (Osbourne 2006: 22). Although the unicursal path of the labyrinth brings the walker back to the same place from which they entered, it is now no longer the same 'place' as before. Their interpretation of the path has changed and hopefully so have they. This 'spiralling' is however subject to elongation and curtailment through the undulating pattern of the labyrinth, which, although broadly heading towards the centre, does so in a circumspect manner. As a consequence, the labyrinth walker always approaches their destination indirectly, interpretation occurring not as a steady growth but instead as a more eventful series of twists and turns that invariably help to narrativize it. In all my labyrinth walks, the centre has always appeared seemingly out of nowhere, hidden within the repeating meanders of the path which encircles it.

This is where the ritualistic aspect of the walk manifests itself, as although it is a path that we only retrace once, its compact design forces us to repeatedly contemplate the path walked and the path about to be walked as they flow side by side. The labyrinth's centre is skirted numerous times, the centre being both revealed and further concealed through the reiteration of its perimeter. It therefore lends itself to a sense of consecration of this centre and with this a need to sacralize this abstract space into place.

Placing the labyrinth

Whether traced with one's gaze, fingers or feet, the labyrinth offers a journey in a multitude of forms. As already mentioned, within this elegant design lies a pleasing ambiguity that has led to numerous studies regarding its elemental and archetypal qualities (Kociatkiewicz and Kostera 2015: 57). Such an ambiguity extends to the labyrinth's centre, which has become symbolically equated with an extensive number of mythic and real-world locations. Pertinent to this study is the means by which this obscurity enables the labyrinth to move and multiply spaces.

In his seminal *Mazes and Labyrinths*, Nigel Pennick references a number of Scandinavian labyrinths named after fortified cities that were overthrown, such as Lissabon (Lisbon) (1990: 35). Here, the walk into the labyrinth became not only a means to imaginatively visit a city that no longer existed as it once did but also a reminder perhaps as to the fluid nature of platial identity. Elsewhere, citing Alfred Gell, anthropologist Tim Ingold highlights the impenetrable weaving pattern of the knot which would adorn the shields of Celtic warriors (2016: 57). Such labyrinthine designs are doubly protective, both in that they guard the centre, but also in that they deflect attention away from the 'real' centre that they are symbolizing. The body of the warrior and the settlement they protect are tied together, each instance of the knot pattern strengthening and extending the reach of the protected site. Inverting this, the labyrinth has also been perceived as a great container, in which its centre becomes symbolic of a fortification or prison. The Cretan labyrinth, which housed the Minotaur, is the most famous of these and was allegedly modelled on the maze to the Underworld (54). The mythic status of this elaborate prison is magnified by the fact that there is still uncertainty as to where it was located on the island of Crete. There are at least three places that have a claim to it, meaning that like many of the labyrinths discussed later in this chapter, it exists as a serious of copies without an original (Connor 2009). Rather than acting as the original site of Daedalus's prison, these possible Cretan labyrinths act as non-sites to the myth of the original.

For some labyrinths there can never be an 'original' place of origin, given that they attempt to map concepts and abstract ideas born from philosophy and mysticism. The complex patterning of the Buddhist mandala is one such design, the tracing of it equating to an imagined walk of contemplation (Bloos and O'Connor 2002: 222). Jean Hani equates the labyrinth with the web as 'a universal symbol of the world' which 'represents the complications and difficulties we encounter during our human existence' (2000: 16). One can perceive such a web-like labyrinth within the kabbalah (tree of life) of Judaism, used to support 'the search for deeper allegorical meaning in the words and letters of the Torah' (Bloos and O'Connor 2002: 222). In such instances the application of Smithson's dialectic becomes a little unstable because the openness of some of these sites extends beyond geography and time. In fact, such sites cannot be wholly detached from the non-site because their vastness means they invariably contain it. As a consequence, the non-sites that point towards them act as a means to microcosmically distil these sites into a symbolic pattern that allows us to imaginatively situate ourselves outside of them.

Ingrid D. Bloos and Thomas O'Connor discuss the significance of the labyrinth within contemporary narrative therapy, which broadly 'believes that humans construct stories to make sense of their experience' (2002: 225). For them, the labyrinth offers the capacity to build 'alternate stories', its expansive role as a 'universal symbol' allowing the walker to acknowledge their place within a much longer life journey and to locate a sense of place within it. While Smithson does not address universality, his non-sites are 'removed from any sense of self' and are devoid of 'scenic meaning', enabling the observer to attempt to shape their own non-trip to the site (Pettena 1996: 297). Within the labyrinth, the walker has the opportunity to symbolically re-enter their own life from a different direction or locate themselves within a journey of a much larger cosmic scale. However, the labyrinth has also historically been utilized to strengthen a dominant narrative, in which the capacity to develop 'alternate stories' is underpinned by a specific ideology.

The substitute pilgrimage

The largely dominant narrative underpinning the medieval church labyrinth stems from the general perception that it provides a 'compressed' (Solnit 2002: 70) or 'substitute pilgrimage' to Jerusalem (Köhler-Ryan 2013: 87). This is where the non-sited qualities of the labyrinth really manifest, through an imagined journey to a remote place. The utilization of the labyrinth in this capacity was aided by Roman emperor Constantine, with his casting of specific geographical locations as 'inherently sacred', providing actual consecrated places for people to journey to (Wiles 2003: 39). This degree of specificity is one of the primary distinctions between that of the 'saunterer' and the pilgrim. The saunterer (holy lander) ambles aimlessly under the pretence of going to the Holy Land (la Sainte-Terre), while the pilgrim walks an often prescribed route to a specific consecrated location (Thoreau in Katsilometes 2010: 193). Although the first of these types of walking could be dismissed as being merely idle, unlike the steadfast conviction of the pilgrim, Bessie Karras Katsilometes reappropriates the saunterer as a means to find one's own Holy Land and centre of 'self-knowing' (2010: 193). This immediately lessens the significance of the sacred as being something collectively tied to a specific location and more towards an internalized and individual sense of it. The saunterer therefore never arrives at a sacred place in a literal sense, but finds fulfilment in the prolonged act of 'arriving', the distance between them and their own sense of the sacred in a state of flux. This is particularly significant when looking at the later replications of medieval labyrinths and how the resiting of its sacred place within the modern labyrinth movement has led to a shift towards Katsilometes's definition of sauntering.

The rise and adoption of Christianity throughout the Roman Empire led to the subsequent Christianizing of many pagan symbols, including the labyrinth, which became a popular motif (Ullyat 2011: 110). For Jean Villette, such a process of appropriation was eased by the fact that at their core, 'both pagan and Christian [ideologies] have a single complicated path within them leading laboriously and inevitably to a final destination' from birth to death (2000: 10). The aforementioned abstract and unicursal quality of the labyrinth design made it simple to recontextualize within the Christian church, in which the heroic myth of Theseus became an allegory for Christ's own journey. For Craig M. Wright, the embedding of the pagan labyrinth within the Christian church deliberately conveys the superiority of the latter over the former (cited in Ullyatt 2011: 111). Tony Ullyatt deliberates on this further, suggesting that alternatively it points towards the Christian church's need to 'embrace the mystical meaning of the labyrinth' (2011: 111). He also suggests that the 'relational interaction' between the two-dimensional labyrinth and the three-dimensional church 'symbolizes the flatness of human existence unless it, too, is embedded in, and surrounded by, God's overarching presence' (Ullyatt 2011: 111, 113). This perspective resonates with the 'contained' and 'closed limits' of the non-site, here evidenced literally by the Christian church building and the dominant narrative it articulates for the pilgrim.

The context of the labyrinth was therefore rewritten, allowing it to become a means to 'promote the beliefs of the Western Church' for over a thousand years, its ability to do so contingent on anchoring the labyrinth's centre to the centre of the world itself (Ullyatt 2011: 110). For the Classical Greeks, this centre was Delphi, but through the Christianization of pagan symbols, this became relocated to Jerusalem as the naval of the world (Wiles 2003: 24). At the centre of the medieval labyrinth, one is supposedly able to centre themselves within Jerusalem and therefore in alignment with 'a microcosmic symbol for the cosmos itself' (Hani 2000: 17). As per Smithson's dialectic, the 'three-dimensional and the two-dimensional trade places' as Jerusalem and the labyrinth's centre converge within a single space (Tilley et al. 2000: 42). The affixing of the medieval labyrinth's centre to a specific location on earth gave the divine a degree of tangibility but also provided the pilgrim with stability, at odds with 'the meandering path around it' (Hani 2000: 17).

Medieval maps such as the *Hereford Mappa Mundi* also depict Jerusalem at the centre of the world (Köhler-Ryan 2013: 99), emphasized by the use of the quartered circle as a symbol for the city during the medieval period. This acted as a compass for the rest of the world to orientate itself around and as a sacred place for pilgrimage. Around the same time, Benedictine monk Matthew Paris's itinerary maps encouraged non-trips for the pilgrim, in which users plotted their own route to Jerusalem, unfolding sections of the map as they went (98). Here, 'the viewer is able to reconfigure the spaces of Christian Europe, alter the routes, and refashion the meanings to be derived from them' (Connolly 1999: 599–600). Such maps provided agency for the pilgrim in plotting their own labyrinthine route, but through a Christianized depiction of the landscape, in which Jerusalem becomes the inevitable centre. The earlier loss of Jerusalem to Muslim forces in 1187 meant that maps such as these were crucial in ensuring that the city remained at the centre of Christianity (Connolly in Köhler-Ryan 2013: 98).

Establishing a non-trip between a church labyrinth and the distant city of Jerusalem would therefore be a difficult undertaking, given that, for Robert Smithson, there was a limit as to how far a non-site could be from its site (in Toner and Smithson [1970] 1996: 235). While maps and small labyrinthine decorations could encourage this imaginative journey, it was the large-scale pavement labyrinths which facilitated a kinaesthetic engagement with the non-site. The cathedrals became substitute destinations, providing a means to imaginatively and symbolically visit the Holy Land. The adoption of the name *rues de Jerusalem* instead of 'labyrinth' in the High Middle Ages cements the labyrinth as being a substitute pilgrimage, but also emphasizes the Jerusalem in its centre as both a heavenly and earthly place (Köhler-Ryan 2013: 92). Although these walkable labyrinths were physically accessible, plotting an imaginary journey towards a symbolic or heavenly Jerusalem was a real test for a pilgrim. This is where the medieval labyrinth 'lends itself to performance and enactment', through the pilgrim's concrete belief in being able to conceive their walk as a journey (97).

Chemin de Jerusalem: The Chartres narratives

The most well known of these medieval labyrinths lies within the Cathedral of Chartres, which is the best preserved and one of the largest of its time, and also lies at the centre of the modern labyrinth movement (Villette 2000: 11). After the medieval period, understanding and usage of church labyrinths began to fade. The 'constant movement of crowds [...] apparently disturbed the clergy', leading to the destruction of a number of French labyrinths (5). In addition to being a disruption for some, Helen Curry also highlights 'the influence of the scientific revolution, which led to a weeding out of older, "pagan" traditions' (2000: 32). The earth-centred 'map of the cosmos' aligned neatly with Jerusalem as the aforementioned naval of the world, but the arrival of Copernican science began to disrupt this (Katsilometes 2010: 194). Furthermore, the labyrinth's ability to 'facilitate' the walker's journey towards the divine may have been met with distrust by some religious leaders who advocated for priests to be such mediators (Curry 2000: 33). By the eighteenth century most of the medieval labyrinths had been destroyed, with Chartres somehow managing to remain intact (Katsilometes 2010: 194).

The Chartres labyrinth has had numerous names, including the aforementioned 'chemin de Jerusalem', 'meandre' as well as 'daedale', which gestures to its Cretan antecedent (Matthews 1922: 60). Despite its popularity, this labyrinth actually represents one of the more recent returns to the labyrinth tradition. In 1194 the cathedral suffered a devastating fire which required significant repair and provided the opportunity for the labyrinth to be constructed. This was believed to have taken place within the relatively short reparation time of 29 years (Bloos and O'Connor 2002: 223). There are countless analyses of the geomantic significance of the labyrinth's design and its location; however, before discussing some of these it is important to note the significance the labyrinth had within the cathedral's renovation. Jean Villette cites historian John James's account of this particular period, which heavily implies that the centre of the labyrinth itself determined some of the architecture of the cathedral's redesign, namely, the locating of the high altar (2000: 11). What is significant about this is that it cements the reciprocal relationship between the labyrinth and its surrounding location and that it played a crucial role in defining the cathedral as well as the reverse. The imbrication of the two suggests that collectively they function as the non-site for the pilgrim's journey and that the efficacy of the pilgrim's non-trip is contingent on an awareness of this. With this in mind, Renée Köhler-Ryan turns to the Chartres Cathedral itself to provide contextual information that would instil within the walker 'a further appreciation of the meaning that the story of salvation carries' for them (2013: 91). Within its stained glass windows lies the narrative of 'creation, redemption and salvation' acting almost as a primer or aide-memoire of the dominant narrative for the labyrinth walker to relate to (Köhler-Ryan 2013: 91). Although Köhler-Ryan assumes that the pilgrim has prior knowledge of the significance of the cathedral's adornments, it is reasonable to assume that at the very least the building's function as a site of Christian worship would invariably characterize their journey.

While Köhler-Ryan is certain that the medieval labyrinth pattern was designed as a 'substitute pilgrimage' to Jerusalem, evidence suggests that other symbolic journeys may have taken place. One of these, which ties to many of the aforementioned themes of the labyrinth's dominant narrative, is that the walk is a recreation of Christ's walk from the Praetorium to Golgotha (Villette 2000: 9). This is obviously echoic of the custom of following the Stations of the Cross, which became replicated outside of Jerusalem when it became inaccessible (Pennick 1990: 135).[1] However, it appears that this alternative site was not as popular as the journey to Jerusalem as a whole, perhaps because it implies a more specific journey to be mapped onto the path.

What could have also complicated the Christian journey narrative within Chartres was the presence of a brass plaque that used to be located within the labyrinth's centre. Melted down to make ammunition for Napoleon, this plaque allegedly bore the familiar image of Theseus locked in combat with the Minotaur (Villette 2000: 6–7). This myth, like many of the pagan customs, had been reappropriated as an allegorical image of the defeat of Satan by Christ in his visit to hell between his death and resurrection (Köhler-Ryan 2013: 93). The removal of the plaque signalled the removal of explicit references to pre-Christian locations, inadvertently strengthening the linearity of the pilgrim's non-trip to Jerusalem as a singular site. Yet there was a time when the identity of the Chartres labyrinth's centre was very much a multifaceted one, accommodating the heavenly city of Jerusalem, Christ's tortuous walk from the Praetorium to Golgotha, the World of the Dead and the ancient prison of Crete.

Veriditas and the modern labyrinth movement

In the mid-1990s the Chartres labyrinth became decoupled from its original location, undermining its medieval function and the dominant Christian narrative that had previously been ingratiated within it. At the centre of the modern labyrinth movement is Lauren Artress, a priest and psychotherapist who had been introduced to the meditative qualities of the pattern by Jean Houston at a Mystery School seminar (Artress 2006: 2). Houston, a proponent of the Human Potential Movement, had adopted the pattern based on her experience of reading a short story by Gerald Heard entitled 'Dromenon'. The tale concerns an archaeologist who is 'brought into a psychophysical state of ecstasy and spiritual awakening' after tracing a labyrinth in an English cathedral (Houston in Curry 2000: x).

This sense of 'awakening' something that precedes the very foundation of the cathedral within the narrative emphasized less a journey to a specific location and more the act of unravelling the 'knot of the self' (Heard 1944: 189). As a consequence of this, Houston's utilization of the labyrinth draws principally from pre-Christian rituals, focusing specifically on ancient Greece and the 'magical dance' performed by a group of *kouretes* which facilitated a rebirth within the place surrounding it (Houston cited in Curry 2000: x). It would appear that for Houston, this dance traced out a labyrinthine pattern that if followed could allow for others to enact this sense of self-transformation and 'the dance of a larger life' (in Curry 2000: x). This perspective draws attention to the etymology of *dromenon*, meaning 'a thing re-done and/or pre-done, and done collectively at regular intervals' (Harrison in Friedrich 2008: 162). From this perspective, the labyrinth is a site of re-enactment, but also a site of potential action. For Houston, the pattern described within Heard's narrative is synonymous with that of Chartres, although, strangely, explicit reference is not made to it at all within the story.

Houston's pairing of Heard's 'Dromenon' with the Chartres labyrinth inspired Artress, then Canon Pastor at Grace Cathedral in San Francisco, to visit Chartres in 1991. On arriving at the cathedral with Dean of Grace Cathedral Alan Jones and five others, the group discovered that the labyrinth was inaccessible.[2] Ironically, the labyrinth's prominence within the cathedral has led often to a neglect, in which it is obscured by seating for various religious services (Figure 2.1). Disappointed at this unforeseen occurrence, Artress and a small group took it upon themselves to remove the seating in order to walk the labyrinth. Jones reflects on this encounter, stating that he 'felt the ambiance of the cathedral change from a place for tourists to a sacred space for pilgrims' (1998: n.pag.). This would seem to imply that he felt that the labyrinth's function was not being realized by the religious authority of Chartres Cathedral and that this temporary reconfiguration of the space by Artress and others acted as a reclamation or reasserting of the labyrinth's role within Christian worship. Artress's 'need to explore the ancient authenticity of the Chartres labyrinth', akin to the archaeologist of Heard's narrative, compounds such a view, implying a desire to tap into a function of the labyrinth which predated its medieval construction (2006: 5). In Jones's (1998) description of this intervention, it is quite telling that Artress's actions are described as a product of 'vision and courage', suggesting that they perceived a risk in challenging the established rules of this space. Renée Köhler-Ryan views Artress's intervention as one of assumed 'propriety authority', in which a way of walking was imposed upon the space (2013: 93–94). The fact that the group arrived with cameras and tape measures (Artress 2006: 4) indicates that they were just keen to duplicate the labyrinth itself, further signifying that its surrounding environment had little or no bearing for them on the walking of future replications.

Although there were some initial tensions between the security staff and the walkers, these quickly dissipated and in the ensuing years a strong partnership was fostered between their respective cathedrals, beginning with a temporary tapestry replication of the Chartres labyrinth at Grace Cathedral at the end of 1991. Three years later, its popularity led to it becoming a permanent stone fixture within the cathedral, prompting a perceived sense of twinning between both cathedrals. This was bolstered by Père François Legaux, Rector of Chartres Cathedral, becoming an honouree Canon of Grace Cathedral, with Jones occupying the same role at Chartres (Veriditas 2018). The size and location of the two labyrinths in their respective cathedrals is so uncannily similar that on first glance it is quite difficult to discern the original from the replica. From this, Artress later founded the non-profit organization Veriditas (1995) as a means to train and support labyrinth facilitators within North America, South America, Europe and Australasia. While it utilizes labyrinths of different types, the Chartres labyrinth remains prominent in its work. The organization's arranging of annual pilgrimages to worldwide locations, including Chartres and Grace Cathedral, cements the aforementioned twinning of the two places.

Although the medieval city of Chartres is still acknowledged within the titling of this particular medieval labyrinth design, it is Grace Cathedral in San Francisco that has become a catalyst for its replication and mass production. Different variants of the Chartres labyrinth design can also be purchased through Veriditas' website in a variety of colours. Other companies, such as The Labyrinth Company, feature the Chartres Replica™ as one of their featured designs, 'scaled from a computer-aided design rendering of the 42.28 ft original, field-checked against the actual labyrinth at Chartres Cathedral' (Labyrinth Company 2018: n.pag.). Robert Ferré's *Chartres Labyrinth Construction Manual* (2014) is one of a number of resources that provides detailed instructions in how to build your own Chartres labyrinth. The mass production of this pattern again highlights how for Artress this sense of the 'authentic' is not to be found within the aforementioned imbrication of the labyrinth and the cathedral but through deciphering the design of the labyrinth itself.

The Mystery School seminars and the Veriditas workshops are a reinterpretation and re-imaging of labyrinth rituals, emphasizing the individual's 'walk inward' to 'our own centre' (Artress 2006: xi, 2). Köhler-Ryan views this utilization of the labyrinth as egocentric, its meaning being 'self- rather than God-centred'

(2013: 94). She takes issue with Artress's claim about a lack of a 'significant tradition of interiority' in the West, highlighting that such a simple binary between west and east cannot be readily applied (Köhler-Ryan 2013: 94). While Köhler-Ryan argues for 'setting the labyrinth back in its place' (2013: 101), Artress is concerned with 'Reclaiming the Body' (2006: 140). This is where the distinction between the original Chartres pattern and Veriditas' appropriation of it really start to manifest, as one proposes transportation to a distant location and the other transformation of the self.

Two non-trips to the sacred

What follows now is a critical reflection of my own experiences of walking the Chartres labyrinth and a temporary replica of it. Framing these journeys within Smithson's dialectic has proven helpful not only in understanding the aforementioned schism between the original function of the Chartres labyrinth and its replications, but also the manner in which walking as an aesthetic act can facilitate a sense of journeying towards the sacred.

Attention and intention

It is important to note that my first experience of the Chartres labyrinth was through a replication of it on canvas at Lancaster University's chaplaincy (Figure 2.2). This was part of a day-long event coordinated by Veriditas and led by Anglican priest and labyrinth facilitator Di Williams. Williams is the founder of Still Paths, a UK-based labyrinth resource and consultancy, who, like Veriditas and Jean Houston, also adopts the Chartres pattern as their logo. She began the day with a presentation on the labyrinth's lineage, drawing out shared principles that have informed her approach to facilitation. Before walking the labyrinth, we were set exercises to prime us for the walk ahead, largely centred around establishing an intention or reason for walking this path. This may take the form of a question that we wanted to answer and would be projected onto the labyrinth's centre. For Williams, walking a labyrinth also requires a particular degree of attention, referred to as 'soft focus', in which the surrounding environment and the rest of the fellow labyrinth walkers would exist on the periphery, at instances bleeding into our experience of the walk. This degree of attention was particularly crucial in Lancaster, with us walking a labyrinth that was not a permanent fixture of this location. Tony Ullyatt shows how temporary labyrinths such as this highlight the permanence of the surrounding environment and interweave its 'location and primary function' into the walking experience (2011: 112–13). In Lancaster I was

FIGURE 2.2: The Chartres labyrinth replica (2014). Black and white photograph. Author's own.

conscious of the religious overtones of the environment of the chaplaincy and also the manner in which fellow walkers reflected on their experience; however this did not so much shape my process of attenuation with the labyrinth, because the 'multifaith' status of the environment meant that it was never explicitly tied to one dominant narrative (Chaplaincy Centre Lancaster 2018).

When walking the original Chartres labyrinth some month later, I tried to prepare in the same manner that Williams had taught us. However, if a 'sacred place must be "uncrowded" [...] to allow for projection of fantasy and the evolution of myth', then the mass of tourists criss-crossing the cathedral floor made the process of attention difficult (Ostwalt 2012: 89). This was expected though, with my walk in Lancaster being one of private study and my visit to Chartres being part of a public visit as a tourist. If the tourist observes and the pilgrim participates (Artress 2006: 35), then I was caught between these two respective modes of attention as the chairs started to be taken away and a queue of people began to form. Irrespective of the personal intention I had for walking the labyrinth here, it was difficult to ignore the overwhelming Gothic architecture that dwarfed me. The labyrinth's medieval function as a Christian means of pilgrimage was ever present, and I quickly became aware that it had a different intention to me. Irrespective of my ignorance of the labyrinth's geomancy and some of the finer subtleties of the cathedral's iconography, one could not detach the Chartres labyrinth from its surroundings. This perspective clashes with Ullyatt's view that the labyrinth as a whole is a temenos 'separate from its environment by virtue of its delineation, design, and construction' (2011: 114). The portability of the labyrinth walked in Lancaster afforded me the opportunity to recontextualize and relocate its centre for myself, however, in Chartres, the pattern is literally bricked into the foundations of the building, its 'closed limits' necessitating a walking of an already trodden path (Smithson cited in Kaye 2000: 95).

The journey in

When Williams raised her arm to let me into the labyrinth in Lancaster, I really felt a pronounced sense of crossing a threshold from one plane into another. She had briefed us beforehand on some ways of walking that would allow us to complete our journey uninterrupted and would accommodate the different paces of the group. All of us slowly paced with a few metres between us, providing adequate breathing space but also allowing for the inevitable meetings and partings of the same people as we would occasionally walk side by side travelling in opposing directions. In Chartres, such moments were just as enjoyable to experience, but overall the pace was less measured and more staccato, due to the aforementioned differences in attention. For instance, one woman ahead of the group would stop at instances and prostrate herself on the floor, her eyes looking upwards with the murmuring of a prayer to herself. In Lancaster, Williams had explained that it was absolutely fine to overtake another walker, provided we did so at specific points in the path. However in Chartres, I felt uncomfortable with the idea of passing this particular walker because I perceived her as having better understood the function of the labyrinth. As a result, the walking of the group began to resemble queuing, echoing more touristic habits of movement. My perspective of the labyrinth as an interior space was also lessened by the people who would walk across its dividing lines, reminding me of its flatness. In Lancaster, I had fortunately been able to retain this sense of interiority, affording me the ability to deliberate on my intention with little interruption. This meant that when the centre suddenly appeared in front of me, it genuinely felt as if I had journeyed into the heart of something. Yet as I looked out and observed the whole labyrinth a sense of exteriority also manifested, taking in the fellow walkers swirling around me, with the sense of centripetal force enabling me to centre myself.

In the centre of the labyrinth at Chartres, the sense of having covered a greater distance than the labyrinth's radius was evident, but I did not possess the sensation of having travelled beyond the walls of the cathedral itself. Even in her 'intense experience' at the labyrinth's centre, Helen Curry's own sense of journeying from her body was a temporal non-trip as opposed to a geographical change in location (2000: 74). Equally in Lancaster, I cannot categorically state that I felt I had walked to a specific site, although I still felt satisfied with a sense that my intention had been met. For Smithson, the site's location is one that can never be ascertained completely, existing always as 'some place', yet he does emphasize that this is a 'physical' place, something that I found difficult to perceive in my sauntering in Lancaster (in Kaye 2000: 95). Renée Köhler-Ryan has recognized similar responses in participants who have walked replicas of the Chartres labyrinth:

> Almost everyone *felt* something when walking the labyrinth, but few could really explain what or why. Without any centre but the self, few could situate themselves within a greater narrative of meaning. This confusion is a crucial point, for anyone who travels forgets the value of his or her surroundings at their peril.
>
> (2013: 104, original emphasis)

The 'surroundings' that Köhler-Ryan refers to are those of Chartres Cathedral, and I would agree that they had an overwhelming impact on my walk of the original labyrinth. However, the 'greater' or dominant narrative they exercise upon the walker is one that I struggled to follow. This may have been because I was attempting to apply the Veriditas method of walking the labyrinth, which has more of an emphasis on establishing an alternative narrative devised by the walker themselves. It also could have been due to the fact that the spiritual significance of Jerusalem did not resonate with me in the same way as it would have others who were walking the labyrinth.

Return and reflection

The journey into the Chartres replica had led to the emergence of the centre, whereas the return journey became an emergence of the self. Although satisfied with the experience, I realized quite quickly that I would not be able to find the same centre again. This was all the more heightened by the temporary location of this specific labyrinth, in which the path would soon be rolled up and taken to another space. If the sacred act can determine the sacredness of the location (Wiles 2003: 27), then what of this remained within Lancaster chaplaincy once the labyrinth was removed? It lacked the permanence of the original labyrinth in Chartres, which, serving as a substitute pilgrimage site, is strengthened by a perception of walking a well-trodden path. My own difficulty in walking this particular labyrinth stemmed from me attempting to engage in a non-trip between it and the replication of it I had walked some months before. This was something that ran counter to the function of the original Chartres labyrinth and cathedral, which sought to direct my intention and my perception of the sacred elsewhere. Although there 'is virtually no wrong way to move through the labyrinth', moving beyond it does seem to require specific preparation (Curry 2000: 61).

Both approaches to the Chartres labyrinth and its replicas therefore necessitate two different types of walking towards the sacred. Veriditas emphasizes a means of sauntering that is led by the 'heart and the gut' as Williams referred to it. An intention is made without a sense of knowing where the walker will end up, prompting them to feel their way along the path and trust themselves to devise an alternative narrative. Through this wandering one happens upon a sense of the sacred on their travels, using the labyrinth as a means to provide a sense of direction that can be reflected internally. The stripping away of its non-sited qualities allows for the prospect of recontextualization and re-placement by the walker. However, walking the original Chartres medieval labyrinth is directed by a collective sense of pilgrimage to a single location, in which one reflects 'upon their membership' within a community (Köhler-Ryan 2013: 89). A familiarity with scripture and maps of the period can provide necessary context for the non-trip, in which the walker perceives themselves merging their own path with an already established route.

Leaving the labyrinth

This chapter has evidenced that Robert Smithson's concept of the non-site is an effective model by which to comprehend the medieval labyrinth's ability to facilitate imaginative travel to an elsewhere sacred site. The non-site is the very thing that preserves the sanctity of places, acting as a reliquary for the 'array of matter' which directs attention towards it (Smithson cited in Kaye 2000: 95). Existing as idealized maps, scripture, fragments of hearsay and myth, the 'utopian' ideals (Ostwalt 2012: 90) often associated with sacred places are preserved within the 'No Place' of the non-site (Smithson cited in Kaye 2000: 95). The medieval labyrinth acted as a means for the pilgrim to filter through all this information at their own pace, conscious always of the overarching dominant narrative of the Christian church that surrounded them. This is where the labyrinth's imbrication within the church building becomes all the more important, highlighting how, like the galleries which house Smithson's work (Linsley 2002: 53), the church is always a non-site. For the pilgrim, such a walk requires a different test of endurance to that of a traditional pilgrimage, in that it requires them to perform Jerusalem – a place they may never have visited before.

Expanding studies of the labyrinth beyond that of its medieval iteration, the non-site is also helpful in understanding some of the debates which centre around the reappropriation of this sacred path within the modern labyrinth movement. Lauren Artress's initial replication of the Chartres labyrinth has led to numerous copies existing as permanent or temporary structures within and without places that will exert different associations with it (Ullyatt 2011: 112). The two-dimensionality of these pavement labyrinths has enhanced their portability, meaning that organizations such as Veriditas have been able to subsequently complicate the non-sited qualities of the medieval labyrinth. They encourage the walker to develop their own alternate narrative for the labyrinth and with this perceive their own sense of the sacred in its centre. It is the equivalent of replicating Smithson's non-sites without any of the contextual information that gestures to their site of origin, attention instead placed on the object itself and the universal and mythic qualities it possesses.

After all, the labyrinth as a design has a long-established history of reappropriation, in which the sacred places it purports to symbolize have often shifted location. It also possesses the ability to gesture to multiple places simultaneously, enhancing its allegorical and universal qualities. The Chartres labyrinth's former depiction of the ancient Greek myth of Theseus and the Minotaur evidences the Christian church's reappropriation of the labyrinth pattern, but it also highlights how important the allegorical function of the Cretan labyrinth was in sacralizing Jerusalem for the pilgrim. For Smithson, the site is always pluralized and multifaceted, which gets to the heart of the potential paradox of the original Chartres labyrinth, gesturing to a single location through several different places. These parts remain 'scattered', with the walking of the non-sited labyrinth acting as a process of assemblage (Smithson cited in Kaye 2000: 95).

There are of course some complications with applying Smithson's model, stemming primarily from his method of accruing the non-sites themselves. In his works, there was always an implication that a journey had been made to the non-site with materials or documentation brought back to the gallery space. The labyrinth, conversely, is often devoid of material totems or artefacts from the site in question. This may be due to the physical inaccessibility of the site or simply because it is gesturing to a place that cannot be accessed through any other means than by an act of faith or imaginary travel. Sacred places such as the World of the Dead, heavenly Jerusalem and, indeed, areas of the self cannot be 'walked' to in advance. However, once visited through the labyrinth, Smithson's dialectic can be more readily facilitated and the reflected site can appear all the more closer.

NOTES

1. Pennick also discusses the Dominican mystic Heinrich Suso who developed a meditative means by which to imaginatively visit each station in turn. Termed 'pathworking' or 'guided imagery', one can establish here a type of mental travel akin to Smithson's non-trip.

2. This appears to be quite a common occurrence with Bessie Karras Katsilometes also finding the labyrinth inaccessible.

REFERENCES

Artress, Lauren (2006), *Walking a Sacred Path: Rediscovering the Labyrinth as a Spiritual Practice*, New York: Riverhead Books.

Bloos, Ingrid D. and O'Connor, Thomas St. James (2002), 'Ancient and medieval labyrinth and contemporary narrative therapy: How do they fit?', *Pastoral Psychology*, 50:4, pp. 219–30.

Chaplaincy Centre Lancaster (2018), 'Home', https://www.chaplancs.org.uk/. Accessed 18 July 2018.

Chaudhuri, Una (1997), *Staging Place: The Geography of Modern Drama*, Ann Arbor: University of Michigan Press.

Connolly, Daniel K. (2009), 'Imagined pilgrimage in the itinerary maps of Matthew Paris', *Art Bulletin*, 81:4, pp. 598–622.

Connor, Steve (2009), 'Has the original labyrinth been found?', *Independent*, https://www.independent.co.uk/arts-entertainment/architecture/has-the-original-labyrinth-been-found-1803638.html. Accessed 18 July 2018.

Curry, Helen (2000), *The Way of the Labyrinth: A Powerful Meditation for Everyday Life*, New York: Penguin Compass.

Ferré, Robert (2014), *Chartres Labyrinth Construction Manual*, St Louis: Labyrinth Enterprises.

Friedrich, Rainer (2008), 'Drama and ritual', in J. Redmond (ed.), *Drama and Religion*, Cambridge: Cambridge University Press, pp. 159–224.

Hani, Jean (2000), 'Labyrinths', in J. Villette (ed.) and M. Miller (trans.), *Notre-Dame de Chartres: The Enigma of the Labyrinth*, Chartres: Cathedrale de Chartres, pp. 16–17.

Heard, Henry Fitzgerald (1944), *The Great Fog and Other Weird Tales*, New York: Vanguard Press.

Ingold, Tim (2016), *Lines: A Brief History*, London: Routledge.

Jones, Alan (1998), 'Letter from Alan Jones', *Veriditas*, https://www.veriditas.org/Letter-from-Alan-Jones. Accessed 13 July 2018.

Katsilometes, Bessie Karras (2010), 'My spiritual journey: Circling the spiral', *Psychological Perspectives*, 53, pp. 189–206.

Kaye, Nick (2000), *Site-Specific Art*, London: Routledge.

Kociatkiewicz, Jerzy and Kostera, Monika (2015), 'Into the labyrinth: Tales of organisational nomadism', *Organisational Studies*, 36:1, pp. 55–71.

Köhler-Ryan, Renée (2013), 'The beginning that is already an end: Finding the significance of labyrinthine travel', in A. Norman (ed.), *Journeys and Destinations: Studies in Travel, Identity, and Meaning*, Cambridge: Cambridge Scholars Publishing, pp. 87–108.

Labyrinth Company (2018), 'Chartres Replica™', https://www.labyrinthcompany.com/products/chartres-replica. Accessed 13 July 2018.

Linder, Mark (1999), 'Sitely windows: Robert Smithson's architectural criticism', *Assemblage*, 39, pp. 6–35.

Linsley, Robert (2002), 'Minimalism and the city: Robert Smithson as a social critic', *RES: Anthropology and Aesthetics*, 41, pp. 38–55.

Matthews, William Henry (1922), *Mazes and Labyrinths*, London: Longmans, Green.

Osbourne, Grant R. (2006), *The Hermeneutical Spiral: A Comprehensive Introduction to Biblical Interpretation*, 2nd ed., Downers Grove: InterVarsity Press.

Ostwalt, Conrad (2012), *Secular Steeples: Popular Culture and the Religious Imagination*, 2nd ed., London: Bloomsbury.

Pennick, Nigel (1990), *Mazes and Labyrinths*, London: Robert Hale.

Pettena, Gianni (1996), 'Conversation in Salt Lake City', in J. Flam (ed.), *Robert Smithson: The Collected Writings*, Oakland, CA: University of California Press, pp. 297–300.

Serra, Richard (1994), *Writing, Interviews*, Chicago: University of Chicago Press.

Smithson, Robert ([1968] 1996), 'A provisional theory of non-sites', in J. Flam (ed.), *Robert Smithson: The Collected Writings*, Oakland, CA: University of California Press, p. 364.

Solnit, Rebecca (2002), *Wanderlust: A History of Walking*, London: Verso.

Tilley, Christopher, Hamilton, Sue and Bender, Barbara (2000), 'Art and the re-presentation of the past', *Journal of the Royal Anthropological Institute*, 6:1, pp. 35–62.

Toner, Paul and Smithson, Robert ([1970] 1996), 'Interview with Robert Smithson', in J. Flam (ed.), *Robert Smithson: The Collected Writings*, Oakland, CA: University of California Press, pp. 234–41.

Ullyatt, Tony (2011), ' "Gestures of approach": Aspects of liminality and labyrinths', *Literator*, 32:2, pp. 103–34.

Veriditas (2018), 'Veriditas history', Veriditas, https://www.veriditas.org/Veriditas-History. Accessed 13 July 2018.

Villette, Jean (2000), 'The enigma of the labyrinth at Chartres Cathedral', in J . Villette (ed.) and M. Miller (trans), *Notre-Dame de Chartres: The Enigma of the Labyrinth*, Chartres: Cathedrale de Chartres, pp. 4–12.

Wiles, David (2003), *A Short History of Western Performance Space*, Cambridge: Cambridge University Press.

Zimmermann, Jens (2015), *Hermeneutics: A Very Short Introduction*, Oxford: Oxford Press.

3

In Peril and Pilgrimage: Exploring the Experience of Suffering in Journeys Endured

Simon Piasecki

This chapter represents something of a new direction, for me at least. For some sixteen years I have been interested in the impact of diaspora on the nature of identity: in the physical sense the crossing of a territory, often fleeing across mountains and at night, the leaving and arrival, and in the spiritual sense the death of one thing and the birth of another. With this chapter, I shift from the need to endure a perilous crossing, to the wish to do this as an act of absolution or a seeking of enlightenment: a pilgrimage. The chapter only really opens that frame, introducing some of my intended objects and hypothesizing simply that in respect of pilgrimage, a sacred place is essentially activated by the journey to it. Having said this, it is also my aim to question the primacy of that sacred space over the embodiment of the journey itself. These elements are not mutually exclusive of course, but traditionally the journey is to and in service of the sacred space; but if we reverse this view, then we appreciate the cruciality of movement and endurance in spiritual transformation, while the space of arrival witnesses, 'publishes' and indulges this. One intention of this chapter is to problematize the opposition between the secular and the religious in the context of endurance and pain, but since this is a crucial element of transformation, we shall also see that the physical pragmatism of a secular journey may lead to a realization very similar to that of the religious pilgrimage.

I also wonder here whether the term 'spiritual' is inseparable from the 'romantic'. The latter is not often an esteemed term, indeed as an art student it was somewhat of an accusation that questioned the integrity or authenticity of work; it implied unnecessary embellishment, sentimentality and impracticality. Spirituality is also a contested term, particularly in its implications for healthcare, which is relevant here when one considers the pilgrimage on a basis of need, wish fulfilment and transition from one place in life to another. Pattison and Swinton considered the contestation of the value of spirituality in nursing, concluding that its cruciality is also formed out of the very subjectivity that causes it to be contested in the first place, even the ontology of its actual existence. Rejecting the pragmatism of post-religious pragmatism, in the context of healthcare, they tell us that 'the task is to listen and to understand the function and direction of the language of spirituality, not to question its validity or right to exist and be used' (Pattison and Swinton 2010: 229). To understand the function of spirituality as a term in respect of this chapter, we should refer its presence to the direction, difficulty and embodied imperative of endured travel. I will embrace the term, even the subjectivity of its romance. I rather enjoy the implication of a romance of hardship, because it has a long history, through many cultural systems of oral storytelling, both religious and secular. I will shift my mode then between the formal and academic, and the deeply personal and creative. In early 2019 I took Lowland Leader training across Anglezarke Moor in Lancashire. We immersed ourselves differentiating lichens, discovered the spot of a Lancaster bomber crash, talked about the Industrial Revolution and came to the ghost hamlet of Higher and Lower Hempshaw's, its ruins lying in abandonment. These things are all at some level romantic and all food for the spirit, earned by miles of placing one foot in front of the other. We walk and we generate meaning.

Walking is the most fundamental of human actions; we place one foot in front of the other and in so doing take ourselves on potentially huge journeys at a pace that allows us to observe. Writing about the Camino de Santiago, Keith Foskett says that 'if [walking] weren't so normal [...], then I would consider it a revelation' (2012: 4). In 2009 skulls and bones from early hominin humans were found in Georgia, which reveal their migration out of Africa some 750,000 years earlier than *Homo erectus* as previously thought. Evolutionary primacy favoured the ability to travel and walk large distances over cognitive intelligence in the early development of mankind. Early human ancestors' success in survival was predicated on their ability to walk rather than the size of the brain. In this sense we can observe that nomadism was a key evolutionary strategy for humankind.

There is a constancy to nomadism, however, that might belie the importance of a particular space, but while we have always travelled, we have also always venerated particular venues and for many different reasons. For example, on a personal level it may be that we hold our birthplace in particular endearment, and any trip to that place revives memory and the 'ache' for it – a nostalgia, a return to the mother. But we also collectively agree on the veneration of certain spaces, again for historical reasons: sites of events that are commemorated. These may be battlefields, but may equally include sports stadiums or simply places where something significant has occurred. Tony Walter considers the fact that the Royal

British Legion formed a Pilgrimages Department in the 1990s, aimed at tours for widows to their loved ones' graves abroad. While this activity is not surprising in itself, Walter observes that the use of the term 'pilgrimage' differs decisively from commercial operators' 'battlefield tours' and recognizes therefore the intentionality of tribute, the presence of grief and the recognition of the widow as pilgrim (2001: 65–69). In the conclusion of the same book, Ian Reader considers hardship and recognizes that while this might exist less in the travel associated with some contemporary pilgrimage, in an age of convenience, there remains the form of emotional hardship associated with the emotional pain of visiting sites of grief and loss. The pain of this should not be underestimated; Reader regards it as 'often vital [to] the development of a pilgrimage' – but can it also be viewed as a public act of penance (2001b: 225)? Pain, both mental and physical, was intrinsic to medieval pilgrimage, and while this is more ambiguous in contemporary and secular contexts, it certainly still plays a role. I will come to this later.

There is no precise contemporary definition of pilgrimage, but clearly a visit undertaken as tribute is not explicitly penitential, while in the context of pilgrimage something endured usually is. But what then is endurance in this context? I would regard pilgrimage as an effective example of Merleau-Ponty's post-Cartesian view of mind-body unity because the two are inseparable; that is to say, from this perspective, any work taken out on the body is also work taken out on the mind. Parallel to Sartre's *Being & Nothingness* (2003), Merleau-Ponty refers to the context of a 'being in itself' and a 'being for itself' (we might think of this as body and then mind) as constituting the 'very essence of existence' and continues with the observation that 'by taking up a present, I draw together and transform my past, altering its significance, freeing and detaching myself from it' (1970: 455). This describes very well for me the efficacy of the pilgrimage, particularly as a meditation. By 'present' in this context I am referring to the importance of the present moment in a pilgrimage, the context of placing one foot in front of the other, the meditational practice of 'nowness'.

I noted in Simon Reeve's fascinating documentary series *Pilgrimage* the number of people on pilgrimage interviewed that described themselves as secular, but also referred to one's inability to escape Self while on the journey (O'Mahony and Mitchell 2015). When Reeve asked what they thought about and felt, the answers were seldom concerned with joy, but much more with the process of guilt, of anger and of loss and a wish to renew. Pilgrimage is a running towards oneself, not away, and the honesty of introspection, the psycho-mirror created by the steady and long footfall of a walk, is an endured space at least inasmuch as we have to face ourselves.

There is a tension between the status of the specific route and the final sacred space in pilgrimage. Some pilgrimages, such as the Kailas yatra in Tibet and

Shikoku Island pilgrimage in Japan, are circumambulatory. Having travelled in the high Himalayas, I read multiple books concerning what is considered a mystical mountain in Tibet, a place of pilgrimage for a fifth of the world's religious population – Mount Kailas, sacred according to Hinduism, Buddhism, Jainism and the older Bonism. In Kailas, we might consider that the sacred space is untouchable, since it is the Kailas mountain that the route surrounds. To complete a *kora* around it takes a Westerner up to five days, walking to altitudes of 18,600 feet (the Everest base camp is at 15,000 feet). Pilgrims die around the mountain on an annual basis because of being ill-equipped and unprepared for the extremes of high-altitude walking. At the most extreme level of pilgrimage, Tibetans perform a prostrated circumambulation of the mountain, laying themselves flat out on the ground throughout the journey. The journey takes the pilgrim up to the plateaus, where cloud burials take place, and across the *Vajra Yogini* field of metaphoric death, where the ground is strewn with the cast-away symbols of attachment and pilgrims can often be seen to rehearse their own death, lying still among the boulder field. Reaching Kailas is in and of itself the largest hurdle, and I wrote an article recently about the pilgrimage concerning the number of pilgrims that die annually, many en route and some around the mountain itself (Piasecki 2019). During 2018 some five hundred pilgrims were trapped due to bad weather on the route back from Kailas, and a similar event had occurred in 2017: in 2017 alone some twenty pilgrims died, many of acute mountain sickness (altitude sickness) that causes cerebral and pulmonary oedemas.[1]

The travel writer Colin Thubron (2012) wrote an engaging account of the journey in *To a Mountain in Tibet*, which while secular and observant in style, contains an unexpected account of his reflections of family, loss and pain while conducting the route, set within or conjured by the spiritual constancy of the pilgrimage. There is a sense that here is a stillness and the permanence of rock stands as a metre to the state of constant change that constitutes life in its journey to death.

Thubron talks about the secular pilgrimage today in the context of self-absolution as a matter of personal survival, although 'a journey', he says, 'is not a cure' (2012: 9–10). Perhaps so, but there is also a huge contemporary growth in secular participation across well-known religious pilgrimage routes. Thubron also reflects that there is an aspect of travelling to a place beyond one's own history and certainly this creates a reflective objectivity; I have a place that I have visited throughout my life, and each time I stand on this particular hilltop, about once a decade, its timelessness raises my own awareness of change (2012: 10).

Like Kailas, the Shikoku Island pilgrimage in Japan is also circular, but while its 88 temples are numbered, the pilgrimage can start wherever the pilgrim chooses, or perhaps disembarks; the point of Shikoku is the completion of the circle, which is eternal. Shikoku, like the Camino de Santiago, concerns distance, being around 750 miles, while the Kailas yatra is 54 miles. Having said this, the journey to Kailas itself is far longer and more remote. Endurance there also concerns surviving at extreme altitudes, and, as I mentioned, every year pilgrims die en route to the mountain. At Shikoku, the *henro* (pilgrim) walks with the spirit of Kōbō Daishi to whom the pilgrimage is dedicated and wears the motto of the pilgrimage: 'We two – pilgrims together' (Statler 1984: 24). Pilgrims wear white clothing, the colour of death, and collect the red temple stamps en route as they visit each temple. While the walk has no single destination, it does require a completion of the circuit. These days some complete it in parts over more than one year, while others use transportation, the physiological ease of which seems to undermine something of the ascetic objective.

The physical endurance and suffering involved in great walks can be read in the musculoskeletal impact on the body. Hopper describes the medieval pilgrim, found and disinterred from his tomb beneath Worcester Cathedral's bell tower in 1986. He wore sturdy thigh-length boots and carried a seven-foot staff, known at that point as a *bourdon*. His physiology itself bore signs that described the use of this staff: he had well-developed shoulder muscles, in particular on the right side, and Hopper adds that there is evidence of inflammation of the shoulder joint, pointing perhaps 'to constant use of the staff and repeated lifting, throwing forward and pushing down on the right arm and shoulder'. This is consistent with long hours of walking, but Hopper adds that 'the heel of the right hand, which would have incurred direct pressure from such a movement, shows evidence of arthritis' (2002: 81). There is something here of the efficacy of repetition in spiritual practice, particularly of a devotee. These physiological marks are evidence of hundreds of hours of repeated movement, that one foot after the other.

Finally, Hopper adds a commentary on his feet, describing the 'take off' movement consistent in walking that deploys a large tendon connected to the big toe; 'in the case of the Worcester Pilgrim, this has formed a significant groove in the bone, much more than usual' (2002: 83). I believe that Hopper is referring here to the halluces longus extensor tendon, and injuries or inflammations associated with this are common among ultrarunners. I enjoy this comparison because I am certainly making a case here for marathons and ultra-events positing a contemporary equivalence to pilgrimage. Diana Webb, also describing the Worcester Pilgrim in her book *Pilgrimage in Medieval England* (2000), points out that he would not have been capable of walking far at the time of his death, in his sixties, but was buried and therefore likely known as a distinguished pilgrim. 'In earlier life', she notes, 'he had been robust and muscular' (Webb 2000: 212).

The Worcester Pilgrim was in his sixties at the time of his death, and his burial, adorned for pilgrimage, might suggest that he had been very active in this regard as an older man. In their paper titled 'Physiology and pathophysiology in ultra-marathon Running', Knechtle and Nikolaidis (2018) describe the typical ultrarunner statistically as being 45 and educated; as I spoke to ultrarunners myself at the beginning of the Midnight Mountain Marathon at Brecon Beacons, I certainly observed that age was a significant factor. These rather weathered runners struck me in much the same way that Butoh dancers and Body Weather training practitioners have in the past: their bodies are lean, thin even, and the muscles sit in an almost transparency of tone at the surface of the skin. One woman in her late fifties told us that she commonly ran 50-mile races cross-country and lived in a mountainous place. With age comes endurance rather than speed, it seems. One embraces the familiar aches, pains and injuries almost as an embodied kinship. For my own part I suffer from a crumbling fracture of the sixth vertebrae and conduct daily exercises to keep it in place, but the pain, which can be considerable, is so familiar it seems a part of my identity. Do I still suffer it then, or is the experience something else?

That the Worcester Pilgrim was an older, arthritic man, buried in his pilgrimage attire, with his *bourdon* at his side, brings me back to Shikoku Island in Japan. It is still a common practice for Japanese pilgrims to be buried in their full attire, which, as I said earlier, is white (although these days most will wear contemporary hiking trousers and shoes on the lower half). Ian Reader describes the traditional clothing for a Shikoku pilgrimage, with the *hakui* (shirt) symbolizing the burial shroud and therefore being fastened on the opposite side to normal, as with the traditional dressing of a corpse. He adds that the broad-brimmed hat, so effective in rain but impractical for modern transport, symbolizes the coffin. Like our Worcester Pilgrim, the *henro* walks with a traditional staff, the *tsue*, which represents the body of the Kōbō Daishi and the foot of which is washed each evening in symbolic washing of the saint's own feet. The staff is also symbolically the pilgrim's own grave marker, and in previous times literally, if they died en route (Reader 2001a: 107–36).

The hero walks in the presence of death on the Shikoku pilgrimage, facing impermanence in the eternal circle of constant change. In this sense, undertaking the pilgrimage is also a relinquishing of the grasping of life. The Shikoku pilgrim's journey represents in itself a fourfold journey to enlightenment that mimics Kōbō Daishi's own story until his death; Reader includes a useful description of this route as a process of travel (2001b: 110),[2] whilst Statler reminds us that the route can be started at any of the temples, so long as the circuit is completed (1984: 26).

Notwithstanding the Shikoku and Kailas pilgrimages, it is tempting to think of pilgrimage as being to somewhere fixed, because of the final sacred space, the object, which is also of course often synonymous with the institution, such as the church. Kailas and Shikoku Island are still places to be reached in and of themselves, and that stasis, that settled permanence, can therefore take on a definite primacy over the issue of movement, and yet it is the movement that is surely the most transformative spiritual aspect, while the space of arrival 'publishes' the fulfilment and the completion and confirms the indulgence.

Focusing on the nomadic, Careri (2005) points out in *Walkscapes* that the earliest architectures of any permanence (monoliths, barrows, circles) were between settlements, rather than within them and as such referred to impermanence and human movement, positioned en route as places of convergence from multiple origins. These were the earliest pilgrimage sites.

These Neolithic sites were consecrated spaces of worship that often also venerated the dead, that is, threshold sites. Recently I visited Newgrange and Knowth in Ireland, both huge burial temples. Before the carved entrance stone of Knowth is a phallic stone, surrounded by a field of stone eggs, and it is believed that these eggs were the pilgrimage offerings of couples wishing for a healthy child, an assumption of its significance perhaps. But this raises also the relationship of the sacred space to an inherent intention for liminal travel; the idea that we will leave, walk and somehow attain something in arrival that makes the journey an essential facet of our experience of that sacred space. If that journey has degrees of difficulty, then the attainment or realization is higher. I imagine the difficulty of carving and carrying those stones to that hillside, distant on foot, as I said, from any settlement, coupled with the pain of a childless marriage and the indulgence of fertility requested. I imagine this childless couple undertaking such a journey and generate a feeling of solidarity with their penitent action – I had recently run a mountain half-marathon with my wife at Brecon, albeit for different reasons, coming down hand in hand (I will write about this shortly). My imagination of this childless couple, as I stood looking at those egg-shaped stones, was of course wholly romantic, but isn't the ardour of the pilgrim also the romanticism that drives the harsher physical reality of their endurance? Pilgrimage places the romance of the spiritual in partnership with physical asceticism. I linked romance to spirituality in the introduction, but it can be reasonably argued to have an etymological link to pilgrimage anyway. Partridge tells us that 'romance' is derived through middle English and French from the vulgar Latin *rōmānicē* (in the roman way), but more fascinatingly, for me, he also suggests that the word 'roam' may derive similarly because of the 'pilgrimages to Rome', although he accepts that there has been some scorn for this (*c.*1958) (1966: 567, 572). This is one of those tantalizing moments in research, to discover that pilgrimage, roaming and romance *might* share a root in language. Certainly the etymological link between 'romance' and 'novel' originates with verses of adventure in the fourteenth and fifteenth centuries; Partridge does tell us as much in his etymological dictionary. Adventure implies a journey.

The liminality of movement, of the journey, has long been associated with philosophical exploration, and this is no truer than in religious texts that present the notion of becoming in respect of their iconic protagonist: the lives of Christ, Muhammad and Buddha all involve the journey as a crucial vehicle to revelation, dissemination and conflict. The penultimate component of the Passion is a journey under great duress, up to the place of crucifixion, and is often played out within promenade performances of 'The Stations of the Cross', wherein the movement of the audience is as of an embodied realization of the meanings of the Passion. Peterson's guide to this combines maps and architectural description of the stations with spiritual meditation and prayer; presented as a walk, it shifts back and forth from religious instruction, meditation and prayer to factual description of the locations, closing the gap between a physical and metaphysical tour of the Passion (1998). But I should take greater care with my application of the term 'liminal' here, if only because the most influential work on pilgrimage in publication, or at least the one most often cited in other works, is *Image and Pilgrimage in Christian Culture* by Victor and Edith Turner (1978). The Turners take care to define the 'liminoid' separately to the 'liminal'. If the liminal is regarded as a mid-stage cultural ritual, a rite of passage as such, then the liminoid is more 'optional', undertaken by choice, perhaps in free time, and is therefore, according to the Turners, associated with more complexly developed cultures (1978: 231). I am reminded here too of Coleman and Eade's theory of voluntary displacement in *Reframing Pilgrimage: Cultures in Motion* (2004). I might well refer, in a more generalized way, to the liminal qualities of a journey, as many performance studies scholars do, but this context of the liminoid is particularly useful here because the matter of choice is at the heart of pilgrimage. Reading Hopper's research on the medieval period, I was struck by how relevant to modern times the problems of wishing to undertake a pilgrimage in the fifteenth century are. Hopper gives the example of Brother Felix Faber (also spelled Fabri), who made two pilgrimages to the Holy Land and recorded his journey closely. He writes about the difficulties faced before leaving, which would remain familiar even today:

> Moreover it was a serious matter for me to ask for leave for so long and so unusual a wandering, and it appeared to me to be almost impossible to obtain it. Nor could I form any idea of how I should raise the money for such an expensive journey.
>
> (Fabri 1892: 3)

The context of personal choice here is crucial and Faber's problem was to account for how a personally auspicious gain was in the interest of others. The other, rather serious, consideration here though is that of chosen danger. To travel has long been associated with taking risk. In its pre-dissimilated Latin form, 'pilgrim' comes from *peregrinus*, and I am interested in the preceding three letters forming 'per'; I have written about this before, with original reference to Careri and am not surprised at the relationship to the pilgrim. 'Per' is variously connected to the journey across or rather through space and of course is also contained in peril, experiment, experience and performance. Careri points out that there is also a natural link to terms that confer a state of knowledge, such as 'well-travelled' (2005: 41). Looking again at my rather coveted copy of Eric Partridge's etymological dictionary,[3] the 'per' prefix, essentially meaning 'through', has an interesting coexistence in a very broad base of languages from the Sanskrit *pari*, old Persian *pariy*, Hittite *para*, Greek *peri* and even Russian *pere*. This notion of 'throughness' does not necessarily always equate to danger directly until we return to the Latin *periculum* and the Greek *peria*, both meaning 'to try' or 'attempt' (Partridge 1966: 485). When we take a contemporary view of a pilgrimage, however arduous, it is useful to recognize that such a journey also involved mortal danger through other lands during centuries past.

Returning to the Latin word *peregrinus*, the 'r' was dissimilated into an 'l' in late Latin, forming *pelegrinus* and meaning simply 'foreigner' (Harper 2018: n. pag.). Therein lies the implicit peril of a long journey to the sacred; to leave ours and to travel through theirs, to negotiate permissions. Pilgrims would often bear emblems in the medieval period that declared their spiritual and non-threatening objective. Famously, the pilgrims of the Camino de Santiago would wear the scallop shell, and this spread to other routes. Such a declaration could also create a fear of divine retribution in those that considered an attack upon them while undertaking a sacred task.

There is fellowship in pilgrimage, despite any original intention to undertake a journey of reflective solitude; certainly as the popularity of pilgrimage increased in the fifteenth century, so did the attraction of its social aspect (Hopper 2002: 11; Stopford 1999). Along with this of course came criticism and the satirical humour described so richly in Chaucer's *Canterbury Tales* (Morris 1985). Chaucer's observations draw out the absurdity of celebration and comfort in the refinery and behaviour of some of his pilgrim characters, including the richly furred monk, the proud bejewelled nun and the wife of bath dressed in fine scarlet: 'in felaweshipe wel koude she laughe and carpe of remedies of love she knew perchaunce, for she koude of that art the olde daunce [*sic*]' (Morris 1985: 5). Chaucer underlines this critical satire by setting characters such as these against the piety and poverty of others. He illustrates very well that while many undertook the pilgrimage, not all observed or even recognized the efficacy of basic discomfort, whether physical or mental, so were any indulgences earned at all?

Most of the contemporary accounts that I have read, including Colin Thubron's circumambulation of Mount Kailas, refer to fellowship as something found but not sought, particularly in the context of a need for self-reflection. This is evident in Thubron's account but also in the key documentaries concerning pilgrimage (O'Mahony and Mitchell 2015; Smith 2015), wherein the social fellowship of travellers is always an irresistible support; they meet along the way, in hostels and camps or in Thubron's case, because they are employed as guides and support. There is also a freedom to be found in being able to confide freely in a stranger, whom there is no obligation to see in the future, and I imagine that routes such as the Camino de Santiago in Spain are a constant space for the exchange of personal testimony. Martin Sheen's fictional portrayal of Tom Avery, walking the Camino in Emilio Estevez's *The Way* (2011), is a moving study of such fellowship overcoming its own resistance in the grief of a father who has lost his son.

The Camino de Santiago is one of the world's oldest continuous pilgrimage routes and certainly existed as such before the Christian context; the route follows the line of Milky Way and, in pre-Christian Celtic history, was most likely undertaken as a walk to the 'ends of the earth' where the sun set over the sea (Hopper 2002: 50). Hopper also suggests that a symbol appearing in the stone-masonry of churches along the route can be interpreted as the sun. This syncretic quality is not surprising though; as with the walk around Kailas or Shikoku, the pilgrim climbs upwards towards the sun, towards the heavens, and is removed from the contexts and rhythms of their regular mortal life. Hills still hold this quality for the weekend walker, the climber, the explorer.

While we refer the pilgrim to holy places, the term also has more secular origins, etymologically speaking, as I described earlier; I am as interested here in reasons for undertaking extreme travel as I am in religious travel. I will perhaps economize the two as spiritual, if we accept that the journey is as key as the arrival, if not more so. I wonder whether the sacred place in and of itself cannot reveal an aspect of potential realization in the visitor without the endured journey to it. The journey then, the endurance of it, is a necessary process in order to gain a level of enlightenment, whatever we believe that to be. For the ultrarunner this is embodied, but no less spiritual in its potential and achievement, and equally a secular walker of the 500-mile Camino de Santiago, stretching from France across the Pyrenees into Spain, will experience something meditative through their aches and pains, just as a religious pilgrim will. The final object, the bones of the apostle St James in Santiago de Compostela, might hold a different import for each, but as the point of arrival after four weeks of arduous walking, it is a spiritual achievement as much as a physical one; the path is necessary.

The most common historical motivation for undertaking the Camino was for redemption, the forgiveness of all sin; the pilgrimage was seen as one of only three that could forgive all sins, the others being Rome and Jerusalem, and after the Muslim armies took control of Jerusalem, the Camino reached its zenith between

900 and around 1350 (Mitchell-Lanham 2015). But this notion of the forgiveness of sin, the indulgence, is arguably not exclusively wrapped up in the remains of St James, but rather in the redemptive suffering of the journey endured, as if one is physically and psychologically paying a price as it were. The walk is long enough for knees to swell, feet to hobble and tendons to become inflamed. There is therefore also typically a journey from energy to its opposite, from comfort and confidence to pain and unsurety and therefore from self-belief to disbelief. These secondary states have to be transcended then if the Camino is to be completed, and it is this transcendence in the diminishment of ego that brings a new understanding and peace to many people. The source of this transcendence is also a communion of spirit with mind, body, weather and landscape; the harmonizing effect as the walker overcomes, finds a rhythm and experiences the care of other pilgrims along the way. A sense of catharsis and love for the beauty and tragedy of life emerges for many and naturally, for the religious, this is a closer proximity to God.

Mitchell-Lanham reflects that during the walk, the word 'camino' is itself deployed to ask for directions or distances and becomes in itself 'semi-sacred' to the pilgrim inasmuch as it stands for that embodied endurance by the end of the journey (2015: xi). Walking huge distances concerns pain and the overcoming of it, and this decisive act bridges the physical and the meta-physical, wherein the *camino* (path) of sand and stones and hills and mud becomes also the inner *camino* of regret and struggle, of pain, beauty and a wish for truths. In the documentary *Walking the Camino* (Smith 2015), there are many spiritual reflections that are not exclusively religious in the Christian context. I was also struck by the number of people that take a pilgrimage, not because they are religiously dedicated, but rather because they have lost a loved one. This is not to deny the specifically Christian context and origin in any way but rather to say that there is a deep human efficacy in the undertaking of pilgrimage, which can be transcendent in a spiritual context, if not a divine one.

In their edited study *Pilgrimage in Popular Culture*, Reader and Walter (2001a) conclude that contemporary pilgrimage has evolved away from the aspect of penitence, with, for example, transportation replacing walking, even in the Japanese circumambulation of Shikoko Island. They make the point that in the medieval era, ascetic hardship was synonymous with the pilgrim, but in the contemporary pilgrimages their book covers, 'and certainly within secular forms [...], the idea of hardship appears to be almost entirely absent, at least in physical terms' (Reader and Walter 2001a: 225). Since its first publication though, in 1993, I would reflect that there has been a phenomenal development of endurance-based fundraising, often performed by people that have lost someone or wish to raise money for the unwell: fun-runs, marathons, triathlons and ultra-events, such as marathons on mountains, at night. I wonder that the development of this is synonymous with the growth of the online business because of course the availability of materials and events is now as immediate as the fundraising itself, sited in specialist social media formats such as Justgiving, or standard online crowd sourcing.

Many people approach these events as amateur athletes, but many also approach them as a physical challenge that embodies an offering to the lost. There is penitence in this because there is often guilt in loss – a helplessness concerning whether we could have done more, a wish perhaps to have said or unsaid things, but also a sense that a physical undertaking gains indulgences against the causality of suffering; it is as if what we ritually endure physically stands in contestation or even battle against that which we have no power over. However secular in nature, fundraising attempts of this nature are deeply spiritual and cathartic. This difficult and self-endangering passing of the body through space concerns 'the necessity for a tangible, visible object' to achieve atonement (Hopper 2002: 30). After I lost my stepfather, whom I loved dearly, to leukaemia, my wife and I did this ourselves, signing up with Brutal Events to run the midnight half-marathon up the Brecon Beacons and raise money for blood disease. I had no idea if I would make it; more-over, the majority of our training had been on flat ground. I certainly suffered the event but was also driven greatly by the 'presence' of my father in a place that he loved; it is not unreasonable to say that we were drawn up ridiculous inclines by loss, memory and a genuine sense of fighting the unfightable. However, we were also drawn by a beautiful sunset and magnificent landscape that felt themselves like a tribute to him, a lovely man; it is this aspect of landscape that creates a space of objective reflection, as we repeat our steps like the stanzas of a prayer, breathing rhythmically through the object of aching pain and burning lungs, feet crunching, knees pounding. As we dropped into the final stretch along the single road of Talybont-on-Usk, pub-goers and spectators applauded. We held hands, in loss and solidarity, I think, and stumbled across the finish line, in quiet disbelief that we had made it at all and a catharsis of tears for my father. We also raised a thou-sand pounds, and while that money is contributed as a real and active resource to charities working to combat illness or support the sick, there is also the aspect of the votive offering, the coin tossed in the well and the wish made to the unseeable, the unknowable, the unfightable. There is pain and regret in such an undertaking.

Returning to Partridge's etymology the listing for 'penitent' directs us straight to that for 'pain'; there is a huge variation of words evolving from the Latin *poena* – the old French *penal*, the middle French *penalité* but also *punnisant*, which is of course the root of the modern English 'punishment'. But the Latin *poenīre* also evolved through *paenitēre*, meaning 'to cause to repent', and so in middle French and English became 'penitent': '*me paenitet*, it causes me regret or repentance' (Partridge 1966: 463). The more Gallic Old French *peneance* became the modern 'penance'. I cannot resist adding that the Latin *poena* that we started with became the Old English *pīn*, meaning penalty or pain from whence Partridge tells us *pīnian* (relating to 'pinion' perhaps?) meant to torment and to suffer torment. From this we also derive other words of sufferance, such as to 'pine'.

While penitence is clearly at the heart of human motivation for the pilgrimage, the devout can also earn indulgences. In Rome Catholic pilgrims may, on auspicious dates, be offered a plenary indulgence, removing all of the temporal punishment of sin after death, in return for worship at the correct places, confession, voluntary work and an offering made. This is penitential inasmuch as the body endures in order to make the requisite offering. Of course, while the efficacy of fundraising is clear, the religious offerings also maintain the institutions of religion – pilgrimage has always been lucrative and this generated a huge industry in medieval relics, which continues even today. Like the fundraising for charities, money is given to support morally good work. In medieval Santiago de Compostela, Hopper tells us that only cash and jewellery were acceptable (2006: 49).

Whatever this monetary offering, in pilgrimage there is also a proportionate 'worthiness' gained by a long, arduous route and means of travel; an absolution. From the theological standpoint a pilgrimage serves to absolve through the endured journey, reaching towards spiritual enlightenment, achieving an auspicious blessing through an act of endurance that visits and therefore serves the sacred place. In the medieval context the pilgrimage may even have been ordered by a higher office; as early as 853 AD 4-year-old Alfred (the Great) was sent to Rome by (and possibly with) his father, the Saxon King Aethelred. The arduousness and peril of that journey is difficult to imagine now.

From a secular perspective there is an equal power in achieving the ends of an endured journey, perhaps simply the first half-marathon of a new runner or the growing community of ultrarunners. Certainly there has been an increase in the past decade of online fundraising for events of this nature, often associated with the illness or death of a loved one, as mentioned earlier. We raise impressive amounts that correlate with a need to reconcile ourselves with powerlessness in the face of illness, an expression of defiance against the nature of things. While the money is pregiven, the endurance of difficulty is now intrinsic to a feeling that we have done something with our whole physical and spiritual beings in a meta-battle of our morality against that which is without cognisance. In its attempt to communicate with the incommunicable, this is quasi-religious.

What develops also contains the possibility of a physical addiction, growing in scale and challenge; having run that first half-marathon last June, over the Brecon Beacon mountains, I talked with fellow runners who considered it purely practice for the 50-mile runs that they regularly undertook; lean, weathered people with knotted muscles. Perhaps this development of ever greater challenges is subject to a law of diminishing returns and the liminal gain is relative to the perspective of the individual. While writing this I realized that the most moving example of gain was so close to me that I had not considered its clear relevance, because it concerns my youngest children.

For 53 years children, young Scouts, as a matter of fact, have taken part in the Cheshire Hike, navigating themselves across the county over a two-day period. This sounds modest until we consider the relative scale of its achievement. The hike is undertaken by teams comprising of two children each, carrying full packs weighing 13 kilograms, including camping and cooking equipment. The juniors, 11-year-olds, walk 40 kilometres over two days, self-navigating the byways and footpaths using compass and map. My son started out this way and continued until at age 15 he undertook the senior-plus challenge of 60 kilometres. My younger daughter has now followed suit on the junior and intermediate routes. They train for some months prior, building up their physical resilience and learning to follow grid-referenced routes, pacing and compass bearings. While the training is adult led, the destination of the actual hike is kept strictly confidential until the day of the event. On that day, parents must drive their child to a starting point and leave. The children have their equipment checked and weighed and have to plan their route under close inspection, but at their individual start time they are simply sent on their way. Five hundred children are sent out in twos, from three starting points, on routes across Cheshire, parents and leaders alike placing their trust in the children's self-sufficiency for the first time in their lives. They walk, they make mistakes, they retrace their steps, adding miles on in some cases, and they are counted through sporadic checkpoints at 6-kilometre intervals. From the parent's perspective, which I have experienced, this is all rather traumatic; contact is prohibited and so we go about our weekend, worried, aware of their synchronicity moment by moment, on some pathway or in their thin sleeping bag on a cold night. Their arrival at the finish is therefore an emotionally charged event for the parents, as the children emerge from the countryside, often limping and mud-ridden. There are really two liminal realizations to this 'pilgrimage'. For the parent the realization that their child can cope on his or her own acts as a rite of passage; they have grown up in some fundamental aspect and astonish us as we see them anew. Children tend to take things rather more in their stride, and the development in them is more subtly realized, but no less impactful; they have taken responsibility for their navigation of unfamiliar space, for food and shelter.

Their arrival at the finish line is certainly marked by exhaustion and parents are far more excited for them than they are at that moment for themselves; they just want to sit! Some have fallen in streams, some are covered head to toe in mud, many have suffered severe blisters. It is all very moving. The site of course is not sacred intrinsically, usually a school field with an arena roped off. The children, having arrived, are brought together into this arena to be applauded by families and awarded neckerchiefs. In this fashion something important is consecrated, and perhaps the slow effect is both a growth in confidence and collaboration but also an extended spatial consideration of their relevance 'out there'.

In this way, as with the Camino de Santiago and the meta-death of Kailas, something is left and something else is born anew. These kinds of pilgrimages are a gestation that leads to a re-emergence, only after a process of formation, forging if you will, through degrees of sufferance. What is certainly difficult for the parents whose children undertake the Cheshire Hike is to relinquish the helping hand that would ensure their success. The children themselves have to cope with the prospect of *not* completing the route; some simply need a little talk at the base camp and a slightly firmer urging off into their second day. In this way, in 2018, I saw a young Scout, tired and lacking self-belief, in tears at the prospect of beginning that second day of walking, receive a few words from leaders at the camp that were enough for her to decide to try. As I arrived at the closing ceremony in the late afternoon I was deeply moved to see that not only had she found the courage and tenacity to complete her walk, with her teammate of course, but they had won both the shield and medal for their junior category. The evident transformation was not lost on any of us, not least her parents I suspect, and this was very much a big moment for a small person.

Ultimately we walk alone in life, in an embodied sense at least, and this is a difficult truth for the parent, but the efficacy of suffering (or pain if we wish for that link to penitence) has both a physical and a mental aspect. In pain on the walk the pilgrim faces mortality, thinks and walks, as I wrote earlier, towards themselves, which is not necessarily a pleasant or easy undertaking. In sixteenth-century Japan, the master swordsman Yagyu Munenori wrote that as the foundation of thoughts, 'the mind is initial. The mind is prior. The very first thought is the initial act. Therefore it is the initiating initiative. This is the ultimate. The very first thought is the foundation of all acts' (2003: 44). Munenori illustrates the evident recognition of the power of 'right' mind in a physical endeavour, but refers this to a phenomenological decision in the present moment – mind the 'initiator'. Evidently it was the mind of the young Scout, who found herself in physical and mental difficulty, that initiated action despite this on that second day. But the post-Cartesian view of Merleau-Ponty removes mind as the primer, because the body and mind are in unity, because all knowledge begins in embodiment and suffering therefore becomes knowledge. Rebecca Solnit (2002), who writes so prolifically on walking, reflects on pilgrimage in her book *Wanderlust*. She discusses here a reconciliation between the spiritual and the material, since 'pilgrimage unites belief and action, thinking with doing', and while we remain bewildered about 'how to walk towards forgiveness or healing or truth, we do know how to walk towards an object' (Solnit 2002: 50). While the premise of a pilgrimage might differ, then, the necessity of the journey remains as a crucial and intrinsic activation in the pilgrims' final proximity to the (sacred) object of their travel, whatever or wherever that may be. I'm reminded again of Pattison and Swinton's (2010) defence of the crucial, cloudy subjectivity of spirituality in its application to nursing, because it serves the destination, which in that case is recovery and, like any journey, is something to be endured.

Ultimately, as we walk, we generate meaning out of the meaningless of nature, we compose and recompose those stories and connect our aches and pains to the catharsis of a 'liminoid' transition (Turner 1982), a meta-death intending to raise or renew us. The endured journey is by its very definition a romance, published as it were by its destination at the point of completion. In this very real sense, the route itself, with its latent history of footfall and suffering, becomes the genuine sacred space.

NOTES

1. This was variously reported by news agencies such as NDTV: https://www.ndtv.com/india-news/kailashmansarovar-yatra-over-500-pilgrims-stuck-while-returning-from-kailash-mansarovar-1878678 (www.ndtv.com); Business Standard: https://www.business-standard.com/article/current-affairs/two-pilgrims-dead-1-500-strandedalong-kailash-mansarovar-route-in-nepal-118070301268_1.html (www.business-standard.com); and India.com: https://www.india.com/news-travel/kailash-mansarovar-yatra-faces-yet-another-hurdle-gets-suspended-3228513/. Accessed 16 December 2020.

2. Temples are numbered and split between four provinces, some close by and others up to 60 kilometres apart. The fourfold process begins with *Hosshin* wherein the mind becomes awakened to the path to enlightenment (temples 1–23), followed by *Shugyō* which provides the spiritual and ascetic training necessary to awaken the mind (temples 24–39). Then *Bodai* represents the dawn of realization (temples 40–65) before full enlightenment is achieved with *Nehan* (temples 66–68).

3. Partridge's *Origins: A Short Etymological Dictionary of Modern English* (1966) was first published in 1958 and, despite the title, is a large volume that traces words through a huge number of linguistic origins, including those as broad as Manx and Finno-Ugric, but also more obviously Anglo-Saxon, Latin and Old German.

REFERENCES

Careri, Francesco (2005), *Walkscapes: Ela Andar Como Practica Estetica/Walking as an Aesthetic Practice*, Barcelona: Editorial Gustave Gili, SA.

Coleman, Simon and Eade, John (eds) (2004), *Reframing Pilgrimage: Cultures in Motion*, London: Routledge.

Estevez, Emilio (2011), *The Way*, USA: Icon Productions.

Fabri, Felix (1892), *The Book of the Wanderings of Brother Felix Fabri*, trans. A. Stewart, vol. VII, London: Palestine Pilgrims Text Society.

Foskett, Keith (2012), *The Journey in Between*, Kindle ed., n.p.: Createspace.com.

Harper, Douglas (2018), *Online Etymology Dictionary*, http://etymonline.com/index. php?term=pilgrim&allowed_in_frame=0. Accessed 20 May 2018.

Hopper, Sarah (2002), *To Be a Pilgrim: The Medieval Pilgrimage Experience*, Stroud: Sutton Publishing Ltd.

Knechtle, Beat and Nikolaidis, Pantelis T. (2018), 'Physiology and pathophysiology in ultra-marathon running', *Frontiers in Physiology*, 9:634, June, https://www.ncbi.nlm.nih.gov/ pmc/articles/PMC5992463/. Accessed 1 June 2019.

Merleau-Ponty, Maurice (1970), *The Phenomenology of Perception*, trans. C. Smith, London: Routledge.

Mitchell-Lanham, Jean (2015), *The Lore of the Camino de Santiago: A Literary Pilgrimage*, Minneapolis, MN: Two Harbours Press.

Morris, William (ed.) (1985), *The Kelmscott Chaucer*, Ware: Omega Books Ltd.

Munenori, Yagyu (2003), *The Life-Giving Sword*, trans. W. Scott Wilson, Tokyo: Kodansha International Ltd.

O'Mahony, Damien and Mitchell, Chris (2015), *Pilgrimage with Simon Reeve*, DVD, UK: IMC Vision Ltd.

Partridge, Eric (1966), *Origins: A Short Etymological Dictionary of Modern English*, London: Routledge and Kegan Paul Ltd.

Pattison, Stephen and Swinton, John (2010), 'Moving beyond clarity: Towards a thin, vague, and useful understanding of spirituality in nursing care', *Nursing Philosophy*, 11:4, pp. 226–37.

Peterson, John (1998), *A Walk in Jerusalem: Stations of the Cross*, Harrisburg, PA: Morehouse Publishing.

Piasecki, Simon (2019), 'A mountain as multiverse: Circumnavigating the realities and meta-realities of a Kailas pilgrim', *Performance Research Journal: On Mountains*, 24:3, pp. 16–23.

Reader, Ian (2001a), 'Dead to the world', in I. Reader and T. Walter (eds), *Pilgrimage in Popular Culture*, New York and Basingstoke: Palgrave, pp. 107–36.

Reader, Ian (2001b), 'Conclusions', in I. Reader and T. Walter (eds), *Pilgrimage in Popular Culture*, New York and Basingstoke: Palgrave, pp. 220–46.

Sartre, Jean-Paul (2003), *Being and Nothingness: An Essay on Phenomenological Ontology*, London: Routledge.

Smith, Lydia B. (2015), *Walking the Camino: Six Ways to Santiago*, Victoria, AU: Umbrella Entertainment.

Solnit, Rebecca (2002), *Wanderlust: A History of Walking*, London: Verso.

Statler, Oliver (1984), *Japanese Pilgrimage*, London: Picador.

Stopford, Jennie (ed.) (1999), *Pilgrimage Explored*, York: York Medieval Press.

Thubron, Colin (2012), *To a Mountain in Tibet*, London: Vintage.

Turner, Victor (1982), *From Ritual to Theatre: The Human Seriousness of Play*, New York: PAJ Publications.

Turner, Victor and Turner, Edith (1978), *Image and Pilgrimage in Christian Culture*, Oxford: Basil Blackwell.

Walter, Tony (2001), 'War grave pilgrimage', in I. Reader and T. Walter (eds), *Pilgrimage in Popular Culture*, New York and Basingstoke: Palgrave, pp. 63–91.

Webb, Diana (2000), *Pilgrimage in Medieval England*, London and New York: Hambledon & London.

PART 2

BREATHING

breathe (v.)
'to draw air into and expel it from the lungs; to inhale and exhale (a scent, etc.)',
*c.*1200, not in Old English, but it retains the original Old English vowel of its
source word, breath. To *breathe (one's) last* 'die' is from 1590s. To *breathe down
the back of (someone's) neck* 'be close behind' is from 1946.

(etymonline.com)

4

Acting Atmospheres:
The Theatre Laboratory and the Numinous

Ilaria Salonna

Preamble about the importance of atmosphere in laboratory work

As we talk about the atmosphere in acting technique, it is fundamental to determine first how to conceive the space for this activity. The space I refer to in this chapter is the one consecrated to the creative work of the actor. This space of creation, where everything is *in fieri*, process and pure potentiality, extends beyond the borders of the place of the scene or rehearsal room, while it involves, at the same time but on different levels, the individual life of the artist and the people 'present there'. The performance on stage is still a far moment on the working timeline, as well as the aim of formalizing the artistic material into a *mise en scène*, for which *les repetitions* (rehearsals), as they are called in French, are to start. In the rehearsal room, the artists are training the technique of transferring on stage the original potentiality of the process of creation, always active and new, but at the same time with the aim to be objective and repeatable.

This creative work relates mainly to the theatre laboratories tradition that sometimes is also defined under the movement of the Great Reform of Theatre[1] which started at the beginning of the twentieth century. In this tradition, research and pedagogy play a primary role, while the realization of a theatre production has secondary importance. The performance open to an audience is rather conceived as a moment for showing research results outside the space of the laboratory. The working space becomes a symbol for the creative work, while this finds its own reasons in the process of creation itself, which cannot be confined to the physical space of a room and quantifiable working hours.

More than a place, the theatre laboratory is a methodological approach to artistic work. This idea is the main trait of this tradition and does not concern only the training as an application of the master's teachings and rules, but it is rather the constant and genuine research in 'dialogue' with those rules and principles previously applied or just discovered. The theatre laboratory work is based on an inductive process, which has the visible aim of advancing in the knowledge of the artistic practice. In this case art can assume the connotation of the Greek word *technè*.[2]

The stress on the process and the continuous questioning of the artistic research in the theatre laboratory can be approached from the culture of laboratories in general, both scientific and para-scientific, such as those of the alchemists. The comparison of theatre laboratories with those of alchemists is already known (Schino 2013). Antonin Artaud, as well as Jacques Copeau, refer to alchemists in their writings. The same comparison can be applied to the pedagogical and artistic work of all the reformers of the theatre in the twentieth century: Stanislawski, but also Limanowski of the Reduta Theatre in Poland in the same years; later Grotowski and others who, directly rooted in the aforementioned tradition for cultural and historical reasons, made the laboratory the centre of their activity, closed to the public and grounded in the cooperation of an ensemble of people.

In the book *The Formation of the Scientific Mind*, about the obstacles to the development of scientific thinking, Bachelard mentions the alchemist laboratory as an example of a more genuinely research-oriented attitude than the rigid positivistic assumptions of modern sciences. He underlines the 'psychological resistance' (Bachelard [1953] 2002: 55) of the culture of alchemy against the objective scientific thought of modern sciences. Bachelard's critic rationalism, which he called the 'philosophy of no', the title of one of his books, challenges the dogmatism of the positivistic idea of science. He pays attention to poetic and para-scientific thinking, where the thought never stops to question the reality. The stress given to the continuous dialectic based on obstacles to the rational thinking, is according to Bachelard, the characteristic of the scientific mind. This dialectic has the form of a rhythm that is present in all materiality.

According to Bachelard, we perceive matter as the rhythm of the chemical exchanges in it, which find their consistency in frequencies and vibrations. Beside the scientific evidence of the vibrating character of the matter, Bachelard underlines an important philosophical principle that can have a resonance with acting and performance: we can see the presence of a natural process only from the effects generated by it. That is why he suggests the study of all materiality through 'rhythmanalysis'. According to Bachelard, rhythmanalysis 'stems from a general metaphysical view' ([1950] 2000: 139) and opens also a perspective on the intersection between theory and practice, as well as between thought and embodied action.

As in the alchemic culture, also in the tradition of theatre laboratory, the research on materiality plays an important part. A relevant example is Jerzy

Grotowski's work with the performer's body and physical actions. Grotowski focused a lot of his attention and energies on the preparatory work of actors, which was inspired by 'all the major actor-training methods of Europe and beyond' ([1967] 1997: 28). Exactly as in the principle pointed out by Bachelard on rhythmanalysis, Grotowski believed that what is visible in the natural process of the performer's action consists in a rhythmical score of impulses. Like Grotowski, for whom 'a man in an elevated spiritual state uses rhythmically articulated signs' ([1967] 1997: 31), Bachelard suggests that 'we shall moreover have a better sense of the rhythmic movement of life if we take it at its summits', because 'the higher the psyche rises, the greater its wave movement' ([1950] 2000: 144, 145).

Bachelard believes that there is always a moral implication in the alchemists' research, which requires complete honesty on the part of the one preparing an experiment:

> We believe that were we to look at all the advice which abounds in the practice of alchemy and interpret it, as it seems still possible to do, in its objective and subjective ambivalence, we would come to establish a pedagogy that is in some respects more truly human than the purely intellectualist pedagogy of positive science. Indeed, alchemy is on the whole not so much an intellectual initiation but rather a moral one. [...] This spiritual enlightenment and moral initiation do not constitute a mere training course intended to help positive progress to be made in the future. The best themes of moral contemplation and the clearest symbols of a scale of inner perfection are to be found through working, in the slow and gentle handling of matter and the alternation of dissolving and crystallizing, like the rhythm of day and night. Nature can be admired in extension, in heaven and earth. And nature can be admired in intension, in its depth and in the play of its mutations of substance. Clearly though, this kind of wonderment, wonderment that goes deep, is bound up with the meditation of an inner life. All the symbols of objective experience can immediately be translated into symbols of subjective culture.
>
> ([1953] 2002: 57)

The continuous oscillation between objective and subjective dimensions is a key point in the value of alchemic culture. The alchemists embody an attitude for which research is a raison d'être, the main purpose of the work:

> Never were the qualities of self-sacrifice, integrity, patience, scrupulous method, and relentless labour so closely bound together as in the work of alchemists. Nowadays, it seems that those who work in laboratories can detach themselves more easily from their work. Their emotional lives are no longer mixed up with their scientific lives. Their laboratory is no longer at home, in attic or cellar. They leave

it in the evening just as one leaves an office, and they go home to their families, to other cares and other joys.

([Bachelard 1953] 2002: 58)

Associating the alchemic culture to theatre laboratories means upholding the sense of a deep and committed research, with a strong collaborative ethos of all laboratory members, necessarily honest in feelings and without egoistic compromises. This attitude builds up the laboratory community, which is not just the physical space in which the members come together.

As Latour explains in his anthropological analysis of the 'laboratory life' (Latour and Woolgar 1986), which I here extend to the theatrical context, those who do not share this specific attitude, even if they are physically present in the same space and interactive with the others, de facto are not part of the laboratory and do not contribute to its life. The space of the laboratory is rather the atmosphere of the creative work, the 'sacred area' in which some people in their differences find a common ground for shared research. Such a space lives on in those who come into relation with it, both inside and outside the bounds of a physical place.

The distinction inside-outside is fundamental in the definition of the relations between the community of the laboratory (ensemble) and the rest of the society. A particular role is given to language and the possibilities to speak 'outside' the laboratory about the work done 'inside'. A paradox appears: the laboratory work is based on research, but the process of research in itself cannot be told, but rather lived. It is possible only to communicate the results of this process. This paradox is more evident when the focus of attention is on elements such as atmosphere, which are related to the living presence, but they are also the object of technical research in the laboratory. It is essential to acknowledge this liminal character of atmosphere in relation to acting technique, in order to talk about it.

Having been myself a member of the laboratory of Anatoli Vassiliev, I would rightly consider the Russian director to be part of the theatre laboratories tradition. For decades, along with his work as theatre director, he conducted research and developed with his actors a system on dramaturgy and acting technique.[3]

Atmosphere and the space as living presence

Atmosphere is a spatial category, and it is usually accompanied by the use of verbs related to the space, such as to fulfil, to flood out, to surround. In daily life, it is common to talk about atmosphere in relation, for instance, to the air or the climate of a place, a certain historical period, a personal memory and so forth. Beside the original Greek word, in many languages there is more than one expression referring to atmosphere, thus showing all the nuances that this concept can assume: for example, the word *stimmung* in German, *milieu* in French or *nastrój* in Polish.

Spatiality is the keyword for understanding why atmosphere is so fundamental for a consideration of feelings in general, and for the way to bring them out in acting technique in particular. Even if considered as a spatial category, there is a distinction between atmosphere and physical space. When perceived atmospherically, the space is assuming the character of a living entity that breathes, interacts and embraces objects and people: 'Atmospheres are evidently what are experienced in bodily presence in relation to person, things or in spaces' (Böhme 2017: 17).

Following Mikhail Chekhov's point of view on acting, that is, the actor's point of view, any creative action is impossible without feeling the space atmospherically. In order to support this thesis, I consider the neo-phenomenological thinking on atmosphere by Hermann Schmitz and Gernot Böhme.

The aim of framing the acting technique of atmosphere with(in) neo-phenomenological thinking is twofold: on one hand, it can offer a strong theoretical base to the technical process of creation of an atmosphere, which for the actor is lived but at the same time perceived as an external object; on another hand, it underlines how the artistic practice in the laboratory can be effectively a work of research that can be complementary, and not opposed, to the reflection of theoreticians. In this respect, and as we said, the work of laboratory finds in the creative atmosphere of research its own reason for existing.

There are two analogous points concerning atmosphere in the neo-phenomenological analysis and in acting technique: the primary importance of the feeling of one's own presence, and the idea of a pre-categorial and pre-linguistic set of shared images and perceptions that form the vital impulse.

To feel one's own presence is to perceive oneself in an 'affective situation': this is the atmospheric feeling, which is at the coincidence of the five moments: here, now, to be, this one, me (Schmitz [2009] 2011: 54). The happening of this coincidence is the 'primitive presence', which recognizes as its own any affective engagement. According to new phenomenology 'emotions are atmospheres poured out spatially that move the felt (not the material) body' (Schmitz 2011: 247). In neo-phenomenology there are two dimensions of the bodily experience: the felt body (*Leib*) and the material one (*Körper*). The atmospheric feeling is felt in one's own body, the felt body.

The etymology of *Leib* is from *Leben*, to live. The felt body has a peculiar dynamic based on a vital impulse. If we concentrate on the dynamic of the perception of our own felt body, it is possible to feel that the vital impulse is made up of forces, mostly of contraction and expansion, which are interwoven but also reciprocally autonomous. The vital impulse is not only felt individually, but it can create a common communication, always based on the felt body level of perception. The communication at the level of felt body is furthermore opened and addressed by the vital impulse when it connects figures separated in the space, for instance, in the exchange of gazes (Schmitz [2009] 2011: 55, 58, 59). In acting, this type of communication is not only the condition of empathy, but it works rather as tuning, creating a channel of direct exchange, a sort of affective 'highway' (Richards 2009: 130).

New phenomenology finds inspiration in Rudolf Otto's critique of the rational. The metaphysical feeling of the numinous, as defined by Otto, shows one of the most fundamental points of the new phenomenology of Hermann Schmitz, which consists in the exposure of oneself without limits to the influence of atmosphere. The numinous is the specific feeling of the holy that Otto associates with the experience of being in the presence of a *numen*: 'the numinous is thus felt as objective and outside the self' ([1923] 1958: 11).

As pointed out by Griffero, 'A theory of the spatiality of feelings cannot but acknowledge its debt towards the theory, also aesthesiologic, of the numinous' (2014: 73). Some places can have a numinous atmosphere more than others, but for sure any place possesses a certain atmosphere, numinous or not, and this is felt always as something impossible to escape from. Rather, it imposes a certain 'authority' from the point of view of a prevalent aesthetic quality (Griffero 2016: 97). In the Latin tradition, *numen* or *genius loci* were the terms used to refer to a living metaphysical presence inhabiting a place, also called the spirit of the place.

Identifying one's own atmospheric feelings with the presence of a *genius loci* can imply some unconscious associations between one's individuality and the place itself. However, this does not mean to perceive the space as an extension of one's own individuality, thus excluding the idea of extraneity. Feeling the space atmospherically places the subject in a special 'disposition' (Böhme [2001] 2010: 130) for which the inside is open to the outside and vice versa. The atmosphere, even in a close relation with the space, implies that the subjectivity discovers itself in the vastity of an external extension, rather than being conceived as a pre-existing objective structure (like for the Kantian transcendentals) separated from the environment. This relation explains the physical resonance of the perception of a living space, while coming to a psychological state in which the aesthetic feeling corresponds to a quasi-religious feeling, a sense of devotion (Griffero 2016: 226).

Atmospheres show the externality of feelings. They are in the space and can be perceived outside and collectively, although they are *quasi*-objective, while the atmospheric feeling can be felt only by the individual.[4] Atmospheres show instead how any subjective feeling is effused in the space outside the limits of one's own body. This is in contradiction with the common assumption about the supposed interiority of emotions and feelings and the Kantian definition of space as a transcendental category.

The subjective is instead reconsidered here in an anti-psychologistic sense, thanks to the centrality given to atmosphere. According to the neo-phenomenological point of view, atmosphere is at the very basis of the process that leads to the ordinary perception of things. This process has the characteristic of a movement of material condensation,[5] from something vague to something concrete and defined. Once the atmosphere has been perceived as feeling of oneself in the here and now of an affective situation, it loses its vagueness, especially its pervasive presence in the space. The passage from the atmospheric feeling to the concrete thing as an objectual pole of perception happens in any perception (Böhme [2001] 2010: 193).

The awareness of the presence of something or someone else comes after the condensation of an atmospheric feeling. This process of condensation happens even in the frame of acting technique. An action expressed in a gesture or in a word is then perceived as something external that has presence in the space, a 'voluminosity'. Böhme explains how this is according to the classic ontology:

> In the classical ontology of the thing, form is thought of as something limiting and enclosing, as that which encloses inwardly the volume of the thing and outwardly limits it. The form of a thing, however, also exerts an external effect. It radiates as it were into the environment, takes away the homogeneity of the surrounding space and fills it with tensions and suggestions of movement. In the classical ontology the property of a thing was thought to be its occupation of a specific space and its resistance to other things entering this space. The extension and volume of a thing, however are also externally perceptible; they give the space of its presence weight and orientation. The volume, that is, the voluminosity of a thing, is the power of its presence in the space.
>
> (2017: 19)

After a series of different perceptions, this voluminosity becomes something that can have an interrelation with us and bring a renovated awareness of our subjectivity. This process is characterized by the continuous shifting between objectivity and subjectivity, and it is based on distance, differentiation and condensation. Thanks to the differentiation between our felt body and the thing, we can start to perceive it more concretely as a new physical reality in relation with our material body (körper).

The word or the gesture enacted by an actor, and thus perceived externally as 'objectivity', can be considered 'the concrete thing'. In the frame of acting technique the concrete thing that becomes an object with which it is possible to interact becomes also a new atmosphere. In the theatre play, this point could be assimilated to the realization of the dramatic composition through gestures and words, as expressive signs of the action of the play.

In the condensation into a localized object, atmosphere becomes ideally an object of ecstatic contemplation and loses its proper spatial character. Therefore, appearances of the physical reality become 'ecstasies' of the perception. This word is not taken in its original sense of something going out of itself, but in a spatial sense, where it is possible to be contemplated in its presence, thus going out into the space of its own presence and sphere of activity. Being the fundament of the process of perception, the atmospheric feeling brings out these ecstatic forms: 'They are themselves spheres of the presence of something, their reality in space' (Böhme 2017: 19).

The dynamic of the process of perception reaches a point at which there is a sudden change in the way of perceiving: at some point, from the feeling of atmospheres, the perception becomes a way of reading signs. They are just appearances, although from them it is possible to deduce the physical reality. In this way to perceive becomes the first level of an active apprehension of the world.

The neo-phenomenological theory of perception sees in the atmospheric feeling a way to build physical reality. Against the idea of perception as passivity, this theory shows that, on the contrary, perception can be active and has its basis in the atmospheric feeling of presence. This has very much in common with a specific doing (or not doing) of the actor, which is possible to find paradigmatically in the acting technique of atmosphere.

Atmosphere in acting technique

Atmosphere is a staging tool together with composition, scenic movements and rhythm. It is connected to the staging of the performance, but also to the rehearsals, when we talk about the 'creative atmosphere' necessary to the ensemble. Sometimes the atmosphere of a performance can be built according to different techniques such as lights and music. In the frame of theatre art, atmosphere is usually connected to the *mise en scène* rather than with acting technique directly, unless the technique of atmosphere is consciously applied by the performer. In his writings on the technique of acting Mikhail Chekhov presents how to create an atmosphere in acting.

The famous actor and pedagogue considers atmosphere as one of the most fundamental elements in the working process towards the development of a character. Chekhov has a partisan point of view on the technique of atmosphere, because for him it is possible to achieve only by the most sensitive and gifted performers.[6] According to Chekhov, in the technique of atmosphere lies a challenging perspective for the theatre artist, especially in a time ruled by materialism and mechanicism: 'The great mission of the contemporary actor', he says, 'is to save the objective Atmosphere in the theatre and with it to rescue the human facet of his profession' (1991: 35–36).

The technique of atmosphere is a fundamental skill for Chekhov, also because of the natural interplay we have with atmospheres in life. According to his point of view, actors should exercise the technique of atmosphere by becoming more sensitive in experiencing them and acknowledging their quality in life rather than on stage:

> The Actor must apprehend all those Atmospheres with which he has come to contact. Atmospheres for the artist are comparable to the different keys in music. They are a concrete means of expression. The performer must listen to them just as he listens to music.
>
> (Chekhov 1991: 27)

Chekhov considers atmosphere as something related to the 'living', something alive that is always present in the space, determining its quality. Atmosphere is necessary because 'the space, the air around the actor, will always be filled with life, and this life – which is the Atmosphere – will also keep him alive as long as he maintains contact with it' (1991: 29). This makes atmosphere a key element for avoiding an imitational way of acting.

In the technique of acting by Mikhail Chekov there are at least two levels of atmosphere: the irradiation of the feeling of oneself, and a further level corresponding to the presence of somebody else there. The atmosphere cannot be casual but should be created by the actor according to the dramaturgy of the play. In the realization of the dramatic composition, considered by Chekhov as the 'artistic frame', verbal action alternates with pauses that are equally relevant to words for the development of the play. In the dramatic composition the pause is 'the expression of the inner life', and hence atmospheres are living in the pauses (Chekhov 1991: 132, 138).

In acting technique of atmosphere, the moment of irradiation happens always in the pauses of the verbal action, when the actor perceives his/her self-presence, thus starting to influence the surrounding space. This irradiation generates an atmosphere. An irradiation pours out with the feeling of being in a certain affective situation.

This movement of irradiation starts from an inner centre of the body towards the outside. Chekhov explains that among the different forms of acting 'the strongest inner activity is a complete Pause'. Against the idea that pause means a stop of the action, Chekhov underlines that it is on the contrary 'a moment of absolute Radiation', where the actor's doing is shifting from a visible exteriority to the inside. The flow of the dramatic action is kept in those invisible tensions present in the pauses. Thanks to that, 'from the point of view of Composition and Rhythm, everything becomes a kind of "music", where everything moves, fluctuates, interweaves'. From the point of view of rhythm and composition, 'the Pause disappears only in those cases when the outer action is complete, when everything becomes outwardly expressed'; from the point of acting, on the contrary, making a pause means limiting 'the outer action'. While exposing a certain perception of oneself, the actor widens it out of the limits of his/her own body (Chekhov 1991: 137).

The pause is connected with the atmosphere:

> Both are inward, must strongly radiate from the performer, and are rooted in the realm of the feelings. Actors know from their own experience that if they succeed in creating a good significant Pause on stage, the Atmosphere emerges immediately and fascinates the audience. Conversely, if there is a strong Atmosphere on the stage, the actor instinctively uses every opportunity to 'hold a Pause', which will strengthen the atmosphere and so attract the audience's attention.
>
> (Chekhov 1991: 138–39)

The actor entering on stage, silent or not moving, can influence the air in the space. The actor's work on the behaviour or the physiognomy corresponds on stage to a pause. Both behaviour and physiognomy are externalized expressions of an 'internal' feeling. This shows the paradox that the technique of pause and atmosphere brings forth, which in turn creates the problem of explaining what 'doing through not doing' is. While in the famous work *The Paradox of the Actor* by Diderot the paradoxality concerned the dialectic of reason and feeling, here the paradox is rather about materiality since the actor can actually make visible and material what is invisible and immaterial.

Chekhov proposes concrete exercises in order to potentiate in acting the link between the objective material of the dramaturgy and the actor's feelings. For creating an atmosphere, he suggests this sequence: '1. Imagine the air around you filled with a certain Atmosphere; 2. Become aware of the reaction within you; 3. Move and speak in harmony with the Atmosphere; 4. Radiate it back into the space around you.' According to Chekhov the performer must prepare the atmosphere in order to make possible and intelligible the interplay with the audience. The performance is actually, as Chekhov says, 'a mutual creation of actor and audience and the Atmosphere is an irresistible bond between actor and audience, a medium with which the audience can inspire the actors by sending them waves of confidence, understanding, and love' (1991: 34, 28).

From the point of view of the actor's doing, it is possible to see, on one hand, the atmospheric feeling and, on the other, the atmosphere by which everybody present is ravished or even infatuated. In the technique of atmosphere in acting this distinction is kept by the 'feeling of oneself', and by the composition and rhythm of the dramatic action. According to the technique of atmosphere, acting starts from the perception of an affective situation.

The actor is the initiator of an empathic process in which a shared atmosphere is the condition of the theatrical event. Chekhov writes about an objective atmosphere interacting with the individual feelings of anybody present. To act an atmosphere is to realize a movement of radiation that, starting from 'the feeling of the presence of oneself', called the *samočuvstvie* (самочувствие), reaches out to the spectator. The actor should be able to irradiate it outside and create a connection with the spectator. The spectator empathizes with the actor's 'feeling of oneself' that irradiates an atmosphere, thus making the actor perceive to be surrounded by it. Atmosphere becomes something perceived as objective, and again, a new potential centre of irradiation by which, by the same principle, even the spectator together with the actor feels to be surrounded.

Moreover, as shown by the pauses, atmospheres have to be considered important from the point of view of the whole composition of the play. In fact, atmospheres do not concern only the 'feeling of oneself' of the actor playing, but also the meaning emerging from the content of the dramatic composition. The actor's doing must be informed by the whole composition: 'As soon as the actor absorbs the network of the Composition of the play, he begins to feel, while rehearsing or acting, that all scenes or moments in the play are present at each moment.' The laws of composition 'extend their threads from each point of the play to all the others, binding and holding them together. Following threads, the audience will inevitably follow the Composition itself, experiencing it as a complete whole, just as the actors do on the stage while performing' (Chekhov 1991: 133, 134). At the end of this path, inside the theatrical action, the spectators can also have a specific 'feeling of oneself' that transforms itself into an atmosphere as common territory shared by them and the performers.

Atmosphere is the 'milieu' (ambiance) connecting the fictional reality of the play with the concrete presence of an individual in the physical space of the rehearsal room. This milieu occupies all the space of the scenic action, although not the scene conceived in a physical, solid sense. The space is filled by a certain 'life'. In this sense what before was an empty and anonymous room becomes the place where the action takes place, not only for the performers but also for those watching them.

The creation of the milieu as an organic living space can transform the place of the performance, commonly shared by the audience and the actors. A very effective definition by performer Thomas Richards comes to mind: it is the feeling to be 'in the territory of something third' (2009: 130). This appears as the surprise of being present in front of an additional and excess of presence, generated by a performative action which discloses the objective sense of atmosphere. When an atmosphere is perceived, it is a space full of 'something' that can have a meaning or a personal quality of the subject. It is the felt resonance of a perceived living space. This something concrete and external is already a sort of second stage, an evolution, of the atmosphere generated by the presence and the action of the performer. It has a specific connection with the meaning of the text, which has a metaphysical value.

However, the action involved is of a physical nature. This externality felt individually (or individual feeling felt externally) is an atmosphere with a numinous quality. As Otto explains, the experience of the *numen praesens* is a mystery:

> Taken in the religious sense, that which is 'mysterious' is – to give it perhaps the most striking expression – the 'wholly other' (θάτερον, *anyad, alienum*), that which is quite beyond the sphere of the usual, the intelligible, and the familiar, which therefore falls quite outside the limits of 'canny', and is contrasted with it, filling the mind with blank wonder and astonishment.
>
> ([1923] 1958: 27)

The most 'spontaneous reaction to the feeling of the actual *numen praesens*' is to keep silent. When reflecting on the means by which the numinous is expressed in art, 'the "nothingness" and the "void" of the mystics' are its modes of expression: 'For "void" is, like darkness and silence, a negation, but a negation that does away with every "this" and "here", in order that the "wholly other" may become actual' (Otto [1923] 1958: 69, 70). As we could see, the pause in the technique of atmosphere refers to this emptiness and silence and requires the most subtle of skills from the actors, that is, the ability 'to do without doing'.

My experience in the laboratory of Vassiliev: How to do without doing?

Acting atmosphere is showing a way of doing without doing. In my notes I transcribed Vassiliev's words:

> We do less and we obtain a lot. If we do a lot, the result will be less. This is about the secrets of dramatic art. What is this 'less' that generates 'a lot'? From that 'less' starts the study of this art. Everybody can do 'a lot'.[7]
>
> (n.pag.)

A rectangular empty room with two rows of chairs along the longer walls: a working space, completely clean, without scenic elements and objects, with natural light coming from the windows. In the rehearsal room everybody present participates actively, and there is no division between who acts and who beholds. Watching is an act too, and everybody is called to action, responsibly and with full attention and will. This is an essential part of the discipline required in the creative working space.

Creation can happen only if there is a certain atmosphere allowing it (Knebel [1961] 2009: 142).[8] This atmosphere can exist only thanks to discipline and almost religious devotion to the working process. It is not a soldierly military discipline based on the obedience to principles of organization or authority. It is rather a discipline of a different kind, in which freedom and respect of the individual work have to be above all exercised by the collective of participants, director included. This discipline is very rigorous, and it is only in this delicate balance between thoroughness and anarchy that the creative work of acting can be realized. Thoroughness and anarchy are the two keywords that could describe Anatoli Vassiliev's laboratory work (Lupo 2006).

When working with Vassiliev, for the first time in my life I was facing personally the rigor of a method and at the same time the drive of a constant creative work and experimentation. I followed him for three intensive years on a full-time basis. This work was often continuing outside the spatial boundaries of the rehearsal room, in the collective analysis of the texts or in the preparation with other colleagues of what 'to show' the next day. I experienced acting in my own language (Italian), together with actors from Poland, Russia, Ukraine, Spain, France, Brazil, Israel, Romania and Greece, who were speaking their own. Sometimes we could not understand each other talking, although we could perfectly agree and be together in action, thanks to the grammar we were exploring and discovering alongside the very rigorous work on the dramaturgical action of the text.

How could we act on texts by Anton P. Chekhov, Luigi Pirandello and Plato, using different languages? The answer to this question concerns the essential part of our work: we were together studying the laws of composition and action in these texts, starting from our 'organic nature', that is, our felt body of experiences and desires, in a sort of total awakening and shaking of our beings, not letting our personal and cultural differences limit or block us. The first of our concerns was actually to get rid of all of the possible clichés that could affect the true and spontaneous work towards the action in the play.

We were compelled to not learn by heart the text, but rather to understand through our improvisations the structural line of the play in each act, scene, even fragment or juxtaposition of words. From the structure, our aim was to understand the action and the composition, in order to enact the passage from the literary text to the scenic one. At this level of work – an ensemble work – we were not only achieving artistic goals, but mainly working on a very personal register.

Everybody could explore freely his or her own creative potentialities without any judgement or censorship from our pedagogue.

This programmatic freedom in the work could be even scary at times. 'No boundaries' is a difficult concept to practice when it stops being a slogan and becomes a concrete attitude. In the laboratory with Vassiliev, the sense of limitation in itself was at stake. Actually all participants were deeply questioning themselves and their own personal limitations. Vassiliev was not our ruler, but our pedagogue in the process of the interiorization of the working principles. Unlike in a system centred on external rules and instructions, the progress in our work was kept by the respect of the principles of acting technique we were practicing. Our propositions could be accepted as work or simply rejected. The realization of something acceptable depended always on our personal commitment to the work and was not just a fulfilment of external instructions.

When I played a scene from the text *L'Innesto* (The grafted) by Luigi Pirandello, I had the best experience of how atmosphere works in acting, but also why this for me has something analogous to the feeling of the numinous.

I worked on this scene with a colleague who was playing Zena, while I was playing Laura. We were improvising following the structure of the text, using the method of the *etjud*. This methodology is sought to discover the composition of the text through action, with a spontaneous and personal approach of the actor to the dramaturgical material. The scene 'Laura/Zena' starts with a pause – even if it is not explicitly written. Without the starting pause, the following dialogue could not work, because it would easily become just an empty text, maybe with some colours in its spoken expression, but still empty of its profound meaning.

I remember Vassiliev underlining that I could not really lead the flow of the atmospheric feeling I was producing with my behaviour in the pause because I was not an expert actress yet. What had I to learn that was so fundamental to acting? For sure Vassiliev was bringing my attention to some inner technique that in my previous training as a professional actor I had never heard about.

From something concrete such as a physical gesture, a pause or a behaviour, it is possible for the actor to change the quality of the surrounding air and, at the same time, connect with the deepest and highest meaning of the play. It sounds very abstract, although in reality, this connection is established by the physical acting of the performer. The performer's creation is an organism alive with its own life. The performer opens the way, gives the possibility for it to appear and to live by itself. Being able to control this living and organic process requires deep and subtle skills, those that according to Anatoli Vassiliev make an actor an expert. In my case, I was at the point when I could not only feel myself in the process, but also modify it and lead it according to the dramatic action of the dramaturgy: this was what Vassiliev meant as basic acting skill for a professional actor. However, in respect to my inexperience in this sense, he pointed out that my doing was leading in a good direction towards the true work within the process, which is the very fundament of the development of action. When I started to do something and to speak, I actually broke it, he said.

Every actor knows that a pause creates tension and keeps the attention of the audience. A moment of suspension helps in maintaining a good rhythm of reactions from the spectators, especially when acting in a comic register. However, that is not the same type of pause that generates an atmosphere. That pause can be defined as a trick of the experienced actor, but not of the expert one.

According to my own experience, the creation of the atmosphere started with the sharp feeling of being surrounded by something exceeding my own presence. I was working together with my colleague and this exceedance produced by our interaction in the pause – within our active 'not doing' – became something palpable, external, which could become the new space for our creative work to come to life.

Practicing what is atmosphere in acting opens a reflection on how to conceive space in relation with the dialectic of inside-outside. The presence and the doing (and not doing) of the performer is a constant questioning of this dialectic, which is also a fundamental question for the aesthetics and the philosophical analysis of perception. The technique of atmosphere in acting appears paradoxically as a technique of not doing and of giving space, rather than taking place.

In my laboratory practice as an actor, I experienced that acting an atmosphere makes possible the transformation of the place of the performance into an organic living space shared by everybody present. This transformation shows the paradoxical nature of the performer's doing, which makes the immateriality of a subjective feeling – already born atmospherically outside the body – an objective presence felt individually, and at the same time shared and perceived by everybody.

NOTES

1. The Great Reform of Theatre is a movement of renovation in theatre art which began in 1876 with the inauguration of the *Festspielhaus* in Bayreuth. This movement is connected with the names of important theatre artists that inspired schools and traditions.

2. *Technè* (τέχνη) means art as ability of doing, both practically and intellectually. In ancient Greek language the meaning was extended to both the process of making and its products (*technai*). A famous interpretation of art as *technè* is given by Denis Diderot in the article 'Art' of the *Encyclopédie*. According to this interpretation liberal arts are not conceived as superior to mechanical arts. The main consequence of such an interpretation is that the artist's action is more relevant than the artistic object.

3. Together with his activity of directing, Vassiliev spent four decades as theatre pedagogue and laboratory master. Although he is internationally known as a theatre director, he rehearsed in the frame of laboratory many more texts and plays than the amount of performances he staged.

4. There is a distinction between the atmospheric feeling and the feeling of an atmosphere. The ravishing feeling that has an atmospheric form should not be confused with the feeling of being ravished by this atmosphere, says Schmitz ([2009] 2011: 104).

5. In a certain way the atmosphere is then condensed in a thing localized in the space (Böhme [2001] 2010: 241).

6. 'Actors who outgrow the phlegmatic conception of the stage as an empty space know that Atmosphere is one of their strongest means of expression, as well as an unbreakable link between them and their audiences' (Chekhov 1991: 27).

7. The transcription is: 'Noi facciamo poco e otteniamo molto. Se facciamo molto il risultato sarà poco. Questo riguarda i segreti dell'arte drammatica. Cos'è questo 'poco' che fa nascere il 'molto'? Da quel 'poco' inizia lo studio di quest'arte. Il 'molto' lo sanno fare tutti'.

8. Marja Knebel was the pedagogue of Anatoli Vassiliev during his years of study at the Theater of Art of Moscow. She is the author of different books, such as *The Poetry of Pedagogy* (1971) and the fundamental *Action Analysis* (1961). Knebel, who was born in 1898, trained with Stanislawski in his last years and also with Mikhail Chekhov.

REFERENCES

Bachelard, Gaston ([1950] 2000), *The Dialectic of Duration*, trans. M. McAllester Jones, Manchester: Clinamen Press.

Bachelard, Gaston ([1953] 2002), *The Formation of the Scientific Mind*, trans. M. McAllester Jones, Manchester: Clinamen Press.

Barba, Eugenio and Savarese, Nicola ([2017] 2019), *The Five Continents of Theatre: Facts and Legends about the Material Culture of the Actor*, Brill: Sense.

Böhme, Gernot ([2001] 2010), *Atmosfere, estasi, messe in scena*, trans. T. Griffero, Milano: Marinotti.

Böhme, Gernot (2017), *The Aesthetics of Atmospheres*, ed. J. P. Thibaud, London and New York: Routledge.

Chekhov, Mikhail (1991), *On the Technique of Acting*, ed. M. Powers, New York: Harper Collins.

Griffero, Tonino (2014), *Atmospheres: Aesthetics of Emotional Spaces*, trans. S. De Sanctis, New York: Ashgate.

Griffero, Tonino (2016), *Il pensiero dei sensi*, Milano: Guerini.

Grotowski, Jerzy ([1967] 1997), 'Towards a poor theatre', in R. Schechner and L. Wolford (eds) and T. K. Wiewiorowski (trans.), *The Sourcebook*, London and New York: Routledge, pp. 28–37.

Knebel, Marja ([1961] 2009), *L'analisi della pièce e del ruolo mediante l'azione*, trans. A. Bergamo, Roma: Bulzoni.

Latour, Bruno and Woolgar, Steve (1986), *Laboratory Life: The Construction of Scientific Facts*, rev. ed., Princeton: Princeton University Press.

Lupo, Stephanie (2006), *Anatoli Vassiliev: Au coeur de la pedagogie theatrale. Riguer et anarchie*, Paris: L'Entretemps.

Otto, Rudolf ([1923] 1958), *The Idea of the Holy*, trans. J. W. Harvey, Oxford: Oxford University Press.

Richards, Thomas (2009), *The Heart of Practice*, London and New York: Routledge.

Schino, Mirella (2013), *Alchemists of the Stage: Theatre Laboratories in Europe*, trans. P. Warrington, London and New York: Routledge.

Schmitz, Hermann ([2009] 2011), *Nuova Fenomenologia: Un'introduzione*, trans. T. Griffero, Milano: Marinotti.

Schmitz, Hermann (2011), *Emotions Outside the Box: The New Phenomenology of Feeling and Corporeality*, New York: Springer.

5

Holding Out:
The Sacred Space of Suspense and
Sustainable Ethics

Annalaura Alifuoco

Introduction

This chapter is concerned with the sacred sites of knowledge, which I regard as the spaces that 'hold out' the capacity to engage with contingencies and uncertainties; that allow us to think and create new situations with and through what can be perceived and felt otherwise. It is this feeling that has timelessly activated and animated material bodies of knowledge – including researchers, practitioners and institutions – to mobilize for the imaginative creation of alternatives to the imperative submission to benchmark evaluations, for the sake of surviving, in the competitive knowledge economy market.

In the rapidly changing landscape of academia, there is an insistent demand for the ways of knowledge to change, adapt and transform, and this certainly entails a necessity to engage with the ever-critical present times – cultural, political and ecological. A 'minor' position is advanced by a new materialism that emerges from the desire to locate new objects of knowledge that oppose the epistemic tendencies to divide and classify theoretical trends, disciplines and paradigms. These operations are minor in the sense that they express and requalify minoritarian locations that have historically been negated, neglected or marginalized.

Hence, my aim here is to map out zones of deliberate, daring resistance to the universalist and dualist approaches to knowledge formation that have been the structuring principles of the transcendent and humanist traditions. I intend to do so through the example of a located and contingent practice – or art – akin to the disciplinary and paradigmatic transversalities of new materialisms (Dolphijn and van der Tuin New 2012). The mapping initiatives that overlap in these sites of knowledge materialize in non-exhaustive, qualitatively different but complementary cartographic projects. In Rosi Braidotti's work, the cartographic model determines accurate maps of the embedded and embodied politics of locations. She writes:

> A cartography is a theoretically based and politically informed reading of the present. Cartographies aim at epistemic and ethical accountability by unveiling the power locations which structure our subject-position. As such, they account for one's locations in terms of both space (geo-political or ecological dimension) and time (historical and genealogical dimension). This stresses the situated structure of critical theory and it implies the partial or limited nature of all claims to knowledge.
>
> (Braidotti 2013: 164)

Key to this topographic methodology is the focus on the enfleshment and emplacement of bodies and other so-called objects of investigation, as philosopher Donna Haraway elicits:

> Bodies as objects of knowledge are material – semiotic generative nodes. Their *boundaries* materialize in social interaction. Boundaries are drawn by mapping practices; 'objects' do not pre-exist as such. Objects are boundary projects. But boundaries shift from within; boundaries are very tricky. What boundaries provisionally contain remains generative, productive of meanings and bodies. Siting (sighting) boundaries is a risky practice.
>
> (1988: 595, original emphasis)

The field of performance is a special place indeed for taking such risks. In fact, its strategies map out the desire to navigate subtle, obscure and often risky terrains, the opportunity to test the bounds of what is known, creating spaces to acquire practical wisdom, where another kind of science can discover, generate and overcome its own uncertainties and limitations. This active site, hence, becomes the potential ground to reclaim forms of politics, aesthetics and ethics that transverse and replace humanist (and human) territorializations.

The reclaiming of such unsettling grounds set the methodological scene of my aesth-ethic project here. This epistemic experience is closely linked to the active, transformative operations located in philosopher Isabelle Stengers scientific re-animism: 'Reclaiming means recovering, and, in this case, recovering the capacity to honor experience, any experience we care for, as "not ours" but rather as "animating" us, making us witness to what is not us' (2012: n.pag.). Hence, this chapter seeks to unfold what can be known from 'what is not us' and perhaps 'more than us' in the contemporary, situated practice of performance.

To mark these possibilities, I will retrace the work of performance artist, activist and scholar Nigel Rolfe. Through radically uncertain acts and experiences, the artist situates human embodiment as a materiality separate yet akin to its dwelling place within the world, from which all sacred traditions and resources of wisdom emerge. Knowledge here, I propose, becomes the product of a spatial and 'special' relation that reorients the human in the 'more than human' world, from which it is distinct but to which it nevertheless belongs. A similar special organization has been noted by geographer Yi-Fu Tuan in his enunciation of 'sacred spaces' as relations, primarily of distance, that exercise the function of separation, or 'cutting out'.

For Tuan, the establishment of sacred places is an operation analogous to the geographer's cartographic work of mapping a territory via the activity of differentiating the undifferentiated space; both are attempts at confining nature within demarcated bounds (1978: 84). While resisting the evident humanist impulse to divide and classify, what interests me here is how much space corresponds to a material experience that forms a set of relations. As a result, I want to recognize the transversal qualities of this and the previously cited cartographic notions as distinct but entangled productions.

Hence, I will pay particular attention to formal qualities of Rolfe's 'standing' work as embodied strategies that 'hold out', rather than 'cut out', the position of the human 'outwith' the environment. My suggestion here is that this critical posture formalizes an attempt to contain and sustain an epistemic experience that is not stringently pre-existing or generated, but that instead 'remains generative, productive of meanings and bodies' (Haraway 1988: 595). It does so by holding boundaries and divisions in a state of suspension for the sake of 'weaving relations that turn a divide into a living contrast, one whose power is to affect, to produce thinking and feeling' (Stengers 2012: n.pag.). These, I argue, are the nodal points of uncertainty and possibility that endow space with a lay kind of sacredness that keeps things spiritually alive and animated, and not just for the human.

Why, where, when, how, what for?

'Why, Where, When, How, What For' is the title under which artist Nigel Rolfe's explores the questions posed by *UNLIMITED ACTION*, a one-day symposium on the 'limits of the body, aesthetics, material conditions, institutional practices, pleasure, or desire' within the critical and material practice of performance (art) (2016: n.pag.).[1] In a formal act of sharing, Rolfe distils a collection of images and slides, interspersed with quotes, personal anecdotes and artistic mantra evolving around tactics, materials and gestures used throughout his history of art activism, as well as in more recent manifestations. He belongs to a generation of avant-garde artists who, since the early 1970s, deliberately chose to make and perform challenging work that questioned boundaries long held sacred in both the art world and society in general.

Born on the Isle of Wight, Rolfe moved to the Republic of Ireland in 1974. His history here becomes that of the strongly politicized landscape as he declares his status upon arrival as 'wrong nationality, wrong place, wrong time' and recalls his experience of migration:

> [W]hen I first went there, the British Embassy had just been burnt down in Dublin and my life there was based on drip-drip terrorism every day, every single day. In a small place, all ground is contested. That seem[ed] to me good terms [for] trying to work out a life.
>
> (Rolfe 2016: n.pag.)

In the following decades, his signature ritual actions and material interactions with bodies, elements and objects became a great influence for his and other generations of artists working in performance.

As a pioneer of action art, in the 1970s, he coined the term 'sculptures in motion' to describe his use of the body as 'both a drawing tool and as a performative sculpture, directly confronting and interacting with elemental materials and environments rather than employing the body as the site of the action itself' (Apple 2005: 45). As a result, his physical form, like the found or appropriated sites it encounters, becomes coloured, marked or touched by processes 'in which the artist directs the material employed within a given space, with all the conditions of the process being of equal importance' (Apple 2005: 45). The largely organic elements involved in such aggregations include pigments, powders, mud, wood, earth, fire, water, sounds and the body itself. Together they become catalysts of strong relationships – 'the greatest friendship' he holds (in Dunne and Rolfe 1993: 42) – that test the formal possibilities of duration, endurance and transformation.

In the moment and over time, the vitality – or aliveness (see Alifuoco 2017) – of actions and raw materials are progressed into events, drawings, installations, sounds and still and moving images that broaden the expression of the work and its potentialities. Some elemental motifs return or recur like the white and coloured dusts – *Dust in Face*, (1996), *Dust Bed* (1980), *Dust Breeding* (2008), *Red Dust Drawing* (2010) and more. The alchemy produced by these substances – including their pure and toxic properties – in intimate contact with the artist's body creates a particular aesthetic of minimal yet austere gestures within a ritualized, formalized structure. There is a clear dynamic here between the apparatus of the body and the medium of the pigments. Once rendered operational, the dense atmosphere of the latter seems to override the former's limited and exhaustive capacities, with almost infinite possibilities to intervene in the action and direct the experience.

This quality of unpredictability and risk reinforces the affective intensity of the subtle and intentional gestures of each performance or trace. The applications of physical restraint, mental resilience and spatial awareness overlay the political implications of Rolfe's actions, directed towards his own profound concerns with the urgencies of ongoing histories. In what is perhaps his most seminal work, *The Rope* (1983),[2] Rolfe fully binds his head in a length of twine covered in creosote, a toxic material, as a meditation on the 'smothering, isolation, loss, and failure of the Troubles' (Rolfe 2014) in Northern Ireland. Early video pieces such as *Hand on Face* (1988) or *Dance Slap for Africa* (1983) confront the shifting dynamics of power in an apartheid-transitioning South Africa via the potency of arresting and jarring symbols. 'Red' (2015), a more recent performance, presented within the context of the solo exhibition *The Burning Frame*, offers an intimate exploration of extreme colours and shades, their specific hazard arising from the powerful association with an image of a thief in Haiti shot dead while holding a framed painting.

Such performative interventions do not set out to resolve conflict; rather, they make sense of a consciousness tugging and flowing with the currents of socio- and geopolitical events. They are sited in particular locations and landscapes where space and place – physical, psychic and political – find correspondence in the materials used; their vibrant forces and unseen rhythms. The artist's torturous and 'inconclusive investigation' (Sigler 2012) reaffirms their deep cultural implications and symbolic meanings, as well as the need for new, personal and collective rituals to divine new borderlands for testing how to live, act and relate.

Within the context of *UNLIMITED ACTION*, Rolfe introduces a more mature approach to the work derived from a new set of risks and challenges as expressions of sites and states bordering on crisis. The renewed energy originates from the experience of a spine fracture, nearly leading to permanent paralysis: 'In 2010, I broke my back very badly and I couldn't stand up. Talking about limits [...] if you live daily with enduring pain, nerve pain is one of the hardest to tolerate. A very real limit' (Rolfe 2016: n.pag.). This limit is what forced the artist to confront the spatial and temporal constrains of his primary tool – the body:

[T]he first year after the first bout of surgery I really just liked standing up, I went with my son to the West of Ireland and I stood there by myself in this place with my hands holding out. [...] And I stood there in the dark, all night in this place until the dawn came up; most magic dawn. And left this position.

(Rolfe 2016: n.pag.)

The set for this long-standing feat is the Skellig Islands – remote, craggy and windswept, off the coast of southwest Ireland, at the furthest western edge of Fortress Europe. The artist recalls:

That first period [...] ended a whole set of standing works in 2010 [...] Standing for a very long time, sometimes 30 hours. [...] If you suddenly know that your legs and the rest of you are hung on a very small thread standing becomes such a great thing to do. This place in Ireland with this ancient invested landscape [...] The sense of land and the sense of being in this place measures something much further than land [...] And of course, [...] the interesting thing now in the world [is] that there really [is] nowhere that isn't contested by someone. The whole land out of Europe is contested.

(Rolfe 2016: n.pag.)

Rolfe attempts to reconstruct a possible genealogy for the in-tense relationship between contested spaces, artistic practices and ethical conscience. He begins by situating this work in the artistic tradition of formal expressionism as embodied in Caspar David Friedrich's painting *Wanderer above the Sea of Fog* (1818). Here a solitary figure, painted with his back to the viewer, stands on a rocky elevation, contemplating a grandiose high mountain landscape extending into the distance. This posture demands that a sole man stands in the place of all the others claiming the mastery of all of space. This image calls to mind the grandeur of its sublime – and subliminal – humanist message.

Friedrich's treatment of pictorial space, in fact, has historically been considered the illustration of Immanuel Kant's concept of the Sublime: '*that* [...] *in comparison with which everything else is small*' (1951: 88, original emphasis). In 1790, Kant wrote:

In the immensity of nature [...] we find our own limitation although at the same time in our rational faculty we find a different, nonsensuous standard, which has that infinity itself under it as a unity, in comparison with which everything in nature is small, and thus in our mind we find a superiority to nature even in its immensity [...]. Therefore nature is here called sublime merely because it elevates the imagination to a presentation of those cases in which the mind can make felt the proper subtimity of its destination, in comparison with nature itself. [...] For what is that which is, even to the savage, an object of the greatest admiration? It is a man who shrinks from nothing, who fears nothing, and therefore does not yield to danger, but rather goes to face it vigorously with the fullest deliberation.

(1951: 101–02)

Man and man only is the centrifugal forces of this epistemic vision, and nature only appears to acknowledge and crystallize that dynamism.

The supporting features of this creative disposition trace another lineage in vanguardism with German artist Joseph Beuys's symbolic stance in the 1981 photowork *Defense of Nature (Clavicembalo)*.[3] Here the artist, his imponent figure recognizable from the back as he is wearing his iconic felt trilby hat and fur-lined jacket, stands on a hilly slope looking over the rural landscapes. This image largely epitomizes Beuys's philosophy of aesthetics existing in close, systemic relationship with living matters and environments. Indeed, there are some elements of social, ethical and spiritual materialism that appear strikingly similar across Beuys's 'living sculptures' and Rolf's 'sculptures in motion'. Both artistic trajectories find potent expression in ritual, alchemic and mythological explorations – or materializations – rendered in human, animal and earthen textures, pigments and sounds, and via their processes of transformation.

Notwithstanding these creative intersections, there is something that is crucially discernible between the symbolic production of space of their respective standing procedures. In Beuys's photographic image, the elongated scale and elevated perspective of the central human figure gives it a monumental presence in relation to the surrounding landscape. This visual affirmation of a sublime kind of individual figuration is very much in the German Romantic tradition of Friedrich; we are always aware of the human mind beholding it. The terrain, the landforms, the urban features, the weather, the sky are distressingly continuous and progressively blended into disappearance. The human presence appears highly dignified in deliberation, poised in a self-confident manner or bearing composed in the self-possession of his beliefs and aspirations.

This contemplative stance stands strangely at odds with my perception of Rolfe's inhabitation of space, particularly in his more recent and meditative work, as expressed by his nightly exposure. This formal act of endurance was captured in a photograph taken by Rolfe's son before driving away (Figure 5.1).[4] The still image is completely dark but for Rolfe's hairless head and naked hands singled out by the flashlight. The edges of his iconic black suit blend in with the night. The tautness of his figure is broken by the gentle bow of the head – eyelids lowered, lips parted, brows corrugated in the concentration of the pose – and the candid gleam of hands outstretched, delicately suspended in a cupped gesture. To my knowledge, no other documentation of this episode exists, with the exception of a reflective poem written by the artist and included later in this text, and Rolfe's quiet stillness in the symposium room as he resumes the posture of the subject matter at hand. In this stance, not facing off but inviting, yielding, opening towards a receiving or offering of the self, something else is presented.

At the time of researching for this chapter, I found an image of a performance of his, *Standing* (2011), which bears some relation to this act of formal abeyance. The photograph is taken in plain daylight.[5] The artist stands on the left side of the shot, seemingly sprouting out of the green grass below, only head and hands visible in contrast with his full-black attire (surprisingly less formal than his signature suit).

110

FIGURE 5.1: Nigel Rolfe, *Standing* (2011). Courtesy of Nigel Rolfe.

Notably, the arms are not raised in front but held to the sides, hands facing back-wards. He is seen from the back, at a sloped angle. It is perhaps the effect of this framing or the curvature of his spine, but he also looks slightly lopsided. The still focus of his solitary reflection seems directed obliquely towards an equally isolated figure some distance away, at the opposite end of the frame – a tall and slender tree, set out from the strip of rolling hills behind and higher mountains beyond.

Within this composition, Rolfe's statuesque physique appears hunched and frail, somewhat diminished by the skinny tree – rising well above his height – and the surrounding landscape. This stilled encounter involves 'distance' yet requires an intimate physical involvement; it demands of all those partaking – human and non, in and outside the frame – a greater awareness of the natural bonds and ten-sions that are formed in this environment. Rather than the centripetal perspective of 'man' aloft the rocky peaks, or the centrifugal grandeur of the artist's pose, this scene exists in collateral spread. It hangs in the balance of forms – landscape, space, tree, body – that yield into a relationship that exceeds the individual.

Whether sculptural form or photographic evidence, there is a plethora of ways to read these traces. This and other 'materials' seem to resist the notion of presence and liveness at the core of Rolfe's performance practice, as he urges: '[I]f others are watching or not watching the sense of live for me carries some risk that processes may and can change right there in the moment' (Rolfe 2019: n.pag.). And yet, this condition determines the larger extent to which processes last – endure – beyond the work as seen and done only by the artist:

> be very very present and at the same time somehow not
> you are freezing images in time,
> powerful pictures will be remembered.
> (Rolfe 2019: n.pag.)

Hence, photograph, like video, sound and other detritus, is less an indication of what may have happened and more an invitation to others to find and experience processes wherever they can be found – action, matter, text, but also memory, imagination, intuition.

In considering Rolfe's performance work, visual, aural and written accounts of live events will all be present in this study. Equally, this attempt to 'make sense' of these traces will inevitably conjure other forms, apart from the physical order, that may carry the active elements of performances to those who encounter them outside the bounds of first-hand experience, starting here with my own reimaginings.

At the limits of existence

The formal and sculptural terms of Rolfe's out-standing work introduce a strategic quality of endurance that marks a progression and evolution in Rolfe's work. The sheer, immediate materiality that was the hallmark of the the artist's trajectory project back in the 1970s and through to the 1980s and 1990s bore a streak of heroic narcissism. Aidan Dunne remarks: 'There is in his earlier work a nostalgia, perhaps, for the image of the artist as hero, as a shaman. A Beuysian nostalgia, widespread, pervasive, for ritual, for the certainty of meaning and position that ritual reflected' (Dunne and Rolfe 1993: 42). Now, looking back at this vexed impulse, the artist finds it 'somewhat naive and vain' (O'Byrne 2015). In a recent artistic statement, Rolfe declares:

The last few years I feel I have reached a good and strong plateau, deeper and with better focus than what preceded it. [...] Now, once again, the images are direct and more to the point. There are always metaphors inside the images and the recent work has maintained this but become more expressive.

(2015: n.pag.)

Significantly, the experience of having the spinal injury, overcoming paralysis, recovering from surgery and managing the uncertainty of continuing on, have marked a turning point in his practice. The artist has found a more profound meaning in simple and minimal gestures such as standing, falling (*Into the Mire* 2011), lying (*Track* 2013) and breathing (*Breath* 2017). Ellie O'Byrne suggests that 'his work has become stiller, more focused and internal' (2015: n.pag.), and he often enters a meditative state of absorption, which has become a tool to explore the ultimate border space: '[i]t's about life and death, and transformation', Rolfe says (Zhangyu 2018: n.pag.). This broadened expression of the work becomes 'a foil for death' (Rolfe in O'Byrne 2015: n.pag.), where the term 'foil' seems expressive of both meanings 'to tread on' and 'to frustrate'[6] this ultimate limit. Concerning Rolfe's long-standing and long-lasting feats, the challenge of sustaining the same activity, in the same place, moment after moment, holding out one's foil of a body in a manner that just is, at the limits of being, endures both these activities.

Fading into the darkness of the nocturnal landscape, the attenuated presence of the human remains suspended as if hung in the balance of external forces. I want to approach this active stillness as a formal suspension of space (and time), where being and non-being, human and inhuman, life and death are held together, in place. More precisely, it is the formal and affective aspect of this 'suspense' that I want to pursue here, in the attempt to figure out a space of surrender to un(fore) seen and unexpected relations, which I shall for now call 'sacred'. Underlying these processes are forms of displacements, interruptions and transformations that allow the unexpected to actually 'take place'.

For geographer Yi-Fu Tuan, the notion of place goes beyond the strict terms of location. Instead, he defines place as

> a center of meaning constructed by experience. Place is known not only through the eyes and mind but also through the more passive and direct modes of experience, which resist objectification. To know a place fully means both to understand it in an abstract way and to know it as one person knows another. At a high theoretical level, places are points in a spatial system. At the opposite extreme, they are strong visceral feelings.
>
> (Tuan 1975: 151)

The experience of the outdoors cultivated by Rolfe, I suggest, formally and affectively sustains an analogous, although non-oppositional, ambivalence of space.

113

What is at stake here is a 'suspended relation', both abstract and immanent, that takes the form of what it suspends – a being both within and outwith a space that is not reducible to a fully subjective or objective location. This relation only make sense – *and* feeling – in the context of its emplacement.

In an impulse generated by physical necessity Rolfe sets out, much like an exile or a pilgrim on a quest outside (the self). In his wanderings, he comes to a deserted and darkening landscape 'at the western edge of the European land mass' (Horn et al. 1990: 2). The Skellig Islands are towering sea crags rising from the Atlantic Ocean almost twelve kilometres off terra firma (Figure 5.2). Skellig Michael, the largest of the two, between the sixth and eighth centuries, became a place of refuge for a small settlement of ascetic monks in search of solitude and God. A monastery was founded on this precipitous rock: 'seven hundred feet above the sea, clinging to the narrow ledges of an austere pinnacle, the Skellig Michael hermitage is a visual wonder and a marvelous feat of construction' (Horn et al. 1990: 2). By the thirteenth century, the monastic community had moved to the mainland, but the island has continued to attract devout and secular pilgrims, eager to explore this dramatic site of extreme devotion.

FIGURE 5.2: Daniel Born, Kerry Cliffs Portmagee, Skellig Ring, Foilnageragh, Portmagee, County Kerry, Ireland, 2020. Courtesy of Unsplash.

The storm-lashed rock of Little Skellig, the minor island, though never inhabited by humans, is seasonally swarmed by breeding colonies of seabirds, with their raucous and reeking nesting rituals. The sublime mystique of these insular sites lies within a picture of wildness, outside the bounds of the human world. The romance and lure of these 'deserted' places rest with notions of remote and timeless beauty of inescapable and fascinating otherness. This place is no-place and therefore 'nowhere', the 'edge of the abyss', as the Lonely Planet guide has it (Kay 2016: n.pag.).

Yet, turn this frame inside-out and the vastity of the North Atlantic supersedes the (supposed) centrality of dry land. From here, it is the United Kingdom that looks distant and irrelevant. In this decentralized (minor) perspective, the Skellig Rocks harbour an incomparable active life; endless variety of jagged and speckled boulders; thrift, sea campion and rock sea-spurrey hunkered down the steep ground. Sea mammals hauled out on rocky ledges. Waves and gales splicing coves and sea cliffs, moulding their profile with every blast and gust. For gannets and puffins, fulmars and guillemots this is Skellig Central: rich, fertile, bustling. This shifted centre is the site of extraordinary life, a 'now-here' place of nature stripped to its essential, active components. This no-place realizes itself fully as the place of negation and effacement of all human terms of habitation and occupation.

The artist is an outsider in this world. Isolated from the kinship of 'mankind', he is inspired to enter into a secret and strange contact with a life beyond the claims and sacrality of the human predicament. This exposure requires us to enter (if voluntarily) a state of exile, which is, by its very nature, challenging and disrupting. This condition is deeply resonant of Edward W. Said's later writings on this 'compelling but terrible' experience: '[e]xile is life led outside habitual order. It is nomadic, decentred, contrapuntal; but no sooner does one get accustomed to it than its unsettling force erupts anew' (2002: 149). This potency is not the fruit of the reckless daring of human ambition. Rather, this 'discontinuous state of being' requires that one 'must leave the modest refuge provided by subjectivity' and inhabit instead 'the perilous territory of not-belonging', a solitude experienced 'outside', where *nothing* is secure' (Said 2002: 137–49, original emphasis).

In *Standing*, Rolfe takes residence in the deep experience of this certain nothing-ness, the intensity and fullness of which emerge out of the darkness of night. The night of silence, solitude and indeterminacy is a profound space that refuses to be bounded by the spectacle of certitude drawn by vision. The heart of darkness erodes the physical surface of the world with a vastness that stretches outside visibility, or more precisely, where the visible proceeds up into the invisible and 'nothing' becomes actually present or presentable. The import of this situation gradually dawns on me, although I can only realize this encounter in my mind's eyes. I see a body waiting, shivering slightly, bracing itself for the night. I imagine the physical pull of the vertical line of the spine straining against the full weight of the mass. I figure the arms and hands, sturdy and trembling – patiently, quietly hanging in mid-air. I picture how this situation might act on the senses; cold and hunger, pain and relief, excitement and fear. I get a sense of vertigo; it must be hard not to fall over the edge of this incertitude. I fantasize a spirit of communion with, rather than control over, these wild embeddings – breathings, murmurings, whisperings and silences seeping into the consciousness. I watch these rhythms slowing down to the speed of stones, as the body enters into the trance of this performance.

Attuned and present – between waking and sleeping – the artist physically and dangerously immerses himself in this situation. It is through this expanding field that this endured practice grows and challenges its own boundaries. As the body remains held in a state of control and containment of its bare life, its consciousness can step outside where there is 'nothing' else; the wind blowing across the exposed terrain, the pressure trickling from the open skies, the silence and whispers felt and heard from the elements, the stillness hushed in by the waves of the sea – a looping live score of inhuman voices. And further, it enters into it; into the secret and mysterious life hidden under the darkest crevices, buried deep below the surface of the water; and all the other irreducible spaces between presence and absence that together bear the lightness of night. This 'nothingness' – no-thing other than the presence of the world 'other' – not only can be embraced but must be fully held.

Rolfe gives himself over to the intensities and temporalities of this matter and space, completely in body, and outside of it. Teetering along the brink between abandonment and absorption, oscillating between vulnerability and sovereignty, it is here that this alive performance finds the most thrilling and tense expressions of an extreme life, suspended half-inside and half-outside the human. This configuration finds its corollary in Rolfe's disorienting topography as described in the text that provides one more permutation of this work:

> Outside
> (Stayoutside)   don't be drawn in
> Without
> What is known
> What is easy
> Outside Track
> Not contained
> Free of all constraints
> Make free
> Take risk
> Break-broken-back
> Be Invisible, of the air, of the sky
> Evaporate.[7]

In the introductory notes to *The Sacred Desert*, theologian David Jasper quali-fies the profound space where the extremes of human experience meet and dis-solve. He writes:

> At the very edge of physical possibility, the mind turns inward and the opposi-
> tions which we create between physical and spiritual, body and soul, collapse into
> a *coincidentia oppositorum* that is a Total Presence. Yet this is not the solipsistic
> experience which is so often wrongly ascribed to mystical souls, but a universal
> and potentially shared moment of utter sociability, a true meeting of the one and
> the many.
>
> (Jasper 2004: 6–7)

Jasper's conception of this unbounded relation is borrowed from the writing of theologian Thomas Altizer on *Total Presence* (1980), which is, in fact, nothing other than 'a voice of silence experienced as such an intensity that it is everything and nothing' (in Jasper 2004: 146). This moment of silence finds its totality as an absolute nothingness that can solely be discovered in utter solitude, for it is only in such solitude that the absolute realization of the chiasmic space (which is no place) where opposites meet can be held out.

This suspension, it seems to me, cunningly describes the artist's voluntary isolation and endured exposure, as well as the journeys and extraordinary asceticism of the monks centuries before. The world they encounter is the absolute 'other' upon which the shunned 'inside' reverses out, only for the 'outside' to re-turn in the totality of this encounter. Altizer concludes his book with these words:

> Genuine solitude is a voyage into the interior, but it is a voyage which culminates
> in a loss of our interior, a loss reversing every manifest or established center of our
> interior so as to make possible the advent of a wholly new but totally immediate
> world [...] But the real end or reversal of an individual interior makes possible the
> actual advent of a universal presence, a presence transcending all interior and indi-
> vidual identity, and presenting itself beyond our interior, and beyond every possible
> interior, as a total and immediate presence.
>
> (1980: 106–07)

Rolfe's posture realizes a formal principle that sustains this experience: holding on one hand the extremity of individual exile, and on the other the full dislocating force of the limitless space beyond the self. In the decentred field of losing the self, an irreducible space opens, alongside presence and absence, and takes material form through a gesture of holding out. This is the suspense where the boundaries and limits of human action and performance are negotiated; at the intersections with external, relational forces.

This situation is truly suspenseful as it accepts the risks, the limits and possibilities of being in an intimate confrontation with what Rosi Braidotti in *Nomadic Theory* recognizes as 'the thresholds of sustainability'. As the philosopher lays out: '[e]ncountering them is almost a matter for geography, because it's a question of orientations, points of entry and exit, a constant un-folding' (2011: 309). Engaging transversally with Braidotti's nomadic approach and the formal qualities of endurance, next I want to argue that the artist's unmediated encounters with the outdoors perform a temporary suspension of the essentialized human subject. This situation, in turn, opens the human up to transactive engagements with the outside that facilitate a radical posthuman ethics of expansive and affirmative suprahuman kinships. It is here, I contend, that sites of knowledge become 'sacred' in an actual, political and ethical sense.

Sacred thresholds

Rolfe's *mise-en-abeyance* functions as a perceptual event that suspends ordinary sense experience in the direct and immediate contact with something beyond the experience itself. In *The Varieties of Religious Experience*, psychologist and philosopher William James depicts this perceptual immediacy as a mystical sensation:

> Our senses [...] have assured us of certain states of fact: but mystical experiences are as direct perceptions of fact for those who have them as any sensations ever were for us. The records show that even though the five senses be in abeyance in them, they are absolutely sensational in their epistemological quality, if I may be pardoned the barbarous expression, – that is, they are face to face presentations of what seems immediately to exist.
>
> (1958: 324)

In the cluster of this experience, the artist's wilful abandonment seems to be sustained by a blind faith in what mysteriously and immediately appears – a total presence that blurs the line between the land's marks and his own. Far from a carefree existence, confined in a solitude made of darkness, this utter decentring of the self makes possible 'the advent of a new but wholly immediate world' (Altizer in Jasper 2004: 156). This experience is an intensely corporeal portrait of a threshold stage of life, and its attendant fears and desires, together with a burgeoning climate of isolation, mystery, dread, allure, terror, calm – all together, all at once.

Suspended in a form of still life, Rolfe enters a crossroad or borderland conditions, betwixt and between dusk and dawn, in the mist of the night. This site becomes marked by the ambiguity, paradox and fluidity of a 'thin' place. In the mystical worlds of both Celtic pagan spirituality and Celtic Christianity, 'thin places' are those locales where the veil between this world and the otherworld becomes particularly threadbare and the sacred and the secular seem to meet. In *Reimagining God and Religion*, psychologist Jerry R. Wright gives an expansive account of this dimension:

> ONCE UPON A TIME … according to Irish and Celtic storytellers, the visible and invisible worlds were one. Matter and spirit were intertwined, and human beings and gods and goddesses cavorted together. However, this commingling was confusing to mortals who needed separation to know what was real and unreal. Out of compassion for the human dilemma, the creative Powers hung a great curtain between the visible and invisible worlds (Estes, Audiotape). Furthermore, to encourage the continuing dialogue and relationship between the parties, there were certain places where the curtain remained very thin and certain times when the traffic through the curtain was especially heavy. These highly charged places and times came to be known as thin places and thin times.
>
> (2018: 223)

Rolfe's boundary project exists in the suspension – a holding – of that which was once before suspended – hung, an intimate bond between different life forms. The Skellig Rocks have an emblematic role in compelling and propelling such extraordinary meetings, as Irish studies scholar Catherine Maignant resounds the intersecting legacies coalescing on these liminal sites:

> 'Thin places' can in fact be found anywhere a form of boundary can be identified and pilgrimages to these locations are no doubt justified. One such threshold is that which separates this world and the next. Thus has pilgrimage to Skellig Michael been interpreted as 'a rehearsal for the soul's journey to eternity'. [...] As a symbolic threshold between the Christian and the pre-Christian cultures relating to death and eternal life, it is a favourite spot for Celtic pilgrims. In this case the eternal present even seeks to encroach on the eternal future of death, which is thus partly conquered by the living. It naturally also symbolizes the sought after rebirth to a new life.
>
> (2007: 24)

In this attenuated zone of indistinction, space and time stretch while one is standing still, at the threshold between exile and pilgrimage, internal and external landscape, self and others, the living and the dead. Yet this still life becomes animated by the topographically inflected formations which overlay the embodied experience of physical endurance with the sensual experience of the landscape.

The affective/ing qualities of this environment are made up of experiences, fleeting and absorbing, entrancing and undramatic, repeated moment after moment, and over time. It is a unique blend of sounds, smells, haptic sights, a unique composition of rhythms, of movement and stillness, of boundaries and crossings; it is a subsumed kind of knowing and sensing. The immanent suspension and circulation of such streams takes place by virtue of a spatial duration that is here expressed as an 'affect' of endurance. In Braidotti's radical project, endurance is laid out as an affirmative quality that informs a principle of sustainability:

> Endurance [...] has a temporal dimension: it has to do with lasting in time – hence duration as self-perpetuation. But it also has a spatial side to do with the space of the body as an enfleshed field of actualizations of passions or forces. It evolves affectivity and joy, as in the capacity of being affected by these forces, to the point of pain or extreme pleasure, which come to the same; it means putting up with hardship and physical pain.
>
> (2011: 315)

The suspension enacted by Rolfe, I contend, works hard to maintain these compelling and challenging possibilities without (de)termination. And more. The artist's durational test of sustainability in this case is emblematic of a form of strife 'beyond the preoccupation with his own body's limits and capacities' (Apple 2005: 45).

In the 2018 volume *Performing Endurance*, Lara Shalson sets out to redefine the performance of endurance in the contexts of art, politics and ethics. She distances her approach from existing discourses that generate consensus over a definition of practices that involve pain or duress, and experiences of time and duration. In contrast, she advances a more specific and broader understanding of endurance as the 'form' of an action that structures 'the intentional commitment to a plan whose outcome cannot be determined in advance' (10). The implications of this indeterminacy are significant and material as they are constitutive of endurance as a contingency 'always performed *in relation* to forces that are beyond the performer's control' (10, original emphasis). This constitutive model shifts the terms of agency as enduring is both something 'done' – tolerating or putting up – and something 'undergone' – surviving or remaining in existence. Ultimately, endurance is 'a willful act, but a willful act that confronts in repeated and sustained encounters the limits of individual agency' (10). Shalson's arguments are productive of a model of action that introduces endurance as both a structure and a physical composition. But where she is interested in this sustained practice as the form of a 'doing', I am here invested in relocating this form within

120

a structure of feelings – an 'affectivity' – that directs the intervening processes of relation and transformation.

Rolfe's attempted still life combines both connotations of embodied duress and temporal duration. But more significantly, the intended geographies of this situation locate the physical body as a material, sculptural form encompassed within an affective exchange, intimacy or collaboration with something outside of the artist's own control. This sustained practice – the gerundive use of stand*ing* indicates a processual form – with all the attendant pleasures and pains of encountering unpredictable and numinous forces,[8] indeed bares the impressions of the 'informal formalism' that curator Dorothy Walker recognizes in Rolfe's work. This approach, according to Walker, denotes the artist's engagement in using formless materials to engender form, and the creation of 'open-ended structures' and ambivalent spatial experiences. In the catalogue of the exhibition *Without the Walls*,[9] Walker emphasized the formless aspects of art that the formal characteristics of the artist's work should reckon with:

> For a deliberate formlessness, even paradoxically in the most formalist work, is an underlying connecting threat [*sic*] in all the works in this exhibition, even in Nigel Rolfe's destructive performances. There is nowhere a static structured approach; there is a commitment to process, to continuing, to recurring, which is endemic not only to modern Irish literature, (Joyce, Beckett, Flann O' Brien) but to ancient linear Celtic art.
>
> (Cotter 2011: 121)

What gets passed on between literature, art and here spirituality is a deep engagement with the processual properties of a sustained practice, at the same time with a sense of the special meaningfulness of it as a relation with place and its own vitality.

In *Standing*, this creative action structurally translates into the vertical line of the body interrupted by the inclination of the hands away from it. Held side by side, they hang in the form an empty vessel or an exploring probe; in the act of offering or receiving; in the possibilities of everything or nothing – and both. They contain and open up, like a graceful gift, in a thanking which engages actively 'with' giving. Simultaneously, the head bows down in an attitude that seems concerned with honouring this gesture, while the lowered gaze remains in contact with the emptiness it hands out or contains, as if absorbed in a mutual caress. The formal principles of these entrancing emplacements are consistent with how the psychologist Jerry R. Wright rewrites Carl Jung's impressions on the religious attitude: 'the allegiance, surrender, or submission to a supraordinate factor or to a "convincing" (overpowering) principle' (in Wright 2018: 234).

The abeyance of these postures is induced by the archetypal affective conditions that Jung describes a partial *abaissement du niveau mental*, a lowering of the threshold of consciousness. This in turn 'gives the unconscious a favourable opportunity to slip into the space vacated' (in Wright 2018: 234). The thin border that formally separates the inner consciousness from the outer is suddenly lifted. What reverses unto this open space is a sensuous intimation of, and intimacy with … nothing – made concrete, palpable and felt. In this thin space 'unexpected or otherwise inhibited unconscious contents break through and find expression in the affect' (in Wright 2018: 234).[10] To be precise, in the sense-making of this chapter, these negotiations are performed not so much by the key symbolic and practical roles of bodies, but rather by the processual, moving and recurring affects[11] – in the sense of dispositions or capacities that in-form (give form and expression to) their encounters and exchanges.

Ultimately, the affective and mystical qualities of thin place become actualized in a network of relations that allows for the spaciousness and capaciousness of a more profound experience 'within' and 'outwith' space. What is interesting is that the Celtic belief of the natural world as numinous, in fact, is the creation and expression of meaningful moments of fellowship among people and the non-human environment. Rolfe's sited activities participate in the bonds that were the original function of monastic practices and pilgrim aesthetics, which was – to set the scene for affective and spiritual encounter with the 'other'. The framework of performance, however, seems to offer an alternative form of spirituality more akin to our 'secularized' age in the understanding of the profound connection between human and environment and the recognition of this bond as sacred.

In his article 'Challenges of Spirituality in Contemporary Times', Kees Waaijman (2004) proposes a version of secular spirituality developed outside of the institutionalized forms of belief and traditional religious life and unfolding in the spheres of education, healthcare, management and ecology. He links this spirituality to the 'primordial processes of life; processes of education and learning, processes of work and organisation, processes of care and compassion, processes of becoming home in the environment surrounding us' (Waaijman 2004: 13–14). The perspective of this chapter situates the practice of performance in similar terms: not as *poiesis* as the material creation, production and invention that is the archetypal model for action and objective knowledge; but in the sense of *praxis*, in its original meaning of transformation, exchange, transfer, always in-formation. In this sense, per*form*ance can be qualified as the active form of ambivalent spatial experiences derived from the exchange of formless materials.

To speak of production here is to speak of an exchange between humans and non-humans in the realization of a social life that transforms the event, together with the space. This complex ritual process is in this case achieved through a temporary de-subjectification of the human in a folding and unfolding between inner and outer tensions. Rolfe's spatial exile is ultimately a journey to transformation. The result instigates perceptual processes – differentially sacral or mystical – of transmissible efficacy, community, power and genealogy. To pay attention to this practice may lead us – humans – to actively, socially and politically decentralize our relationship with space and place, through time.

For an ethics of suspense

Rolfe's artistic expressions emerge as a process and consequence of nomadic, ritual and liminal practices that develop in the perceptible suspense of a life at the limit. Endurance here is experienced not simply as physical or temporal state but as an affective condition that informs – gives form to – posture, location and relation. The bodily gestalt affects a situated practice of suspense that is not just incited but also defined by a set of contingent relations. The body becomes in this figuration annexed to the intervening nocturnal landscape and the other entities that inhabit it. The gestural mark formally holds out a threshold consciousness that reveals itself in an intimate contact with the surrounding world. The nomadic nature of this sculptural form mobilizes the processual transience of bodies and boundaries; virtualities and materialities that become actualized in co-creative events through the metamorphosis of sense into matter into sense into matter.

This dynamic relationality of bodies with-in-out-of space becomes incorporated, as it is excorporated, by the repetitive and enduring interplay of reciprocal 'holding' through the intermediate bridge of the night. The feeling and knowledge of the other side of the in-side – the out-side – reveals the threshold of passage, or in/distinction, between interior and exterior, exclusion and inclusion that calls the notion of the 'sacred' into articulate existence. The frame of this practiced intension/extension rests on an ethic principle and impulse realized by Braidotti's eco-ethic project:

> As a limit experience it marks the threshold of (un)sustainability, i.e., it prompts the awareness of fragility and the recognition of contingency. It also propels the subject to act according to this awareness. The result of the confrontation with the limit (the limit experience) is the transformation of the subject's relation to knowledge and to itself as a knowing subject. The limit experience accounts for the conversion of the subject into something else. This is the ethical moment.
>
> (2011: 316)

The artist's formal stand/ing takes the risks (and pleasures) of things changing in the moment, and towards this ethical sensibility. In its vertical form it stands out as a symbol of the distance between the human apparatus and the surrounding nature. Yet, its vertiginous dispositions signal a yielding over of its humanity to other life, to more life, to more than human life. The artist's words mark this ubiquitous situation: 'I'm still outside in the world inside in the work' (Rolfe 2016). In this intimate distance, the many others of this encounter interrupt the continuity of one-self, allowing for space, not only a reprieve from the material contingency of pain, but a new possibility of being otherwise in this relation.

This form of artistic suspension lays bare a qualified cartography that maps out the qualitative shifts necessary for an aesth-ethic of contingency, risk and uncertainty, which appears here as something other than a negative form of knowing and learning. Rather, it invokes the infinity of the great outdoors, which are all around and within. In this sense, it generatively animates a consecrated sphere located between the material density of the everyday world and the numinous, thin spaces of irreducible relationality. Here, the only sacred knowing is not being, not even becoming, but the suspenseful uncertainty that everything can be felt, 'otherwise' than what we know.

NOTES

1. The full title is *UNLIMITED ACTION: Limits of Performance*, at the Whitechapel Gallery, London, on 28 May 2016. The transcript of the audio recording of this presentation will constitute the backbone of my speculative analysis here. From here on, I will refer to this cited material as Rolfe 2016.
2. This piece is extracted from a larger series of performances begun in the mid-1970s under the title 'The Rope That Binds Us Makes Them Free'.
3. *Defense of Nature* was the title of an operation he promoted in the Italian region of Abruzzo in the late 1970s.
4. I am grateful to the artist for providing a copy of this image.
5. This picture is the trace of a performance on the occasion of the Morgeland Performance Festival in the town of Schaan, the largest municipality of Liechtenstein, and can be found in Þröstur Valgarðsson (2016).
6. The term 'foil' originates from the Latin word *fullo*, 'a fuller', and the verb *fullare*, 'to full cloth'. The Old French and obsolete English usages point to the sense of 'to step on or trample down'. See *Online Etymology Dictionary*, 2nd ed., https://www.etymonline.com/search?q=foil. Accessed 10 January 2019.
7. I am grateful to the artist for sending this text directly via email correspondence.
8. 'Numinous' is the term that theologian and philosopher Rudolph Otto (1958) coined for the powerful world 'sacred'; full of terror and fascination. This epithet is generally associated and/or equated with the definition and experience of thin place (see Wright 2018).

9. Held at the ICA, London, in the spring of 1980 and including Rolfe as one of the featured artists

10. Here again Jung is resounded via Wright, whose own reading productively unlocks the affective resonances between states of consciousness and the experience of open or thin places.

11. Perceived as extra-personal and suprahuman, beyond the command or control of the subject but not beyond the physical world of matter.

REFERENCES

Alifuoco, Annalaura (2017), '*Alive* performance: Toward an immersive activist philosophy', *Performance Philosophy*, 3:1, pp. 126–45, http://www.performancephilosophy.org/journal/article/view/87/179. Accessed 15 February 2019.

Altizer, Thomas J. J. (1980), *Total Presence: The Language of Jesus and the Language of Today*, New York: Seabury Press.

Apple, Jacki (2005), 'Special section – Franklin Furnace: A different world: A personal history of Franklin Furnace: Nigel Rolfe', *Drama Review*, 49:1, pp. 45–47.

Braidotti, Rosi (2011), *Nomadic Theory: The Portable Rosi Braidotti*, New York: Columbia University Press.

Braidotti, Rosi (2013), *The Posthuman*, Cambridge and Malden: Polity Press.

Cotter, L. Á. (2011), 'Curating, cultural capital and symbolic power: Representations of Irish art in London, 1950–2010', Ph.D. thesis, Amsterdam: University of Amsterdam, https://pure.uva.nl/ws/files/1426773/85906_thesis.pdf. Accessed 14 January 2019.

Dolphijn, Rick and van der Tuin, Iris (2012), 'The transversality of New Materialism', in R. Dolphijn and I. van der Tuin (eds), *Materialism: Interviews & Cartographies*, Open Humanities Press, pp. 93–114.

Dunne, Aidan and Rolfe, Nigel (1993), 'Work in process: Have home. Have not home less', *Circa*, 64, pp. 35–42.

Haraway, Donna (1988), 'Situated knowledges: The science question in feminism and the privilege of partial perspective', *Feminist Studies*, 14:3, pp. 575–99.

Haraway, Donna (2016), *Staying with the Trouble: Making Kin in the Chthulucene*, Durham, NC: Duke University Press Books.

Horn, Walter, Marshall, Jenny White and Rourke, Grellan D. (1990), *The Forgotten Hermitage of Skellig Michael*, Berkeley: University of California Press, http://ark.cdlib.org/ark:/13030/ft1d5nb0gb/. Accessed 13 January 2019.

Jasper, David (2004), *The Sacred Desert: Religion, Literature, Art, and Culture*, Oxford, MA, and Victoria: Blackwell Publishing Ltd.

Kant, Immanuel ([1790] 1951), *Critique of Judgement*, trans. J. H. Bernard, New York: Hafner Publishing Company, http://www.bard.edu/library/arendt/pdfs/Kant_CritiqueofJudgement.pdf. Accessed 1 September 2020.

Kay, James (2016), 'The Skelligs: A trip to the edge of the abyss', Lonely Planet, https://www.lonelyplanet.com/ireland/county-kerry/skellig-islands/travel-tips-and-articles/the-skelligs-a-trip-to-the-edge-of-the-abyss/40625c8c-8a11-5710-a052-1479d2763244. Accessed 14 January 2019.

Maignant, Catherine (2007), 'Alternative pilgrimages: Postmodern Celtic Christianity and the spatialisation of time', *Nordic Irish Studies*, 6, pp. 17–28.

O'Byrne, Ellie (2015), 'Performance artist Nigel Rolfe is muddying the waters between art and movement', *Irish Examiner*, https://www.irishexaminer.com/lifestyle/artsfilmtv/performance-artist-nigel-rolfe-is-muddying-the-waters-between-art-and-movement-363778.html. Accessed 13 January 2019.

Otto, Rudolph (1958), *The Idea of the Holy*, trans. J. W. Harvey, New York: Oxford University Press.

Rolfe, Nigel (1992), *Resonator*, Dublin: Douglas Hyde Gallery.

Rolfe, Nigel (2014), 'The rope that binds us makes them free', Troubles Archive, http://www.troublesarchive.com/artforms/performance-arts/piece/the-rope-that-binds-us-makes-them-free. Accessed 7 January 2019.

Rolfe, Nigel (2015), 'This is performance art (TIPA) // 29–31 Oct', Peacock Visual Arts, http://www.peacockvisualarts.com/this-is-performance-art-tipa-29-31-oct/. Accessed 13 January 2019.

Rolfe, Nigel (2016), 'Why, where, when, how, what for', transcript, 28 May, *UNLIMITED ACTION: Limits of Performance*, http://www.whitechapelgallery.org/events/%EF%BB%BF%EF%BB%BFsymposium-unlimited-action-performance/. Accessed 12 July 2018.

Rolfe, Nigel (2019), 'Nigel Rolfe, Ireland', Beijing Live, http://beijinglive.org/artists/nigel-rolfe.html. Accessed 12 January 2019.

Said, Edward W. (2002), *Reflections on Exile and Other Essays*, Cambridge, MA: Harvard University Press.

Shalson, Lara (2018), *Performing Endurance: Art and Politics since 1960*, Cambridge: Cambridge University Press.

Sigler, Jeremy (2012), 'Nigel Rolfe by Jeremy Sigler', *BOMB Magazine*, https://bombmagazine.org/articles/nigel-rolfe/. Accessed 10 January 2019.

Stengers, Isabelle (2012), 'Reclaiming animism', *E-flux*, https://www.e-flux.com/journal/36/61245/reclaiming-animism/. Accessed 12 July 2018.

Tuan, Yi-Fu (1975), 'Place: An experiential perspective', *Geographical Review*, 65:2, pp. 151–65.

Tuan, Yi-Fu (1978), 'Sacred space: Exploration of an idea', in K. W. Butzer (ed.), *Dimensions of Human Geography: Essays on Some Familiar and Neglected Themes*, Department of Geography Research Paper 186, Chicago: University of Chicago, pp. 84–99.

Valgarðsson, Þröstur (2016), 'Choreographing stillness', MA thesis, Reykjavík, Iceland Academy of the Arts, https://skemman.is/bitstream/1946/25465/1/MA_thesis_Throstur.pdf. Accessed 15 February 2019.

Waaijman, Kees O. Carm (2004), 'Challenges of spirituality in contemporary times', *Spirituality Forum III*, University of St Thomas, Manila, Philippines, 6 August, https://repository.ubn. ru.nl/bitstream/handle/2066/59845/59845.pdf?sequence=1. Accessed 1 September 2020.

William, James (1958), *The Varieties of Religious Experience*, New York: New American Library.

Wright, Jerry R. (2018), *Reimagining God and Religion: Essays for the Psychologically Minded*, Asheville, NC: Chiron Publications.

Zhangyu, Deng (2018), 'Living in the moment, pushing boundaries', *China Daily*, 2 June, http:// usa.chinadaily.com.cn/a/201802/06/WS5a7905cba3106e7dcc13af81_2.html. Accessed 13 January 2019.

6

The Introspective Theatre of
Spirits Read Foucault:
The Digital Space, the Inner Gaze and a
Sacred Landscape

Silvia Battista

Form does not differ from emptiness [and] emptiness does not differ from form. Form is emptiness, emptiness is form [...] No appearing, no disappearing.

(Sahn 1997: 130)

Introduction

In the seminal book *The Empty Space* Peter Brook refers to 'Holy Theatre' as '[t]he Theatre of the Invisible-Made-Visible [...] a place where the invisible can appear' (1968: 47). He cites a tradition of artists and theatre makers from Antonine Artaud (1896–1948) to Jerzy Grotowski (1933–99), Samuel Beckett (1906–89) and the Living Theatre as a few of the many instances where art has been employed as a vehicle for entering into contact with 'a sacred invisibility' (Brook 1968: 54). That is, a process of accessing knowledge through consciousness states that are separate not only from the scientific gaze, but also from our daily-life perception. Although the conception of holy theatre is often positioned within the scope of the irrational, opposed to the logical, structural and methodical approaches of science, there is a sense of empirical experimentation not only in the concept of a theatre laboratory[1] but also in the terminology used regarding experimental theatre and some forms of contemporary art making.[2]

This chapter looks specifically at the performance *Spirits Read Foucault* (SRF), a practice-research project that I wrote and performed for the first time in 2015,

128

and developed into its final outcome in 2019. This work employs the aesthetics of theatre and practices related to the paratheatrical to investigate the relation between the material and the spiritual, to confront assumptions about the physical body and to question binary approaches that demarcate fixed boundaries for spirituality and materiality. Further, still in theatre, it aims to reveal and record perceptions that are intangible to our daily life apprehension of things through an ethnographic, participative strategy. The ultimate objective is to involve audiences in experiencing aspects of human consciousness and perception that are often difficult to access.

Methodologically speaking, I am interested in bringing together the experiential with a third-person perspective, the semiotic and the phenomenological, to engage with and explore how performance can contribute to the ongoing conversation on spirituality and embodiment in contemporary society and whether it can problematize the fixed, oppositional categorizations of reality that divide spirit from matter, among other things.

So far, this work has benefitted a multidisciplinary community of scholars, but also artists and students. For example, in 2015, it was performed before an audience of 70 theologians and religious studies scholars at the Faith and Civil Society Unit, Goldsmith University, London, during the second annual symposium *Sacred and Secular: Faith and Formation*. The same year, it was presented to an audience of 40 psychologists and psychiatrists involved in psychedelic studies and interested in the role of altered states of consciousness in therapeutic contexts during the third *International Conference on Psychedelic Studies*, at Greenwich University, London; and to 20 artists and scholars at the IFTR conference at Hyderabad University, India. In 2016, a video version of the piece was screened by Dr Anton Krueger to students studying in the Department of Drama at Rhodes University, South Africa, who were interested in learning about mindfulness. In 2019, the online, participative video/performance was launched for an invited audience only.

SRF was adapted differently to suit each format, reflecting the nature of each context and the cultural backgrounds of the recipients. It has been presented as a live, participative performance; as a participative, experiential video screening; and eventually as a participative, individual online performance.[3] Each format required a slight revision of the text. The version of the project analysed in this chapter is the latest online version.

This version is particularly useful to my research trajectory because by engaging with and employing a multidisciplinary set of cultural contexts – performance, digital media, spiritual practice, anthropology and religious studies – it contributes, as practice research, to the field of studies intersecting posthumanism, spirituality and performance. Indeed, located in that liminal area between imagination, theatre, ritual and advanced technology, the experiment is part of my ongoing research into posthuman spiritualities at the convergence between contemporary performance, ritualistic practices and the paratheatrical (see Battista 2018).

The online performance unfolds as follows. A performer, called *Nothing*, is digitally present on the screen, standing under a spotlight in a theatre space and looking at the beholder. A voiceover guides the participant, through a previously devised script, into mindfulness exercises, including observation, intersecting gazes with the digital performer, reflections and internal visualizations, until the narrative reaches a different level of engagement. The participant is asked to wear a blindfold and engage in visions of dismemberment. Within this complex internal/external/digital perceptive system, the participant is guided to dismember the body of the performer, *Nothing*, from the surface of the skin to the bones of the skeleton until *Nothing* is left. It is then and there that reflection on the material apparatus of life is triggered. In the lack of apparent materiality the voiceover asks participants to feel a different order of matter which is intangible, nevertheless material and sensory.

Assumptions and objectives

What is now referred to as practice-as-research or practice-research comprises artistic processes that, by being located in the context of research, problematizes the position of the arts in opposition to science and reveals a much more complex scenario as to what research can be and do. As well as the rehabilitation of the subjective perspective, this entails imagination, affects and many other contexts that, by escaping the gaze of the sciences, become fruitful material to be explored within the arts. This also provides the possibility of dialogue between different spheres of human endeavour and cultural perceptions that can and should all be allowed to contribute to the formations of narratives through which reality 'is' viewed, 'can be' viewed or, more radically speaking, 'could be' viewed.

The potential of the 'could be' is particularly productive in the context of this chapter as it opens research to the paradigm of the sacred, to a diversity of onto-epistemological possibilities that multiply the perspectives of what we understand as physical 'reality'.

It is worth specifying that within the paradigm of the sacred I refer to a paradoxical condition including both separation and indifferentiality. These are both temporal and spatial conditions that, by moving between one state and the other, disrupt the notion of reality attached merely to solid matter. They are discrete bodies moving within discrete, separated environments producing multiple stages of realities through intersecting material formations. To explicate this point further I refer to Rudolph Otto's interpretation of the holy, the sacred. In Otto's view, the meaning of 'holy' lies in its etymological genealogy, for example: 'in Latin and

Greek, in Semitic and other ancient languages, [the sacred] denote[s] first and foremost *only* [an] overplus' of meaning (1958: 5, original emphasis). This overplus of meaning is always and inevitably situated somewhere not only beyond the rational and moral interpretation of the 'completely good', often associated with the idea of divine (*numen*), but also beyond fixed, established, accepted interpretations of reality. Otto's exploration of the sacred questions its singular interpretation, given by a specific moral code, potentially opening it to unexpected and unfamiliar ontologies. My assumption here is therefore that ontology is always a positioned project, always ongoing, on the move. Consequently, the sacred with its association to the unknown, moves too. It changes according to perspectives, positionalities, opportunities: social, cultural, biological, perceptual, spiritual, technological and so on.

Hence, this approach looks at the question of the sacred from a multiangled point of view and a plurality of perspectives; an attitude that is borrowed from both the analysis of Amerindian prospectivism provided by Eduardo Viveiros de Castro in his book *Cannibal Metaphysics* (2009) and from John Caputo's ([2000] 2008) thesis around his inclusive and multiple hermeneutical approach referred to as radical hermeneutics. The former, by looking at Amerindian shamanism, claims 'an anthropological theory of the conceptual imagination, attentive toward creativity and reflexivity that belong to each, single collective human and non-human' (Viveiros De Castro 2009: 31). This encourages the production of differences and alterities by recognizing multiple potential producers of ontological perspectives and conditions of existence. Here, the question of truth is not valuated in terms of universal value, but actually in terms of performativity. In other words, around the question: which kind of ecological formations does this perspective produce and what are the social, political, ecological, spiritual consequences of it?

Radical hermeneutics also opposes any form of essentialism of reality, endorsing a view of knowledge that resists fixity and permanence and necessarily is embedded in non-knowing (Caputo [2000] 2008: 3). However, according to Caputo, it is exactly this sense of impossibility that hovers around the project of knowledge and the sacred itself with its overplus of meanings, which renders necessary the application of temporary, shared categorizations of reality, and at the same time maintains the momentum for further engagement, interpretations and revisions (Caputo [2000] 2008: 5). This is to say that although a certain kind of structural blindness is always at play in radical hermeneutics, it is the same condition of non-knowing that, according to Caputo,

keep[s] us open to innumerable mutations and unforeseeable possibilities, to incalculable ways of being and knowing, doing and seeing, exposed to potentialities of which we cannot presently conceive, to things improbable and incomprehensible, unimaginable and unplannable.

([2000] 2008: 6)

This is why, Caputo argues, nothing should be left outside the project of radical hermeneutics: 'nothing is off-limits, nothing banned from discussion, or beyond question' ([2000] 2008: 7). From this perspective knowledge requires an ongoing research attitude, a continuous development of previous positions through adjustments, as well as a passion for the impossible, the secret and the imaginary (Caputo [2000] 2008: 7–8).[4]

This is not post-structural relativism, but rather the ontological assumption that reality is eventful and open to interpretative positionalities, positionalities that nonetheless are not reducible to each other or negotiable. In other words, each position rather than being relative is solely limited, finite and therefore always inadequate. This also means that in between the categorizations of reality organized around fixed, axiomatic oppositions such as science and art, spirituality and materiality, mind and body, there are many other ontological opportunities to be accessed in order to achieve a less insufficient understanding of what reality can be.[5]

In the effort of unpacking and problematizing polarizing discourses lies also the contribution of this chapter, which by reclaiming performance as a context of discovery and knowing proposes it as a paradigm for the encounter between dissociated practices such as detached observation and experiential, embodied knowledge; analysis and imagination; the text and the body; but also between disconnected spatial conditions: the digital, the physical and the imaginary. It contributes to this effort by focusing on the question of embodiment, the relation between matter and spirit, mind and body. It does that by connecting to the tradition of theatre makers and artists interested in the potentiality of theatre as a laboratory for experimentation with the limits and potentials of human perception, non-ordinary states of consciousness and cognitive processes.

Therefore, *SRF*, by using theatre as a laboratory and the body as a technology, maximizes Bruce Wilshire's approach to the paratheatrical, which he defines as the crossing of the boundaries which divides imagination[6] from fact (1990: 169). Accordingly, I propose a view of embodiment as the axis and the opening of consciousness to an order of materiality that questions what Octavio Paz (1978) referred to as 'the ancient notions of solid matter'.

Furthermore, by guiding the audience into a well-calibrated imaginary act of dismemberment, *SRF* offers to participants an opening towards a 'theatre of cruelty' that, as Antonine Artaud conceived it, is capable of holding in embodiment both the horror of decomposition and the ecstasy of resurrection. What is asked in exchange is the perspective of the participants, their inner world and imagination, which is included in the work by forms of written feedback collected as ACT III. ACT III is when participants are asked to leave a written commentary on their experience. This is a particularly significant part of the work, as it is considered the real theatrical experience of *SRF*. Indeed, *SRF* is eventually an introspective theatre that radicalizes the value of what happens inside the mind, body and being of each participant. All the rest – the text, the performer, the sound – are triggers, vehicles, activators allowing the active imagination of the participant to take over.

Contextualization

The internal order of spectatorship of the introspective theatre that participants are invited to navigate has been studied and explained through various terminologies according to the disciplines and perspectives taken. For example, Colin McGinn (2004) calls it 'mindsight'; Richard Noll (1985) articulates it as mental imaginary; Henri Corbin (1972) as *Mundus Imaginalis*; Carl Gustave Jung (1997) interprets it as active imagination; Peter Schwenger (2008) as 'hypnagogia'; Michael Harner (1990) as shamanic journey, and so on.

The latter is particularly poignant in this context as the premises from which the script and the work generally has been devised are to be found in a shamanic journey that I experienced under the guidance of Zoe Bran during training I undertook in Core Shamanism.[7]

During this journey I saw and experienced myself being dismembered by a group of undefined entities who destroyed my body and ate it. Eventually I reappeared as a firefly. Apart from the poetic reincarnation suggested during the journey, the experience of dismemberment left me utterly shaken and disturbed. I was unsure about how to interpret it, and there was an unpleasant internal fear of 'going mad', of losing control over 'my' psyche and of having experienced a psychotic episode.

The book *Madness and Civilization: A History of Insanity in the Age of Reason* by Michael Foucault ([1961] 2001) supports an historical contextualization of 'madness', providing generative evidences of its cultural, political and social implications. This study provides the historical scaffolding from which to locate the experience mentioned earlier within the parameters of a specific moral code which has located such episodes within the context of insanity and medicalization. Indeed, the fact that the journey I undertook was a spontaneous visualization of my body being dismembered represented a determinant occasion in which the logic of my habitual self clashed with an experience that was highly challenging because of its brutality, to the extent that it ruptured the moral codes of the cultural context I belong to. However, when the journey was concluded, and I talked with Bran about my feelings she assured me that this was not a sign of psychosis and that I was not having a mental breakdown. Rather, she argued that it was a common experience in shamanic traditions wherein it is understood as a sort of initiation to the practice.

Following Foucault's cultural and historical contextualization of the moral codes through which insanity has been identified and treated, I hypothesized that my personal biases and resistance towards such a brutal imaginary experience belonged to a cultural tradition which is prone to medicalize such psychophysical conducts. For example, Noll refers to early historical and anthropological interpretations of shamanic practices of this kind that were in fact described by early anthropologists as psychopathological occurrences or psychotic instances (1985: 445). Accordingly, as Foucault delineates, the question of how 'the hallucinatory sphere' has been contextualized and valuated is always a matter of cultural practices and positioning. Indeed, what is acceptable and what is not, what is functional or dysfunctional, superior or inferior depends on how power relations are established and conducted within the specificity of a culture and its dependent myths and narratives. Hence, it is from there that this complex and deep set of intangible influences, which are the moral principles that a society follows, are established together with the set of standards that determine what is acceptable and what is not, what is real and what is not ([1961] 2001).

For example, in European culture, since the enlightenment, there has been an increasing distrust towards the imaginary. It has come to be regarded from a binary perspective as an aspect of our life that is non-real and therefore opposite to what is real with a capital R=Reality. Indeed, as Corbin reminds us:

> regardless of our effort, we cannot prevent the term *imaginary*, in current usage that is not deliberate, from being equivalent to signifying unreal, something that is and remains outside of being and existence-in brief, something utopian.
>
> (1972: 1, original emphasis)

On the contrary, going back to the journey I mentioned earlier,[8] although the experience I had was imaginary, it was also strangely real in a way that was tangible in and to my body, therefore it is possible to argue that it crossed the boundaries of the so-called mind and touched my body inside. My body was shaken by the physical quality of the experience, like when we have dreams that somehow hold a different quality from the usual. They are able to cross the limit of the dream-like-dimension and enter the landscapes of what we know as reality. These are moments of contamination between spheres of 'reality' that are usually separated. They are instances when the dream leaks into the waking life and the visionary pierces the veil to penetrate the logic of daily life.

This is the aspect of the experience that attracted my attention, triggering not only questions around what kind of experience took place, but also the creative modalities devised for the theatrical piece. Indeed, this experience opened a space, an unknown, sacred space, within the dualistic fabric of my reality and questioned some of the assumptions about where the mind starts and the body ends, exposing a complex system of different spatial materialities.

I would like to conclude this part of the chapter by inviting the reader to reframe or reposition this practice-research project from within the premises of the oppositional constituents of binary thinking, towards the more prolific exploration of the performative aspect of such experiences. In other words, rather than asking 'was that experience real or imaginary?' I would like to involve the reader in an analysis of the following questions: what did that experience do to the participants? What changes did it trigger? And does the experience triggered reflections on the topics mentioned earlier? I believe that focusing my attention towards the analysis of the affective and experiential reverberations of the work will prove to be a much more productive endeavour than the effort of determining whether the experience was real or not.

The analysis that follows is structured around the three parts of the piece: ACT I/The Threshold; ACT II/The Experience; ACT III/The Feedback. ACT II and ACT III will be investigated together.

ACT I: The Threshold

FIGURE 6.1: Still frame from the video *Spirits Read Foucault* (2019). Courtesy of Massimiliano Ferraina.

The performance as experienced by the participants starts with an email that is addressed personally:

Dear ...,

I hope you are well!

This email is to invite you to the individual online vernissage of the work *Spirits Read Foucault*, a project that I started in 2015 and it is now at its final stage.

Spirits Read Foucault has been presented live in UK, experienced collectively through video recorded instructions in UK, Italy, India and South Africa, and now, this individual, digital/online form represents its conclusion. The work as a whole represents a first utterance of what I call Introspective Theatre that is an ongoing research project developing performative experiences wherein external sight is hindered and internal visualizations stimulated.

The work consists of a guided visualisation that includes imaginary blood and cuttings, so if you do not feel that this is something that you would like to engage with at this moment in your life, please let me know. It is absolutely fine to say no.

However, if you decide to experience the work, here are some instructions: you will need around 30 minutes to engage with it; a computer connected to internet; a blindfold; and a pair of headphones.

To start, please follow this order of actions:
• Act One: open the attached document and read the letter;
• Act Two: open the Vimeo link https://vimeo.com/360090466 and enter the password ----------------- and when you are ready and comfortable play the video[9];
• Act Three: when the video is finished write something about your experience in the Vimeo comment box, feel free to write anything that emerges from the guided journey you went through. If you do not have a Vimeo membership and do not intend to have one, please send me your feedback via email.

Bear in mind that at a certain point, during the video you will be asked to wear the blindfold, so keep it at hand. Please do not share this video with anyone else. If you would like someone else to experience it, send me their email address and I will send them a personal invitation. To conclude, if you decide to participate, I wish you an insightful journey and look forward to reading your feedback.

Many thanks,
Silvia

This email sets the tone of the experience and works both as an invitation and as a warning, especially in relation to some aspects of the performance that can trigger traumatic experiences or provoke undesired emotional responses. The email is metaphorically the entry into the virtual, theatrical space of *SRF*, situated at the gate of the experience and allowing participants to make an informed choice and decide, like in the myth of the hero, whether to cross the threshold and start the adventure or to decline the offer. Furthermore, it determines the rules of the journey by providing instructions, information and the boundaries around which the experience is meant to be shared. This experience is ritualistically organized around individually crafted invitations, and this direct relation between the author and the participant is maintained by asking each invited guest to avoid sharing the video with others. If someone else is interested, the person should be referred back to the moderator, who will in turn invite the new participant directly through the same ritualistic route, email and letter.

This choice is strategic in resisting the undemanding and indiscriminate modalities by which experiences are shared via the internet and on social media, and in reclaiming a condition of intimacy and privacy within that same virtual space. In a way, it employs the procedures that characterize the formation of sacred places through protection and separation within the spatiality of the digital environment. This is a form of restraint, of boundaries-making, to contain the limitless potentialities of navigation within the digital space and to create 'a particular condition of clarity and organized attention' towards one experience only (Battista 2018: 39). It is a necessary step when engaging with an experience such as *SRF*, which requires mindful attention and dedication within a virtual, limitless spatial condition such as internet. I find this contradiction particularly prolific within the objective of this experiment that requires the application of temporary perimeters for the expansion of perceptual possibilities. In other words, it is the nature of the laboratory, both scientific and theatrical, to necessitate the establishment of clear boundaries and instructions within which the research is carried out. In this context this requirement operates an exorcising activation of the internet that differs from its usual employment and navigation.

I encourage the reader to think in terms of systems and apparatuses, to reflect on the email as a strategy to create a highly controlled setting within an expansive environment and then to discover a different system within the system where a certain condition is kept stable in order to experiment, in isolation, with the behaviours of certain phenomena. That is, for the experiment of *SRF* to operate within certain physical/virtual conditions, I needed to establish perimeters so that certain aspects of the environment/internet were selected and controlled in order to carry out the experiment within a stable apparatus (Battista 2018).

According to Foucault, an apparatus is essentially strategic in manipulating the relations of forces within a specific system (1980: 196). These relations can be moved in a particular direction, blocked, stabilized or multiplied in order to accomplish specific objectives and in accordance with the specific knowledge from which it is constructed. An apparatus is, therefore, always linked to 'certain limits of knowledge that arise from [the system] and, to an equal degree, conditions it' (Foucault 1980: 196). The internet, as a virtual space, is in itself an apparatus in which contents are shared within a specific system. In this context contents and apparatuses both constitute the specificity of the system in place and, vice versa, the specificity of the system emerges from the influences of both knowledge and apparatus. This is to say that the relation of forces that emerges in a system is produced by a reciprocal loop of influence that reinforms and re-enforces, in time, all of the participative constituents, their perceptions and descriptions of what is real and not real (Battista 2018).

In conclusion, by restricting the modalities by which the internet operates within *SRF*, I produced a different system within the system, a sacred apparatus with specific rules and instructions which opened the virtual space to a kind of experience which is other from the conventional, virtual navigation.

To go back to the email, when and if the invited guest decides to accept the invitation and consequently crosses the threshold of the performance, or of the *SRF*'s system, they are asked to engage with the second stage of ACT I: the opening of the attached letter. This is the symbolic ritualistic act of unsealing the digital, attached, encrypted object, the significance of which becomes evident in time. The letter, in fact, provides the cultural, experiential and personal contexts of the piece. It has been specifically written to provide further perimeters to the experience: the cultural premises of the process of dismemberment in shamanic contexts, its interpretations in contemporary anthropology and psychology. What it follows is an expanded version of the letter, which allows the reader to explore the avenues of studies around this practice.

The letter

SPIRITS READ FOUCAULT – ACT ONE

Dear ...,

In 2014 I had a dream or better a journey guided by Zoe Bran with whom I was training at that time. I had a dream of being dismembered. This experience disturbed me but also made me feel strangely anew.[10]

FIGURE 6.2: Still frame from the video *Spirits Read Foucault* (2019). Courtesy of Massimiliano Ferraina.

Despite that the experience of dismemberment belongs also to classical Greek mythology, for instance, 'Dionysus is tricked and dismembered while still a baby, boiled and placed on a spit by the Titans to then be put back together from the leftover and ashes', this is a mythological experience that is rarely explored in contemporary cultures. According to Noll, however, in shamanic cultures the imaginary brutality of events of this kind and their narrations are of great importance. We are referring here to 'traditions devoted to the deliberate, repeated induction of enhanced mental imaginary [...] for its functional and adaptive value' (Noll 1985: 444). Therefore, these are events that, by crossing the threshold dividing the mental and the physical, represent initiatory rituals functional to allow consciousness to access a plurality of ontological conditions and existences, which are functional to profound, existential passages.

Mircea Eliade argues in the seminal book *Shamanism: Archaic Techniques of Ecstasy* (1996) that the experience of being dismembered is recorded in several shamanic traditions. For example, Siberian Tungus shamans experience visions of dismemberment in different forms when their bodies are cut and blood drunk by evil spirits. The same is recorded among the Buryat, the Teleut and the Eskimo (Eliade 1996: 44). The Eskimo 'speak of an animal [...] that wounds the candidate, tears him to pieces or devour him' (Eiliade 1996: 45). There are recordings of similar experiences in the Tibetan Buddhist ritual *chöd*, traditionally performed in solitude in cemeteries. The practitioner cultivates detachment when visualizing that her/his body has been dismembered. Alexandra David-Neel provides a personal account of the experience of *chöd* rituals explaining how the practitioner, by conceiving the idea of nothingness of the self, realizes also that 'sacrifice is but an illusion, an offshoot of blind, groundless pride' (1937: 123). Her distinct narration of the rite describes endless preparations and, in her words, 'rehearsals' to prepare the practitioner for the perilous undertaking of destroying the illusion of the ego (David-Neel 1937: 121). She describes the beginning of the rite in mythological terms, aspects of which clearly resonate with the experience I described in the section earlier:

> The celebrant blows his bone trumpet, calling the hungry demons to the feast he intends to lay before them. He imagines that a feminine deity, which esoterically personifies his own will, springs from the top of his head and stands before him, sword in hand. With one stroke she cuts off the head of the [celebrant]. Then, while troops of ghouls crowd round for the feast, the goddess severs his limbs, skins him and rips open his belly.
>
> (David-Neel 1937: 122)[11]

Richard Noll tells of the initiatory vision of a Nganasan Samoyed shaman of Siberia, when 'a "blacksmith" dismembered him and also changed his eye' (Noll 1985: 446).

In the tradition of Jungian psychoanalysis, imaginary experiences of dismemberment relate to the process of individuation and are a practice aimed at dismantling self-attachment to a fixed sense of identity or to a specific form of self that we perceive as immutable. It aims to give birth to a new awareness of a liberated, fluid sense of self. For example, Norma Churchill in her account of such an ordeal argues that

> dismemberment is a worldwide function of the psyche, perhaps best known in shamanic traditions. It is an ancient process of the inner self or soul to reveal itself, to expand and grow. To die and to be born anew is one of the oldest ideas of the human mind.
>
> (2011: 83)

She recalls her personal experience of dismemberment when she visualized snakes tearing her torso apart 'making a triumph of blood and brains, sinew and bone' eventually declaring 'I was now only consciousness' (Churchill 2011: 91). These experiences are in themselves initiations to a new life, representing the culmination of existential journeys where the self is confronted not only with physical death but with the death of the ego and the resurrection of a new, connected sense of self.

Psychiatrist Roger Walsh notices how in many rites of passage around the world 'death-rebirth rituals are acted out at times of important life transitions'. Even in Christian contexts, those who go through profound religious conversion 'may have a sense of dying to the old bodily self and being 'born again' in the spirit or in Christ' (Walsh 1994: 23). However, as Richard Noll argues, although Christianity has assembled numerous accounts of visionary apparitions and the Bible is rich with spontaneous visions, contrary to shamanic spiritual traditions there is no encouragement to develop cultivated processes and forms (Noll 1985: 444). There is indeed an important distinction to be made between spontaneous visions and cultivated forms of active imagination. According to Noll 'cultivated imaginary' consists 'in taking the primary material or "raw stuff" of spontaneous imaginative experiences and forging methods of reproducing such phenomena at will that can be taught to selected others' (1985: 444).

SRF is one of these attempts, within the contemporary, cultural context of performance, art and practice-research. It is an experiment allowing the possibility for Western contemporary consciousness to cultivate the imaginary, where the shock of the brutality of the dismemberment experience is held beyond the crisis through the calibration of voice and rhythm. From this perspective, the performance strategies and dramaturgical choices locate the experience simultaneously on both symbolic and phenomenological levels 'where a symbol stands for a semiotic sign which in no way attempts to fully convey and exhaust the object of its signification' (Campagna 2018: 118) in abstraction, but actually attempts to experience it in embodiment by crossing the divide between the signifier and the signified. Indeed, each of the instructions emerge as symbols, but not 'as a product of semiotic convention, but rather as something that dwells within mythic structures like life dwells in a body' (Campagna 2018: 151).

ACT II and ACT III: *The Experience and The Narration*

If compared to the brief and certainly uncompleted overview of the symbols and practices related to the imaginary experience of dismemberment provided earlier, in the context of *SRF* the practice and process of dismemberment follows an unusual direction.[12] Instead of being dismembered, the participant is invited to dismember the performer standing in the theatrical space depicted in the screen.

The performer is called *Nothing*, both a theatrical and performative strategy that refers to a presence that is also semiotically an absence. It reduces the actor/performer to a non-representational entity that refuses even to present themselves.

FIGURE 6.3: Still frame from the video *Spirits Read Foucault* (2019). Courtesy of Massimiliano Ferraina.

Nothing is indeed a mirror rather than an actor, they are a receptacle, a vessel for the participant to project her/him/themselves on. Rather than representing a character, a signified other, or a self, as in the case of performance artists, *Nothing* remains nothing until the participant fills the vessel with their projections. Indeed, although *Nothing*'s appearances offer some cues from which to retrieve some sense of identity, age, gender, class, these cues are too weak to resist the overlapping of projected images. For example, Participant M saw *Nothing* 'as an invitation to discard preconceived ideas of the "self" and uncover alternative understandings which I may have either buried, lost forever or could invent anew'. Participant O identifies the question very clearly when they say:

> It's interesting to watch 'nothing' in a spotlight on a stage: the surface of an identity on display, to be viewed. But *where* is she? I don't know. There and not there. Else-where perhaps. Certainly not visible, not picked up by the spotlight in the theatre.
>
> (n.pag., original emphasis)

It is indeed in the theatre where the spotlight shines on a section of the stage that *Nothing* enacts nothing, offers nothing, represents nothing. *Nothing* is the void, the void as 'a living, breathing indeterminacy of non/being' (Barad 2012) that 'do[es] not exist in space and time [...], [a] ghostly non/existence that teeter on the edge of the infinitely fine blade between being and nonbeing' (Barad 2012). But *Nothing* is also the second threshold of the hero journey of the participant. It is through *Nothing* that they reach the centre of the experience in introspection.

The journey is led by the narrator, an additional entity who refuses to identify themselves as the narrator. As *Nothing* and with *Nothing* they are the technologies, instruments and activators of the unusual observation of the physical void of solidity.

From that point onwards the participants are guided to open an internal condition of spectatorship that is radicalized when they are asked to use the blindfold. The blindfold is a radical perimeter of protection, a sensory deprivation strategy to restrain the participant from the visual distractions of the so-called outside world. However, because before wearing the blindfold participants are involved in mindful observation of *Nothing*, when blindfolded they maintain awareness of their physical, visualized, digital presence and at the same time of their imagined one. This multiplies both images and the crossing gazes of observation between the performer and the beholder, and also between the beholder and themselves. For example, participant D states, 'As I looked into the screen, at first I saw you, but then I quickly realized that NOTHING was Me'; similarly participant E says:

> I connected deeply with *nothing* and burst into tears. The emotions were an externalization of the reciprocity and mirroring I had been experiencing. I became *Nothing* and the boundaries me-you and me-others dissolved.
>
> (n.pag.)

The usage of the digital screen disrupts further the definitive boundaries and identities of the single self, proliferating cross-pollination between externalized and internalized existential conditions. The physicality of the body perceived outside oneself is indeed a digital body (*Nothing*). On the other hand, the body of the participant stands in the physical, solid world of our daily life; however, both the digital and the physical get overlapped in the imaginary. Hence, when participants are asked to wear the blindfold and see the imaginary body internally, it is a dynamic that pierces the oppositional surfaces of the physical, the digital and the imaginary producing in juxtaposition a web of perceptive, hybrid alternatives where the other potentially becomes the self. Here, seeing opens an intersecting field of gazes that resonates with the act of 'seering', the craft of sybils and prophets able to see beyond the boundaries of the visible into topographies of visionary states.

This is an adventure that might reset the order of things as we know them, turn the external into the internal and render things upside down as, according to Corbin:

It is a matter of entering, passing *into the interior* and, in passing into the interior, of finding oneself, paradoxically [...] once this transition is accomplished, it turns out that henceforth this reality, previously internal and hidden, is revealed to be enveloping, surrounding, containing what was first of all external and visible, since by means of *interiorization*, one has *departed* from that external reality. Henceforth, it is spiritual reality that envelops, surrounds, contains the reality called material.

(1972: 3–4, original emphasis)

It is within this process of repositioning oneself in the matrix of existence that participants start dismembering *Nothing*, and it is in that moment that the experience acquires the meanings that the work intends to investigate. As from an Artaudian perspective on cruelty, the act of dismemberment plays the function of awakening the self to the experience, as if the act of dismantling a body in its brutality is able to 'wake us up: nerves and heart' (Artaud 1958: 84). For example, according to participant G,

cutting and removing the skin was very disturbing, but it was also the most vivid act: my throat was dry, my feet and my sweaty hands writhed. The blood impressed me, but I also found it liberating, terrifying, but the body seemed to rejoice in jets.

(n.pag.)

Artaud regards shock as essential in the experience of theatre if it is to revive our understanding and comprehension of reality away from the long and mortal separation of the mind from the body (1958: 86). However, this is not always the case, and the experience might be too demanding for some; indeed, some of the participants devised strategies to carry out the action and avoid the shock. For example, participant C states, 'My mind then created a more graphic depiction of the body. It turned it into a mannequin used in doctors' training – that can be neatly taken apart into its individual components.' In order to cope with the perceptive complexity of the action, participant I chose speed as their strategy and they stated that 'I could then imagine the dismemberment but only at speed and without too much details'. For others there was no escape from the trauma of the experience as, for example, participant F recorded the following:

I felt exposed and hated being the voyeur. And then, to pass to the act of dismemberment: the blood that flowed, the tearing, the anguish of the pain: even to write about it, reliving the imaginative act, it makes me suffer a lot. I can even smell the blood.

(n.pag.)

Here there was no cathartic experience in the act of cruelty. Although this reaction might be a success from an Artaudian perspective, in the context of this project it did not allow the participant to access the last part of the performance. In this case, connections to traumatic experiences, lived or heard, moved the ritualistic context of *SRF* towards the dimension of power relations in the context of punishment. This offers interesting points for reflection on the fragile line dividing technologies of the self from abusive practices as often the technologies employed in context of punishment and torture have similar characteristics with spiritual and ritualistic practices. For example, isolation cells, sensory deprivation techniques, repetitions and the taking away of identity are all strategies employed in both contexts, however with very different aims. In *SRF* intention and agency are the elements that draw apart the perimeters between the two. Unfortunately, the perceptive overlapping of the two rendered the experience that *SRF* offered unbearable for participant F. However, most participants managed to get through the difficulty of this part of the performance. For example, participant E had a deep cathartic experience: 'I connected deeply with *Nothing* and burst into tears. The emotions were an externalization of the reciprocity and mirroring I had been experiencing.'

Others, especially artists accustomed with the cutting and blood of body art, entered completely into the ritualistic aspect of the experience and felt the need to request a slower paced delivery of the instructions. For example, participant D wrote:

> It was interesting that you told us to remove the skin quickly – I did not want to. I want to peel it off slowly, I wanted to see how everything oozed, I wanted to sit holding a knife the way you would when skinning an animal and cut that glue layer and the veins. But when I ripped it off, the most startling image was the eyes, of the face, of the blood and the muscle and the tissue of the face. But it did not frighten me, in fact it felt ominously familiar.
>
> (n.pag.)

Participant N also asked for a different pace: 'Too quickly, too quickly. These things take time. I want to feel the resistance under my knife, the resistance under my fingers as I peel away.' However, eventually, they felt something; for example, participant N continues: 'now I see the flayed body and feel a revulsion not there before. Moist, raw, red and noisy. Ooze. I feel nauseous. Strangely, I smell nothing.' But soon after, an interesting reference to ritualistic practices is offered again by participant N in relation to the pace of the dismemberment:

> The removal of muscles, tissues, vessels and organs is too quick. Do I want to savor the experience? No, not for enjoyment, instead I want to give the process the time and respect that should be attributed to ritualistic practice. To take it all in.
>
> (n.pag.)

They are referring to stylistic and dramaturgical choices in both performance and ritual contexts, including the use of voice and language and the employment of storytelling. All of these were carefully chosen having in mind the variety of people who might be involved. Necessarily, these choices work for some and not for others. For some the description was far too precise. For the more experienced artists it limited the potency of the work. It is worth saying, however, that most of the participants stood in between these categories. For them the experience of dismemberment worked as a devising, dramaturgy aimed at accessing the apex of the piece when the participant is confronted by nothing: the presence of absence. It is indeed the 'nothingness' of what was left in term of physical solidity and its appearances that was the aim of the piece. If the cruelty of dismemberment led participants to perceive the sound of silence, and also, perhaps, a different order of presence, or a different register of materiality, the work succeeded in its intent.

In fact, it is in this moment that most participants come together in a chorus of descriptions, presences, perceptions and feelings. Participant A could 'smell his/her presence and the sound of her breath'; participant B could perceive 'a presence that would fill the space where her/his body was'; participant C could sense 'their physical shape [...] still present at the end – as their spirit or soul'. Participant D talks about energy:

> After the skin, the meat and the bones were gone, in their piles, there was still something. Something I recognized that was beneath all of those layers. It was an energy. Almost turquoise blue on the outside and white on the inside. It was in a line-shape -- but when I looked closer it had mini tentacles of light that came out of it. I tried to erase it, to get at NOTHING, but it remained, staring back at me. I could tell and feel that it was present the whole time, I could remember its gaze -- looking at me through the skin-face of Nothing, the skinned face of Nothing, the Skull face of Nothing and now Nothing. There was an energy always beneath it. As an energy it was the musical note 'A'.
>
> (n.pag.)

An invitation is offered by participant E when stating:

> At the end there was no nothingness. The lack of visual representation doesn't equal emptiness. The matter has different qualities and forms. The presence was there, vibrant and persuasive. Still graspable, still loudly speaking. If only you dare to listen.
>
> (n.pag.)

Participant I 'felt a huge relief when we reached the absence. It was familiar and shimmering like little patches of light almost fading out. I could have stayed there for a long time' (n.pag.). And participant L argues:

> As I could not tell which state was more real or where the person really was now, but still wanted to feel her presence. This paradoxical state felt very profound and moving and I stayed with it for some length of time.
>
> (n.pag.)

Participant Q connected to the energy of her lost friend:

> I thought of my friend, who passed away a few months ago and I smiled. I felt that a big cloud of white smoke or dust has replaced the body on stage. 'They' were still there present, somehow [...] and that felt good!
>
> (n.pag.)

A possible, never-ending, conclusion can be offered by participant O in their call for a plurality of lives in death:

> And the dead live on, of course they do – materially, their materials dispersed and redistributed (most vividly in the sky burials of Tibetans, but literally and actually in the fate of all bodies in death too); also in the memories of those who saw their 'nothingness' as a temporary flaring into appearance of a particular something; and in consciousness, the 'light matter' of the universe that physicists have not yet begun to look for.
>
> (n.pag.)

Conclusion

Grounded in the objective of acknowledging the space in between opposites as a location for discovery, this chapter looks at the philosophical problem related to the relation between form and emptiness, matter and spirit, but also to the interconnection between the digital, the physical and the imaginary. It explores these relations through performance practice as a prolific instrument of investigation. Practice offers an experiential method of exposure to the space that emerges from venturing into what we understand as our internal spatiality through procedures that turn the senses into themselves, wherein touching and seeing are directed within rather than towards the outside environment. In these conditions the self aims to see in introspection, to engage with a different order of visibilities, with a theatre of the inside, a sacred theatre that emerges from the digital through sensory visual restrain such as the ones imposed by darkness. Here, paradoxically, the self becomes both the observer and the observed, the toucher and the touched, the known and the knower within an internal order of spectatorship that opens epistemological possibilities that are otherwise precluded from access. Consequently, I qualify these spaces as sacred because they are producers of a continuous sense of 'un-knowing' which not only disrupts linear and logic modalities of apprehension but also forces the self to accept other ways in which reality is codified, imagined and potentially ordered.

The self might paradoxically discover other agencies or actants inhabiting these emergent internal spaces offering 'a topography of these interworlds [...] explored in the visionary states' that emerge as places 'outside of place, a "place" that is not contained in a place' (Corbin 1972: 4).

Introspective theatre, or the holy theatre of the inside, is a theatre where the imperative remains 'that of never closing language into itself. Never reducing a "thing" to its linguistic dimension, but keeping it always open to its ineffable dimension' (Campagna 2018: 165). The experiment presented here engages with the paradoxical dimension of the *concidentia oppositorum* playing with the possibility of a theatricality and a spectatorship which occurs within, but at the same time touches without. In this complex scenario opposite realities such as the presence and the absence of the body are held together by calibrated practices. *SRF* is therefore a theatrical technology, and as any technology offers a privileged access to conditions of perception that are otherwise rarely experienced. It is a laboratory, a system within systems, aimed at disrupting the conception of the material understood only as a discrete and solid condition, and an opening towards the opportunity to be confronted with a material which is layered, fluid and multiple. This might offer a glimpse of a sacred topography wherein which life emerges alive beyond the perimeters of physical appearances, the boundaries of the visible, and perhaps beyond the veil dividing the living from the dead.

NOTES

1. Here I refer to the term as developed within the context of Jerzy Grotowski's research towards the paratheatrical.

> This signalled a gradual departure from work whose chief objective had been to satisfy the demands and needs connected with further performances in favour of moving towards a process of discovery carried out using theatrical methods

that was as much concerned with the art of acting as with the possibilities of the organic development of the human being.

(http://www.grotowski.net/en/encyclopedia/laboratory-theatre. Accessed 16 December 2020.)

2. I refer to a lineage of artists interested in engaging with what Ronald Grimes and later Richard Shechner referred to as para-shamanic practices, within which the 'focus of theatrical activity has shifted from the "finished work" to the "process of working"' (Schechner 2010: 236).

3. The video was conceived and performed by Silvia Battista and filmed and edited by the film-maker Massimiliano Ferraina.

4. Here Caputo refers to Derrida's sense of the secret as the irreducibility of 'the other' who always 'sits in the spot we can never occupy, speaks from the point of view we cannot inhabit, presides over a secret we cannot share. [...] [This] means that the absolute secret, the structural not-knowing, enters into and is the condition of the "other"' ([2000] 2008: 8).

5. In the past century many reflections were made aimed at bridging the gap between oppositional apprehensions of materiality and reality generally in order to expose the limits of binary thinking and reveal a more complex landscape of cognitive modalities. Although the effort of mapping out a rigorous cartography of all the contributions to the ongoing, multidisciplinary effort of moving away from binary thinking is a task that is far beyond the remit of this chapter, it is my duty to mention at least the contributions that in particular have inspired my practice and continue to do so. For example, Antonio Damasio (2006, 2008, 2010) brings to light the inevitable emotional biases of rational thinking, highlighting their interdependency; Karen Barad (2007) reveals the construction of reality produced by all instruments of knowledge and their apparatuses, scientific ones included; John Caputo ([2000] 2008) unleashes the problem of the hermeneutic circle to demonstrate the difficulties of knowing about anything, the question of truth and the role of imagination; Ann Taves (2009) encourages an understanding of things religious that is beyond the framework of what has been institutionalized as such and expands it to the processes through which things become special; Eduardo Kohn and Eduardo Viveiros de Castro oppose the single point of view of historical anthropology towards a reconfiguration of a multiple perspectivism (2013, 2009); and Federico Campagna (2018) explores the language and codes of magic and the ineffable dimension of existence as the form of resistance to the technologies of production of contemporary corporative organizations of society.

6. In the original text Wilshire uses fiction rather than imagination.

7. Core Shamanism, developed by Michael Harner (1929–2018) is a form of neo-shamanism that argues for the universal, near-universal and common features of shamanism. Although the universalistic claim is problematic, the techniques developed are useful technologies of the self which are highly accessible and effective. For further details, please refer to their foundation in Europe (https://www.shamanism.eu/what-is-core-shamanism/) or in America

(https://www.shamanism.org/workshops/coreshamanism.html). Accessed 1 December 2019.

8. This part will be explored in the section 'ACT II and ACT III: The Experience and The Narration'.

9. If the reader would like to view the video and experience the online performance, please send me a message to my Liverpool Hope University email.

10. The text that follows is an expanded version of the letter I sent to participants. To read the original letter, please follow this link: http://www.silviabattista.com/srf---texts.html. Accessed 1 December 2019.

11. I am aware that her account has been regarded as romantic and several studies have corrected her narratives; however, I find her description of the practice very prolific in its mythological, visionary descriptions and strangely close to the experience I had within the context of the core-shamanic workshop. Indeed, *SRF* is not an investigation into the authenticity of the Tibetan Buddhist ritual *chöd*, but rather an artistic exploration of an internal condition of dismemberment and its potentials for studying the notion and condition of embodiment and the relationship between the spiritual and the material in contemporary, post-industrial contexts.

REFERENCES

Artaud, Antonin (1958), *The Theatre and Its Double*, New York: Grove Press.

Barad, Karen (2012), 'On touching – the inhuman that therefore I am', *differences*, 23:3, pp. 206–23.

Battista, Silvia (2018), *Posthuman Spiritualities in Contemporary Performances: Politics, Ecologies and Perceptions*, London: Palgrave.

Brook, Peter (1968), *The Empty Space*, London: Penguin.

Campagna, Federico (2018), *Technic and Magic: The Reconstruction of Reality*, London: Bloomsbury.

Caputo, John ([2000] 2008), *More Radical Hermeneutics: On Not Knowing Who We Are*, Bloomington: Indiana University Press.

Churchill, Norma (2011), 'Whiteshell woman', *Jung Journal*, 5:1, pp. 81–97.

Corbin, Henry (1972), 'Mundus imaginalis, or the imaginary and the imaginal', trans. R. Horine, http://www.bahaistudies.net/asma/mundus_imaginalis.pdf. Accessed 1 December 2019.

Damasio, Antonio (2006), *Descartes' Error*, London: Vintage.

Damasio, Antonio (2008), 'Conversation with Antonio Damasio', *Performing Medicine*, London: Tate Modern, n.pag.

Damasio, Antonio (2010), *Self Comes to Mind: Constructing the Conscious Brain*, London: William Heinemann.

David-Neel, Alexandra (1937), *Magic and Mystery in Tibet*, London: Penguin.

Eliade, Mircea (1996), *Shamanism: Archaic Techniques of Ecstasy*, Princeton, NJ: Princeton University Press.

Foucault, Michael (1980), *Power/Knowledge: Selected Interviews and Other Writings, 1972–1977*, New York: Pantheon Books.

Foucault, Michael ([1961] 2001), *Madness and Civilization: A History of Insanity in the Age of Reason*, London: Routledge.

Harner, Michael (1990), *The Way of the Shaman*, New York: Harper Collins.

Jung, C. Gustave (1997), *Jung on Active Imagination*, New York: Routledge.

Kohn, Eduardo (2013), *How Forests Think: Toward an Anthropology beyond the Human*, London: University of California Press.

McGinn, Colin (2004), *Mindsight: Images, Dream, Meaning*, London: Harvard University Press.

Noll, Richard (1985), 'Mental imagery cultivation as a cultural phenomenon: The role of visions in Shamanism', *Current Anthropology*, 26:4, pp. 443–61.

Otto, Rudolf (1958), *The Idea of the Holy: An Inquiry into the Non-Rational Factor in the Idea of the Divine and Its Relation to the Rational*, Oxford: Oxford University Press.

Paz, Octavio (1978), *Marcel Duchamp: Appearances Stripped Bare*, trans. R. Phillips and D. Gardner, New York: Viking Press.

Sahn, Seung (1997), *The Compass of Zen*, London: Shambala.

Schechner, Richard (2010), *Between Theater and Anthropology*, Philadelphia: University of Pennsylvania Press.

Schwenger, Peter (2008), 'Writing hypnagogia', *Critical Inquiry*, 34:3, pp. 423–39.

Taves, Ann (2009), *Religious Experience Reconsidered: A Building-Block Approach to the Study of Religion and Other Special Things*, Princeton, NJ: Princeton University Press.

Viveiros de Castro, Eduardo (2009), *Cannibal Metaphysics*, trans. P. Skalish, Minneapolis, MN: Univocal.

Walsh, Roger (1994), 'The making of a shaman: Calling, training and culmination', *Journal Psychology*, 34:3, pp. 7–30.

Wilshire, Bruce (1990), 'The concept of the paratheatrical', *The Drama Review*, 34:4, pp. 169–78.

PART 3

RESISTING

resist (v.)
Late 14c., from Old French *resister* 'hold out against' (14c.), from Latin *resistere* 'to make a stand against, oppose; to stand back; withstand', from *re-* 'against' (see **re-**) + *sistere* 'take a stand, stand firm', from PIE **si-st-*, reduplicated form of root **sta-* 'to stand, make or be firm'.

(etymonline.com)

7

Performing on the Tightrope: Sacred Place, Embodied Knowledge and the Conflicted History of Colonial Modernity in the Welsh and Khasi Relationship

Lisa Lewis

Introduction

The transcultural relationship between the Welsh people and the Khasi people of Meghalaya is rooted in the history of the Welsh Calvinistic Methodist overseas mission to India (1841–1969) and their presence in the Khasi-Jaiñtia Hills. The cultural exchange that this relationship produced had a profound impact on the Khasi people and at the same time created a particular lens through which the people of Wales came to construct their view of India.

This chapter approaches the concept of sacred place as a site of underlying tensions stemming from the legacy of transcultural exchange. The contrasting nature of sacred places involved, from the 'natural' environment (for instance, in sacred forests and groves) to demarcated ritual areas and religious buildings (from monoliths to chapel buildings), reveals the conflicted history of colonial modernity in the state of Meghalaya. What this means for performance is complex, both in terms of the relationship between traditional and contemporary forms of cultural performance, but more specifically for performance-making in the present that sought to disclose the underlying tensions forged by colonial relationships. This second function was the aim of a research project in performance and film by Indian and Welsh scholar-practitioners investigating the Welsh-Khasi cultural exchange.[1] Our intention overall was to examine how creative arts can mediate complex historical and transcultural relationships, and more specifically, how performance, as both method and event, can help us to understand the implications of the Welsh-Khasi transcultural relationship for the present.

One of the central difficulties in attempting to reveal trans- or intercultural influences is the process of pinpointing them (Lewis and Sharma 2016: 81).[2] According to Rustom Bharucha, the intercultural is often so deeply embedded so as to be invisible: '[O]nce importations and borrowings become indigenized, they cease to be "intercultural" after some time. Indeed, they begin to represent new norms' (2000: 32). Bharucha also refers to the idealization of the process of cultural exchange and the related notion that the intercultural 'is somehow independent of larger political processes'. As a consequence, the 'intercultural worker' has to 'disimbricate his/her intervention from existing hegemonies by working consciously, if not subversively, against the grain of assumed norms' (Bharucha 2000: 33). What exactly might 'working against the grain' entail in relation to the Welsh-Khasi connection? In this chapter I attempt to respond to questions of transcultural exchange and its manifestation in performance through the lens of sacred place and explore how we might position ourselves in practice as 'working against the grain'. In three sections, the writing explores contexts, places, and a process of exploratory workshops between Khasi and Welsh performers that investigated ideas of culture as emplaced and embodied.

Contexts

The Welsh Calvinistic Methodist overseas mission (1841–1969) had a profound effect on the Khasi people and on sacred place in the Khasi-Jaiñtia Hills, in what is now the state of Meghalaya in India.[3] In the 2011 census Meghalaya had a population of 2.9 million, with 86 per cent recognized as members of Scheduled Tribes or native peoples.[4] In this 'geopolitically and extremely sensitive area' of India (Datta 2012: 3), a diverse region (Kharmawphlang 2017: 180) considered to be problematically defined as the 'north-east', Christianity is prevalent, particularly in the states of Meghalaya, Mizoram and Nagaland, and tribal communities are identified as Christian (Oomen, cited in Subba et al. 2009: 8).[5] However, despite the prevalence of Christianity, Ka Niam Khasi, the indigenous religion in the Khasi Hills, also remains, and it is difficult to make any numerical comparisons based on census data regarding Christianity and Ka Niam Khasi as the presence of Niam Khasi as cultural practice pervades Khasi society.

The integration of religion with culture does not conform to the traditionally Western view of religion as being emplaced within its own discrete sphere. According to Richard King (2005), world religions have reflected 'assumptions about the nature of religion' due to colonial influence: 'It is not that these religions were simply "imagined" by Westerners without the input of indigenous elite groups, but rather that their representation and subsequent developments within

South Asian culture continue to reflect Western Orientalist concerns and assumptions.' King advocates an approach to religious studies and an approach to the study of India that enables these fields 'to extricate themselves from the Christian categories and secular assumptions [...] [that] continue to influence representations of the Orient, particularly the emphasis that is placed upon so-called "world religions"' (2005: 284). In this model, Ka Niam Khasi cannot be measured against or placed within the metanarrative of world religions. The fact that it has existed alongside and has been intertwined with Christianity for almost two centuries reveals that religious worldviews may be composed of several religious perspectives over time. Indian sociologist T. K. Oomen notes that a 'change in nomenclature of a religious community does not bring about change in their religious beliefs and rituals [...] Thus the religion of Northeast Indian tribes is an amalgam of their primal vision and the new religions into which they are inducted' (2009: 10–11).

The Welsh Calvinistic Methodist mission's belief in the importance of using indigenous languages to educate and evangelize is significant in this context. Literacy, gradually imposed on the Khasi communities as a new knowledge system, was delivered in the Khasi language – 'a revolutionary step' that contrasted with the 'hegemonic roles' taken by the major languages of India in order 'to displace and/or marginalize the mother tongues of Northeast Indian tribal people' (Oomen 2009: 11–12). The difference in linguistic practice in the Welsh missionary endeavour provided space for cultural identification, and despite the overall civilizing ambition of mission, the Welsh Methodists introduced ideas associated with advocating for the 'small nation', possibly in response to their own circumstances as Welsh people (Jones 2005: 158–59).[6] Such a view was far removed from the stance of the Anglicist (as opposed to Orientalist) movement to educate the population of India through the medium of English, although this imperialist view did eventually impact on the medium of education in the Khasi Hills.[7]

Before the arrival of the Welsh missionaries, British rule had already begun to profoundly alter Khasi society. From 1824 onwards, the East India Company had attempted to control the Khasis with 'treaties, engagements and negotiations' that were, according to Khasi historian Helen Giri, 'executed not between equals but between a superior power and an inferior power' (2012: 123). Subjugating the Khasi people became instrumental to the East India Company in their quest for strategic access from the plains of Sylhet through the hills to Assam, based on their desire to exploit the commercial possibilities of the region and to gain a military foothold in relation to neighbouring countries.[8] By 1829, the British had begun their occupation of the Khasi Hills through an 'Agreement' between Dewan Sing, Syiem (chief) of Sohra (Cherrapunji, as it was then), and David Scott, agent to the governor general, North East Frontier, and established their base in Sohra, which became the British hill station in the Khasi Hills.[9] The location of this hill station became significant to the newly formed Welsh Calvinistic Methodist mission's choice of mission field in 1840, and the missionaries resided, initially, within the military compound at Sohra. Keeping to themselves was never the goal of mission, however, and for some of the more radical Nonconformists such as first missionary Thomas Jones, their personal journey in the Khasi Hills represented a shift away from the mission as institution and towards the Khasi community, even when it meant, in his case, the end of his formal ties with the mission.[10]

The Welsh brought with them beliefs and practices rooted in Welsh Nonconformist ideals and Calvinistic Methodist theology. The Welsh Methodist revival of the eighteenth century, one of the most significant social and religious movements in the history of Wales, was rooted in a response to the absentee clergy of the Church of England within Wales and their disregard for cultural specificity. It was a potent movement that affected most of Wales, both rural and industrial communities, and was strongly though not exclusively connected with the Welsh language and a political radicalism.[11] Its adherents were passionate educators and were responsible for some of the most significant educational movements in Wales.[12] According to Welsh historian K. O. Morgan, 'The Welsh democracy was a thriving and creative one. It was its nonconformist leadership and ideology that largely made it so' (1981: 18). This was the ideology that drove the educational and 'social improvement' plans of the Welsh Calvinistic Methodist mission in the Khasi and Jaiñtia Hills.

Nonconformity tends towards an internalized and personal experience of the sacred based on the individual's own relationship with God. When the mission brought this form of Nonconformity to the Khasi Hills, it might have appeared to be relatively benign to the British situated there, but it held within it the promise of a radical and democratic stance which was to prove inflammatory in the history of the mission in several respects, as well as supporting, in several cases, the movement towards Indian independence.

An example of this can be found in the Welsh missionary periodical *Y Cenhadwr (The Missionary)*:

> The British man, in the view of the Indians, is nothing but a stranger in their country; what right has he to govern, and to intervene in their social and political matters? [...] The cry for equality is nothing more than the natural cry, or rather the right, to be acknowledged as a man.
>
> (1926: 43, author's own translation)

This is not to say that over its long history the mission and its members did not collude, even unwittingly, with the imperial aims of the British administration in India. It suggests, however, that questions regarding so-called peripheral entities, geographically and culturally, complicate our understanding of colonial relationships.

Over time, formal education via the Christian missions came to be seen by the population as a modernizing force, with Christianity heralded as a doorway to civilization despite the fact that the beliefs and values introduced by the missionaries were fundamentally contradictory to those of the Khasi community. Indian scholar Nalini Natarajan writes that many Khasi Christians manifested a sense of superiority in relation to orthodox Khasi people considered to be 'pagan' ([1977] 2009: 90–157). This schism was only to deepen over time.

In defence of traditional Khasi culture a group of young intellectuals, led by Jeebon Roy Mairom, set up Ka Seng Khasi (the Khasi society) in 1899, with the aim of combating the erosion of traditional Khasi customs and values by Western influences.[13] This was a pre-emptive move made in the face of cultural annihilation. Part of this defence included the preservation of Ka Niam Khasi, which locates the sacred in divine conceptions of creation and of nature. According to Khasi scholar S. S. Khongkliam, 'The Khasi concept of *U Blei* is the concept of the sacred' (2012: 12–13), but the translation of *U Blei* into English as 'God' is incorrect. Furthermore, according to Sujata Miri (2010), though the prefix *U* is masculine singular, *U Blei* cannot be limited by ideas of gender, and therefore can be addressed as He, She or Them (*U Blei, Ka Blei, Ki Blei*), an aspect which affected early British anthropologists' (and missionaries') perceptions of the religion as plural or animistic. H. O. Mawrie elaborates on this point:

> Being the be-all and end-all, we give Him different names in the different spheres of our life and in the different aspects of His creation. Our Khasi religion is monotheistic and these names connote attributively the absoluteness of God in this Universe.
>
> (1981: 1)

Places

Two primary religious markers are evident in the landscape of Meghalaya: the monolith and the chapel (or 'church'). The stone monoliths prevalent throughout the Khasi-Jaiñtia Hills are placed in groups representing family members, as Desmond Kharmawphlang explains: 'Matriliny, with its association of the *Iawbei* or ancestress and *suidnia* or first maternal uncle, is central to the Khasi religion' (2017: 103), and it is this social structure that is represented in the formation of the monolith (Figure 7.1). According to J. F. Jyrwa these are constructed of three stone uprights, with a horizontal stone lower down and five, seven or nine upright stones and two or more horizontals, reflecting the size of the clan. The central stone representing the maternal uncle is always higher, while the shorter stones represent the younger male members. The flat stones represent the female members of the clan. Jyrwa notes that these are memory stones that form part of funeral rites venerating

FIGURE 7.1: Monolith stones, Khasi Hills, Meghalaya, India. Photograph by Helen Davies.

the ancestors, with the clan *mawbah* (a depository situated beneath the stone) used as repositories for remains. Monoliths can also serve as boundary stones on the edges of villages and *himas* (the region governed by a Syiem), and designate ownership of land or serve a commemorative function. They are situated at a variety of places, including urban crossroads, marketplaces and sacred forests (2011: 83–89).

Khasi converts to Christianity were prevented from cremating and burying the remains of their dead in the clan *mawbah*. According to Pynshai Bor Syiemlieh, the mission also dissuaded them from participating in arrow shooting, dancing, games of chance and other traditional customs (Syiemlieh, cited in Subba et al. 2009: 112). More than an attack on traditional culture, this negation of traditional ways of life was damaging in the context of social relations and was to profoundly affect communities. Khasi historian Cecile Mawlong states:

> Khasi converts were slowly alienated from their own orthodox fellow Khasi brethren and by extension to their roots as well. Inevitably this impacted on their faith in a significant way leading to a gradual discontinuity of the rituals associated with ancestor worship, bone collection and interment ceremonies and also the megalith

building activities. The implication of the loss of this core aspect of their culture is in fact significant.

(2009: 199)

Describing this 'deculturation' that is evident in relation to the megalithic tradition, Mawlong suggests that Christianity 'contributed to the growth of a sense of alienation displayed by the converts among them towards their culture and traditions'. Thus, the diminishing role of Khasi cultural practice in relation to these memory stones impacted the clan structure, as the monolith rituals are intimately bound up with the matrilineal structure and organization of the clan (Mawlong 2009: 195).

Presbyterian churches are prevalent today in almost all Khasi villages, are numerous in urban areas and members worship in large congregations. In architectural terms many of the Presbyterian churches resemble Anglican churches with a tower or spire, others resemble plain (earlier Welsh) chapels[14] and all display the influence of local architecture. Early photographs of the Khasi Hills show stone chapel buildings emerging incongruously above village houses built from natural materials such as bamboo (Figure 7.2).

FIGURE 7.2: *Native Village at the Entrance to Shillong, India; Chapel for Kasia Christians,* *c.*1870s. Photographer: Oscar Mallitte. © The British Library Board (Photo 913/32).

This dissonance between the built and the natural environment in the colonial experience of place is a visual marker of the complex power relations at work and their direct impact on the lived experience of culture. The colonial context within which mission activity advanced was responsible for the changing nature of 'place' – how it was socially and culturally defined – and this had drastic implications for the experience of the sacred in the natural environment, and deleteriously affected the indigenous social networks associated with religious and cultural practices that originally defined such places. For instance, the early mission barred Khasi Christians from attending traditional celebrations such as Shad Suk Mynsiem, a dance that 'explains the roots of the whole being of the Khasi' (Giri 2012: 9). This particular dance encapsulates literally, in terms of movement, Khasi ideas of the sacred rooted in the earth/in nature (Figure 7.3). Its rejection signalled a missionary imperative at work: the removal of cultural/religious practices and beliefs at odds with the social activities deemed appropriate for Presbyterian converts.[15] Similarly, the British administration banned dances that included weaponry, which affected the Shad Phur, a male dance with swords signifying the protection of Khasi home, family and country. This two-pronged attack on Khasi culture ensured the near demise of definitive cultural performances, though they were not to disappear completely and have been revived.

According to Esther Syiem, the negation of Khasi religion and the performances associate rituals instigated a crisis in which the Khasi was '[c]ut off from God

FIGURE 7.3: Shad Suk Mynsiem (dance of the spirit at peace), Khasi Hills. Photographer: by Welsh and Khasi cultural dialogues team. With thanks to the people of Mawlyngbna.

[...] in a state of exile' (2011: 7), an experience already reflected in the originary myth associated with Lum Sohpetbneng, one of the most sacred Khasi mountains. *Sohpetbneng* refers to the umbilical cord or navel of the sky, and the story describes an essential connection between heaven and earth, and the arrival of human beings into 'the lap of mother earth' (Khongkliam 2012: 48). According to Syiem, the story tells of a tree that grew from the peak of the Sohpetbneng mountain called *Jingkieng ksiar* (golden ladder). Via this ladder the sixteen families that lived in heaven moved between heaven and earth. One day, when seven families were tending their land on earth, God removed the ladder, darkness covered the earth and the seven families remained on earth forever to become the originating clans of the Khasi people (the clan being a composite group of all those who have descended from the same ancestress). Thus, the Khasi people call themselves *Hynniew trep/Hynniew skum* (the seven huts/seven families). This origin story is marked by a separation that causes a spiritual crisis. Yet, according to Esther Syiem (2011), this state of exile has been a source of empowerment for the Khasi people, because the Khasi relationship with God is a reminder of the 'imperative [...] the construction of an identity based upon a semblance of the former one'. For Syiem, this exile has facilitated a ' "contrapuntal" [after Said] sensibility' and a condition of plurality. In turn, this 'exilic dimension of the Khasi imagination' was able to adapt to 'the Christian set-up where the oral, though in an entirely different context, is as much a matter of significance and power' (2011: 7). Syiem perceives a form of collective memory associated with the oral, the residue of which provides a parallel influence to that of Christianity. Khasi folk tales, in the absence of written form, became truly internalized and in this way, a parallel oral discourse always existed 'on the sidelines of the written' (Syiem 2011: 4). The steadfast role of oral culture in the performance of everyday life is exemplified by the tradition of offering *kwai* (betel nut), a customary welcome to every Khasi home, and one that persisted even though the missionaries objected to it. Offering and eating *kwai* is a custom embedded in Khasi oral culture and relates to a cautionary tale; consequently, it is a practice that accompanies a deeply held belief. For Syiem, this reveals the impenetrability of the oral tradition: 'the hegemony of the colonial ruler, and by implication the written, was, as in the case of oral societies everywhere, not fully able to penetrate the inaccessible and therefore, unmapped regions of indigenous discourses' (2011: 5). Khasi oral culture is, according to Syiem, founded on a dual awareness, or 'two orders of reality' in the Khasi way of life, represented by the Khasi dictum '*tip briew tip Blei, kamai úa ka hok* and *tip kur tip kha*' (know man know God, earn righteousness and know your maternal and paternal relations). This 'Divine Decree' given to the Khasi people 'reflects the philosophy of the oral in Khasi thought and lays the visionary foundation of a society that must take into account the interpenetration of the spiritual with the physical' (Syiem 2011: 2).

The interpenetration of the spiritual with the physical is evident in the Khasi relationship with the land. Khasi sociologist Rekha M. Shangpliang describes the influence of the matrilineal system on an ecological stance:

> The Khasis live in profound communion with nature. Nature is the pivot around which their economic, social, cultural and religious activities revolve. They sanctify nature and all its elements as gifts from God. The earth is honoured and idolized as *Mei ramew* (mother earth).
>
> (2009: 220)

The sanctified earth in Khasi religion comprises the land, forest, stream, rivers, hills and all that the earth holds. J. Kerrsingh Tariang emphasizes the fact that when Khasis associate 'places and objects such as mountains and hills, forests and groves, with the act of making them serve as "*u Ryngkew u Basa*" [a protective force for well-being], it is not their belief that these places and objects are the abode of God or embody God Himself' (2012: 75). Such places, for instance, sacred groves, are marked as consecrated by prayer or animal sacrifice, and if a tree were then to be cut down from such a place it would be a defilement (76). According to Shangpliang (2009), the abrupt change in ecological stance enforced by British state rule was to have a profound affect. The establishment of a succession of Forest Acts in 1865, 1878 and 1927 ensured British ownership of large swathes of forestry and restricted its use by local people (228–31). This process of enforced land acquisition by the British,

> systematically eroded people's traditional rights over natural resources posing a threat not only to their livelihood but also to the delicate balance between them and their forest. The British looked at the forest as a revenue-yielding property, which could be commercially exploited.
>
> (Shangpliang 2009: 228)

This was to remove a way of life that was dependent on the forest, and which derived its cultural traditions and religious beliefs from living in accordance with it.

Through the sustained attacks on cultural and religious performances, and on the land itself and its social meanings – part of the mores of political and military imperialism – Khasi ways of life were placed in crisis.

Practice as research with Khasi and Welsh performers

How do we make practice in full recognition of these relationships between different experiences of the sacred, and in ways that unfold the historically implicit power structures in the Welsh-Khasi relationship so that they may be seen clearly? This question underpinned our approach to practice. The process of answering it suggested a method for practice as research in a contemporary transcultural context. It was an answer that revealed the ways in which the contact between Wales and India through the Welsh mission complicates the understanding of colonial history and how the traces of this cultural exchange continue to impact on postcolonial identities. While our approach to practice was of the moment, the question we were asking sought answers of the past, and this involved a consideration of being on supposed 'peripheries' of both Empire and Nation – both for the Welsh (Wales being a so-called first colony [Jones and Jones 2003: 57] and at the same time complicit in imperial activity) and the Khasis (with Meghalaya forming part of the Northeast India region made peripheral by political circumstance). It is in this context that Bharucha's 'working against the grain' became a potent reminder of the necessity of uncertainty when devising a performance about transcultural history that is open to its contradictions. Understanding the historical implications of the Welsh-Khasi exchange for postcolonial identities involves staring face on at colonial complicity, and this is not done without careful consideration of our methods of collaboration and working practices.

Through workshops with Khasi performer Lapdiang Syiem and Welsh performer Rhys ap Trefor, we attempted to reach a method of dialogic performance by asking specific questions and seeking answers to them in embodied form. Both professional performers are rooted in their respective cultures and represent two distinct performance traditions at odds with the primary national cultures associated with 'India' and 'Britain'. Both performers understood the implicit significance of orality within their own performance traditions – the oral 'folk' culture of the Khasis for Lapdiang, and the bardic tradition, including the eisteddfod, for Rhys – and had participated in these traditions fully.

Given our different and similar backgrounds could we find a common framework for devising work together in practice based on embodied knowledge, and furthermore, could we construct a way of working that acknowledged difference and similarity at the same time? We thought that through a consideration of the social relationships that constitute and configure social spaces – everything that goes into making space 'place' – we might be able to trace the dynamics of cultural exchange and contestation. But how do we embody our experience of place? How might we reveal this embodied experience of time-in-place as a sensate experience in and through the body?

Initial workshops began with ideas of homeplace, of our relationship with the land and of the language used to discuss ideas of place, home, land, earth and so on. We then considered how we articulate our somatic understanding of these concepts and what associations there might be between these ideas of place and our corporeal experience of them. This embodied knowledge was important for two reasons: in terms of a physical understanding of culture, that is, what the body reveals of culture; second, in terms of constructing images that can affect or that have artistic currency in Khasi and/or Welsh cultures. This was important because we did not want to start from the premise that our cultural gestures and expressions are the same, or that we manifest the same cultural understandings of embodied practices. We began with physical responses to specific words we had discussed and began responding to them on foot. Some words belonged to both performers, some belonged to one more than the other and a few were exclusive:

- *Kynmaw* | *carreg* | stone
- *Ri* | *gwlad/cenedl* | country/people
- *Khyndew* | *daear* | earth
- *Leit bri* | *trin y tir* | to farm
- *Puh lyngkha* | *i aredig* | to plough
- *Krem marai* | *daeargryn* | earthquake
- *Ka shnong ka thaw* | *pentref* | village
- *Maw ngot briaw* | *y garreg a lyncodd blentyn* | the boulder that swallowed a child.

These eventually became trigger words for an embodied response in gestures and movements which suggested relationships with the land, with the earth we tread, with nature, ecologies, landscapes, and their impact on the physical body. None of the performers' movements were explicitly related to notions of sacred place as external entity but for those watching, the motions sometimes hinted at a physical metaphor for colonial mapping or missionary advance. The first set of performance principles were arrived at in this way.

In this corporeal exploration of keywords, we wanted to see whether we could draw attention to the way in which ideas of difference are structured, not in order to negate difference, but to articulate or disclose it. Some differences were based in cultural and environmental circumstances, but many arose that have been historically constructed from matters relating to social and colonial power structures, and these were mainly related to ideas of gender, race, language and national identity. In order to navigate these ideas physically, we worked with balance and counterbalance and the opposition between different movements, their energy, duration and rhythm (Figure 7.4).

We also imagined the impact of cultural connections on the physical body, a factor frequently conveyed through missionary letters. Early missionaries in India lost their partners and children and died themselves, in a succession of seemingly long-drawn-out deathbed scenes, conveyed in fractured narratives by the

FIGURE 7.4: Welsh performer Rhys ap Trefor and Khasi performer Lapdiang Syiem in a workshop on counterbalance, North Eastern Hill University, Shillong, 2017. Photographer: by Lisa Lewis.

intermittent letters that carried their stories home. The onslaught of the transcultural experience is also evident in the history of Khasi Christians who travelled to Wales, such as U Larsing Khongwir, who died in 1863 and is buried in Chester cemetery.

During the workshops on ideas of land and corporeality we also looked at the notion of presence, the often-elusive flow of energy and focus that emanates from performers. Interestingly, in this project, presence is not only a phenomenon in live performance; the concept of presence has been a recurrent element in the archival research. The archive concerned is a vast body of writings, including correspondence, personal letters, notes, diaries, creative writing (poetry, plays, music, hymns), translations, guidelines for translations, folk tales, anthropological writing, travel writing, and also photographs, films, audio recordings, radio and television broadcasts, magic lantern lectures and slides, deeds to land and property, maps, building plans and artefacts.[16] Within the archive, the letter-writing between members of the mission, both Welsh and Khasi, and their counterparts in Wales provides a real sense of distance, both physical and cultural. So much of the history takes place in the silent moments, between letters crossing oceans, and also 'between the lines'. There are moments of stillness between the ebb and flow of correspondence crossing the world by sea and moments of quiet suggestion within the letter as performance of being in/out of place. The thousands of letters written between 1841 and 1969 reveal the tension in this process of waiting, and of a relationship built on a certain presence, of the Other, of the self out of place and of the negation of certain forms of place, including sacred place. Could we consider the epistolic nature of the early mission in terms of place in order to embody it in performance? Additionally, there is the scattered unofficial archive that gradually revealed itself from the wealth of material in cases, attics and memories and oral histories revealed in conversations and in passing.

Embodied responses held by the performers' bodies also revealed something of this repertoire in the performance of traditions and customs passed on into the present. Workshops on language and sound, voice and echo explored both Khasi and Welsh oral traditions. These particular sessions took place in a colonial bungalow in what was once the 'mission compound' in Mawkhar, Shillong, next to the Presbyterian church. The notion of the echo became increasingly more resonant as we worked within the wooden room and could hear our own voices speaking and singing to the accompaniment of choral singing (of familiar Welsh hymn tunes) emanating from the nearby buildings. In the process of transcribing the sounds of oral language into written script the fluidity of the oral is trapped within the structure of grammar and all the cultural hegemonies that accompany it. Early Welsh missionary writings reveal attempts at capturing sounds and meanings that are part of the embodied repertoire in order to transform them into the finite inscription, and the written form would eventually become part of the archive from which authoritative historical discourse is constructed. Conscious of the reduction of culturally specific sounds into predetermined linguistic structures, we explored the voicing of sounds in either culture, including what could be considered to be abstract sounds, culturally specific sounds such as *Hoi! Kiw!* (a customary salutary sound at the beginning of Khasi cultural events and celebrations) and hymns, in particular those that exist in both Welsh and Khasi. We related stories and spoke of poetic forms, for instance, *cynghanedd* (a Welsh poetic form based in rhyme and alliteration) and *phawar* (a Khasi poetic form of rhyming chant; see Syiem 2014: 48–49). The primacy of these oral forms in both cultures, and their prevalence in the performers' repertoires, confirmed for us that oral culture is a spatial practice, and one shared between cultural performers and participants so as to create a meaningful sense of place. The oral is a significant transaction that has a bearing on participants in space, and in this way, it is a transaction between people than cannot be undone. The oral leaves its traces in between people and in place; it is a 'live' text with its own energy and presence.

Finally, we worked directly on the visual archive of photographic images related to 'Northeast India' as colonial site and specifically on the mission photographs and what they were designed to tell about the Welsh and Khasi peoples. One of the photographs explored in this context was the portrait of Reverend William and Mary Lewis with U Larsing (anon, c.1860s). U Larsing Khongwir (1838–1863), one of 'the first Khasi evangelists', was raised by Mary and William Lewis, two of the earliest Welsh missionaries. He was ordained in 1855 at the age of 17 and travelled to Wales with the missionaries in 1861, in preparation for life as a minister in the Khasi Hills. It was in Wales that he contracted pleurisy and died in 1863. The portrait of U Larsing is a microcosm of the mission's goal of converting the native population and a representation of colonial modernity. How could we draw attention to the process of looking in relation to this photograph?

During the workshops on photography we sought the moment of performance within the photographic event, which allowed us to explore time and movement around the framed photographic pose. This stretching of imaginary time around what we came to call 'the gaze event' allowed us to explore a range of possibilities in terms of movements and gestures within the context of the framed portrait. What we imagined the movements to be was not important in itself; rather, it was the exploration of representation enabled by the movements that was crucial – the way that the performers gesture in slow motion, moving through the image, facilitated a re-organization of elements within the frame in the moment leading up to and beyond the photograph as static image. In performance, the portrait of U Larsing in particular allowed us to animate the context of the imperial gaze present in relation to the original image and to question the implications of the image. It allowed us to play with representations of difference, with pursuing juxtapositions in the performance of the photograph in order to subvert the way it is constructed. This process also offered a way of opening up closed archival representation. There is something about the performers' corporeality and presence in live performance and their ability to turn the gaze towards the audience that provides a powerful agency. According to Helen Gilbert,

[T]he performing body's susceptibility to being read within systems of codification would seem to make it an unlikely site of strategic resistance to imperial power. However, it is precisely at the body's moment of entry into theatrical discourse that it acquires the potential to counteract voyeurism.

(1998: 264)

169

In *Performing Journeys*, the moment Khasi performer Lapdiang Syiem turned towards the screen behind her and the photograph of U Larsing with William and Mary Lewis appeared, those of us watching entered a tangle of acknowledged looks and gazes that seemed to deconstruct the conventions involved in the process of gazing upon this image (Figure 7.5). Gilbert refers to Barbara Freedman's 'fractured reciprocity' to explain this self-conscious gaze that draws attention to itself and that 'refuses the closure of imperialist relations of looking' (Freedman, cited in Gilbert 1998: 264).

Through the entire series of workshops, held over two years, we arrived at principles for performance based on the performers' embodied responses to keywords deemed to be important to their cultural lives and responses to archival material and embodied performance traditions. These principles were established between us so that they could be used as a basis for a devised performance to be held in India and Wales in 2019. Entitled *Performing Journeys* (in Wales, *Perfformio'r Daith*), the performance presented Khasi folk tales and Welsh missionary writings, both of which deal with literal and symbolic journeys

FIGURE 7.5: *Performing Journeys* with Lapdiang Syiem and Rhys ap Trefor, directed by Lisa Lewis, April 2019. In the background, the portrait of Reverend William and Mary Lewis with U Larsing (anon, *c.*1860s). With kind permission of the Historical Society of the Presbyterian Church of Wales. Photographer: Andy Freeman.

in different ways.[17] Rather than offering a specific narrative, the performance wove together different forms of telling and performing, in stories, letter, music and physical and visual modes from two cultures, that have had a specific cultural exchange for over a century and a half. What we found through the workshops and the performances is that the interaction between performers, their embodied knowledges and the archival material, presented through film/photography, music and letters, offered a particular view of the more ambivalent and nuanced aspects of the cultural exchange. Responses from audiences in both communities suggested that there is a desire to explore ways of expressing deeply held and often paradoxical feelings relating to the postcolonial condition. This is the tightrope on which we perform (one that is not clearly seen or shown), where we must deconstruct and divulge certain histories and at the same time work towards a recognition of what the power relationships behind these histories reveal about ourselves in the present.

NOTES

1. This research was made possible through a grant from The Leverhulme Trust. 'Welsh and Khasi Cultural Dialogues' was a four-year project by investigators from India and Wales, examining the shared cultural history of the Welsh and the Khasi people of northeast India, and the influence of this history on cultural identities. See website http://www. welshkhasidialogues.co.uk. Accessed 16 December 2020. I am grateful to Lapdiang Syiem for her assistance with Khasi spellings.

2. In the research project we decided to use the term 'transcultural' rather than 'intercultural' in order to reflect the distance involved in the cultural exchange between the Khasi and Welsh peoples in which there is no developed diasporic relationship.

3. Meghalaya was first established as an autonomous state within Assam in 1970 and as a full state in 1972.

4. The Khasi people are designated a Scheduled Tribe within India, which means that they have an administrative system based on traditional tribal institutions recognized by the Sixth Charter of the Constitution of India. The Dhebar Commission on Scheduled Areas and Tribes (1960–61) suggested that a region is defined as 'tribal' when at least 50 per cent of the people dwelling there belong to tribes. The Khasi people are recognized as the indigenous people of the Khasi Hills, according to the definition of 'indigenous populations' by the United Nation's Working Group on Indigenous Populations.

   As the government of India defines all the citizens of India as indigenous, the term 'tribal' rather than 'indigenous' or 'native' is used within the Indian Constitution. The official term 'Scheduled Tribes' is used to refer to these communities nationally, and they are recognized as a separate demographic entity within the census. In 2011 the population of India was 1.24 billion with 104.3 million (8.6 per cent) belonging to Scheduled Tribes.

5. Northeast India is a mountainous region geographically situated next to Bangladesh (to the south and west), Burma/Myanmar (to the east) and Tibet and Bhutan (to the north). The 'North East' is also marked by its history as a colonial region due to its important strategic placement as a corridor between countries and regions, and the nomenclature 'North East' is a reflection of this.

6. Historian Aled Jones has shown that the missionary enterprise in Victorian Wales was bound up in identity issues and concerns of liberal respectability. This was in turn a response to the deeply affecting indictment of Welsh morality in the Report of the Royal Commission on Education in Wales in 1847, which had a profound impact on the way in which the Welsh viewed themselves in relation to the world. The Blue Books purported to be a report on education but was predominantly a critique of Welsh family life, the morality of Welsh women and, above all, the supposedly destructive influences of Nonconformity and the Welsh language. Its effects continue to manifest themselves and are deeply ingrained.

7. 'Macauley's Minute' (1835) established the policy and framework for educating the population of India through the medium of English, a policy that was also introduced in Britain to counter the influence of indigenous British minority languages.

8. These included their need for access to a postal service and to trading, the necessity of instigating good relations and of guarding the border areas due to the threat of invasion from Burma and their desire to reside in the cooler climate of the hill station.

9. In 1858, following the Indian uprising of 1857 against the rule of the East India Company, the Government of India Act was passed, by which the rule of the East India Company ended and the direct rule of the British Crown began.

10. Having been taught to speak Khasi by U Duwan Rai and U Juncha, Thomas Jones codified the language into a written script based on Welsh language orthography and began to translate the Bible into Khasi using the Roman alphabet, a task completed by others by 1891. He was not the first to attempt to do so. Khasi had first been written around 1817 with the translation of excerpts from the Bible into the Shala (Shella) dialect via Bengali script, and in 1831 the Serampore Baptist Mission under William Carey published the 'Khassee New Testament'. It was the use of Roman script by Jones, however, that stuck. Jones was eventually removed from the mission for behaviour that the mission headquarters in Wales disapproved of and died in Kolkalta in 1849.

11. From the 1730s onwards, Methodist leaders in Wales, such as Howell Harries, Daniel Rowland and William Williams Pantycelyn, continued within the Church of England though they developed networks of like-minded people who believed in Calvinist theology and gradually established religious meetinghouses or chapels. This eventually led to the secession of 1811 under the instigation of Thomas Charles and the establishment of the Calvinistic Methodist Presbyterian Church of Wales in 1823.

12. Such as Sunday schools and board schools after 1870 and the first university college in Aberystwyth in 1872.

13. The socio-religious movement of the Seng Khasi was initially an alliance between Khasi intelligentsia, the Bramo Samaj and the YMCA (though the two latter societies left early on due to religious differences). The society strove to assert Khasi religion as a cultural practice central to the Khasi way of life. As part of this cultural revivalism, folkloric material was used to establish and perpetuate group ties and ideas of regionalism and ethnicity.

14. Chapels in Wales were initially modelled on the farmhouses and barns that became the first meeting places for Nonconformist societies. Subsequently, the basic Welsh chapel before the 'façade wars' of the nineteenth century is a plain unostentatious building and not a designated sacred place. Though most chapels are consecrated for use as a place of worship, they are not 'holy ground' in the same sense as a church building, and there are no areas off limits.

15. This was not the case in relation to Catholicism in the Khasi-Jaiñtia Hills.

16. Official archives include the Welsh Calvinistic Methodist Archive (CMA) held at the National Library of Wales, the specialist Khasi material held at North Eastern Hill University Library in Shillong and primary source material held by the Presbyterian Church of India. Some artefacts are also held in the CMA, and there is a missionary collection (Presbyterian Church of Wales) held by Amgueddfa Cymru: National Museum Wales.

17. *Performing Journeys* was performed at Chapter Arts Centre, Cardiff, Wales, and the Khasi National Dorbar Hall, Shillong, India, in April 2019; in 2020 it toured India (Delhi, Jowai, Kolkata, Sohra, Shillong) and Wales (Aberystwyth, Cardiff, Caernarfon, Carmarthen, Clydach, Holywell).

REFERENCES

Bharucha, Rustom (2000), *The Politics of Cultural Practice: Thinking through Theatre in an Age of Globalization*, Hanover and London: Wesleyan University Press.

Cobo, José R. Martinez (1986), *Study on the Problem of Discrimination against Indigenous Populations*, United Nations Department of Economic and Social Affairs, Indigenous Peoples, https://www.un.org/development/desa/indigenouspeoples/publications/2014/09/martinez-cobo-study/. Accessed 24 November 2019.

Datta, Birendranath (2012), *Cultural Contours of North-East India*, New Delhi: Oxford University Press.

Freedman, Barbara (1991), *Staging the Gaze: Postmodernism, Psychoanalysis and Shakespearean Comedy*, Ithaca, NY: Cornell University Press.

Gilbert, Helen (1998), 'Responses to the sex trade in post-colonial theatre', in L. Dale and S. Ryan (eds), *Cross/Cultures 33: The Body in the Library*, Amsterdam: Rodopi, pp. 261–72.

Giri, Helen (2012), *The Khasis under British Rule (1824–1947)*, Shillong: La Riti Publications.

Jones, Aled (2005), 'Culture, race, and the missionary public in mid-Victorian Wales', *Journal of Victorian Culture*, 10:2, pp. 158–59.

Jones, Aled and Jones, Bill (2003), 'The Welsh world and the British Empire, c. 1851–1939', in C. Bridge and K. Fedorowich (eds), *The British World: Diaspora, Culture and Identity*, London: Frank Cass, pp. 57–81.

Jyrwa, J. F. (2011), *Christianity in Khasi Culture*, Shillong: K.J.P. Assembly Press.

Kharmawphlang, Desmond L. (2017), *Folklore Imprints in North East India*, Shillong: Don Bosco Publications.

Khongkliam, S. S. (2012), *Religion of the Khasi*, Guwahati: D.V.S. Publishers.

King, Richard (2005), 'Orientalism and the study of religions', in J. R. Hinnells (ed.), *The Routledge Companion to the Study of Religion*, London and New York: Routledge, pp. 275–90.

Lewis, Lisa and Sharma, Aparna (2016), 'Welsh and Khasi cultural dialogues: Transactions and translations', *Performance Research*, 21:5, pp. 81–84.

Mawlong, Cecile A. (2009), 'Christianity and the megalithic tradition in the Khasi-Jaintia hills: A preliminary study of the processes of deculturation and enculturation', in T. B. Subba, J. Puthenpurakal and S. J. Puykunnel (eds), *Christianity and Change in Northeast India*, New Delhi: Concept Publishing Company, pp. 194–202.

Mawrie, H. Onderson (1981), *The Essence of the Khasi Religion*, Shillong: Seng Khasi.

Miri, Sujata (2010), 'An introduction to the study of tribal religions', in H. O. Mawrie, *The Khasi Milieu*, New Delhi: Concept Publishing, pp. 1–23.

Morgan, K. O. (1981), *Rebirth of a Nation: Wales 1880–1980*, Oxford: Clarendon Press and University of Wales Press.

Natarajan, Nalini ([1977] 2009), *The Missionary among the Khasis*, New Delhi: Sterling Publishers.

Oomen, T. K. (2009), 'Culture change among the tribes of Northeast India', in T. B. Subba, J. Puthenpurakal and S. J. Puykunnel (eds), *Christianity and Change in Northeast India*, New Delhi: Concept Publishing Company, pp. 3–32.

Roberts, Gwyneth Tyson (2011), *The Language of the Blue Books, Wales and Colonial Prejudice*, Cardiff: University of Wales Press.

Shangpliang, Rekha M. (2009), 'Ecological basis of Khasi ethno-cultural traits', in T. B. Subba, J. Puthenpurakal and S. J. Puykunnel (eds), *Christianity and Change in Northeast India*, New Delhi: Concept Publishing Company, pp. 219–31.

Subba, T. B., Puthenpurakal, Joseph and Puykunnel, Shaji Joseph (eds) (2009), *Christianity and Change in Northeast India*, New Delhi: Concept Publishing Company.

Syiem, Esther (2011), *The Oral Discourse in Khasi Folk Narrative*, Guwahati: E.B.H. Publishers.

Syiem, Esther (2014), *People's Linguistic Survey of India. Volume Nineteen, Part II, The Languages of Meghalaya*, New Delhi: Orient Black Swan.

Syiemlieh, Pynshai Bor (1994), *The Khasis and Their Matrilineal System*, Shillong: Author.

Tariang, J. Kerrsingh (2012), *The Philosophy and Essence of Niam Khasi*, Shillong: Ri Khasi.

Y Cenhadwr: Cylchgrawn Cenhadol y Methodistiaid Calfinaidd (1926), March, Caernarfon: Llyfrfa'r Cyfundeb, p. 43.

8

Performing Memorials as
Intervening Grounds

Ruth L. Smith

Introduction

Installed in late 1996, the Sarajevo Roses would begin to deteriorate as soon as the red resin was poured onto the pavement where mortar shell imprints remained from deadly sniper fire during the Siege of Sarajevo (1992–96). Reflecting local sensibility, the Roses evince street exposure and permeability, recalling shell impact and leaving flowers when possible, moving bodies and wiping away blood (Ristic 2018). Their immediacy to mostly civilian death contrasts with the Vietnam Wall, armed services war dead and missing named from the far capital of Washington, DC. Both memorials convey ground orientations that elude finishing. Dedicated in 1982, the Vietnam Veterans Memorial Wall cuts aggressively yet falls modestly into the earth; the wound of the war and the healing of wounds infuse a design that encourages vulnerable and variable expression (Lin 2000). The Roses with their fragile, tentative architecture and the Wall, as it is also known with its durable granite stone, link to other twentieth- and twenty-first-century memorials that direct attention by way of grounds to war deaths, oppression, conflict and appalling violence. Choeung Ek in Cambodia, Berlin Stolpersteine, Plaques of Buenos Aires and the National Memorial for Peace and Justice in Montgomery, Alabama, bear these apprehensions. Unwilling or unable to iterate official civil and sacred practices of monument and memorial that promise resolutions of recognition, rest and assurance, the architectures differently register proximity, reservation, agitation, disappearance, injustice and the incommensurate. There is incompleteness in silences and more to be said. If we regard memorials as intervening grounds, we can consider architectural gestures in their performative effects, rendering more complicated histories of deaths than modern formalism permits and more discursive expressions than already placed proscriptions of ritual and text.

The activity of societal commemorative agency has traditionally been demarcated with ritual and rhetoric conducted at a civil or religious building, marker or burial ground. Edifice and ground establish agreements of their setting that bespeak relations of death and earth, injury and recompense, body and authority, claim and evidence in argument. Combined in seemingly unalterable assumptions, they enmesh sacrifice with hierarchical distributions in state-religious care of those dead associated with the monumental. Yet, deaths and the structures that do or do not identify them change views and communicate changing views, intervening in notions of grounds, at once evoking the religious, the political and the moral. In the United States, panels from the NAMES Project AIDS Memorial Quilt were arranged atop canvas covering the ground of the National Mall first in 1987, assuming official grounds for deaths of people who had been denied recognition and care. Carole Blair and Neil Michel (2007) argue that like the Vietnam Wall, the Quilts democratize death and mourning. In Spain, at a moment of election success in July 1936, Left Partisans exhumed bodies of nuns, priests and saints buried in churches. Instead of leaving the occasion to charges of offense, Bruce Lincoln (1989) presents not background but the large arguments with which actions organize societal order and disorder; the destruction of official architectural burial coheres with revolutionary equality and iconoclasm. These instances demonstrate the social construction of grounds, one ground displacing uncivil terms to claim the civil-sacred, one ground overthrowing the other.

What follows is an attempt to delineate architectural engagement in memorializing grounds where places remain fraught regarding loss and the events of loss; grounds where the horror of deaths stands existent as time has passed. My working premise is that architectural measures respond to and contribute senses of agency with suggestion and insistence, indirection and direction, slippage and conjecture. With this interest, the discursive character of design comes into play, inseparable from disjunctures and lacunae. An approach to intervention with performing and grounds argues for the significance of the linguistic possibility that is not already assigned or anticipated when familiar practices no longer lead and nothing is already held apart. Even in official locations, conditions of loss weaken the avowedly firm monumental, as with the London Cenotaph and the Vietnam Veterans Wall. Other built places manifest distance from or disregard for monumental totality: Sarajevo Roses, Choeung Ek in Cambodia, Berlin Stolpersteine and Plaques of Buenos Aires. In Montgomery, Alabama, the National Memorial for Peace and Justice, recognized as the lynching memorial, summons critical conjunction with Maya Lin's final memorial, the digital architecture of the ecological site to planetary loss 'What Is Missing?'. What intervenes not only comes between but cuts into or moves across to do something, including saying something else.

The sites briefly detailed here grapple with gaps of account and impossibilities of recall belonging to their histories. Difficulties of telling or fracture of memory appear in responses to distorted or suppressed information and point to the phenomenology of social cognition in the built-discursive elaboration of how things happened. Determination and investigation yield faint or definite settings that may permit notating bones, soil from a lynching spot or the person in the area of capture. In ground placements the Berlin Stolpersteine inscribe street addresses and dates of murder where Nazis rounded up Jews and others, now named on stones registering the episode. Memorials and their audiences warrant critical argument for refusals of just evaluation in religious and civil adherence, proliferation of consumption and simulacra of display, delusion and distraction of invocation. And critically, they want to say more with shifting emblems of distress and mappings of death taking place. When W. J. T. Mitchell speaks of images 'wanting' thought and feeling, creating and changing our criteria (2005: 92), we can underscore architecture in current imaginations and articulations, construction intervening with construction.

Performance and grounds

When extensive disruption mars grounds of death, the impetus of architectures mingles and struggles in invention and floundering. Such places live with their historical dilemmas at remove from certainties attributed to ritual legitimation and sanctification and their oppositional stance modern thinkers too readily assign all resistance, for instance, Antigone, as Madelyn Detloff (2007) reminds us. Denial of proper burial has exemplified the dehumanizing of enslaved, displaced or massacred peoples under diverse powers and practices of rule. Current moral and social initiatives compel searches to locate people in their situations of death. A potential construal of built memorial relies on, adds to and guides accessible records, meeting limits and resources with research tools in the hands of those alert to the political geography of disappearance. Their actions bring forward and assign performative aspects available with architecture, perhaps the most overtly rhetorical of the plastic arts as it explicates and queries designations of grounds beyond agreements of ritual codification.

Performance gains latitude beyond ritual in Ludwig Wittgenstein's investigations of grammar and use and Herbert Blau's of actor and stage. Their notions of performing stipulate the shaping powers of the contextual and the exceeding of any move in producing it, unbound by the monumental absolute universal and a priori possession of ground. Exploring the vague and the specific, Wittgenstein's questions emphasize accrued and malleable social agreements in multiple means of searching, moving, guiding and aspect seeing. Senses of thinking-language occur in rules as the inquiry-action of what to do that humans exercise in practices, including when rules falter in connection or fail in circumstance. Rules operate not in isolation but by patterns of cross-referencing, inducing confusion if encountered from another side or loss of direction if with a different language situation or group (Wittgenstein 2009: #202–06). Consider groups working out knowing and remembering in situations outside recognition. Their shock, fear or statement defies fixed comparisons: mute versus representational, material versus idea, feeling versus thought. Unlike the remote yet clear abstraction that the modernist was inclined to assume, argue and build, quandary and contradiction speak to the difficult but necessarily public life of language, the 'civil status' of 'entanglement in our rules' (#125). This notion of civil life describes the architectural performative locating contingently or not finding a way, wondering how to go on (#664).

These memorials want some kind of scene that indicates the not already grounded. As theatre director and theorist, Blau (2002) dismisses generalized conceptions of performativity. Bracketing a hypothetical parley with Wittgenstein's enacting character of language, we get from Blau complementary cues about animating routes of knowing a way and making it up; rather than false or trivial, qualities of contingency are useful to investigate constraint and try to make something significant. Rejecting Victor Turner's universal view which confines theatre and societal seriousness to ritual, Blau calls performance no less serious for being improvisational or a place of play. He releases closed answers of prepared forms in ascribing opening and uncertainty to action, seeing theatre as a public way of thinking, intentionally provisional, crossing limits 'as a reflection on limits', a place of indeterminacy but 'no slack in the void' (Blau 2002: 317–18). Wittgenstein (1993) wonders if ritual lends to the formation of the serious in human culture, but argues against James George Frazer's idea that ritual occupies the literalized originating place of human activity, a claim to prior ground. As with other societal practices, deaths involve agreements of grounds yet grounding agreements come to an end and we start elsewhere or otherwise. For Wittgenstein the end does not come by the proposition or the seeing but more, 'our acting, which lies at the bottom' (1969: #204). Consequently, we may not have grounds but may learn more about what might be true there. Wittgenstein goes on to say, not that there is no truth but that it is not already deposited there, not already grounded (#205–06).

Speculating on death and burial, Robert Pogue Harrison holds that all grounds are burial grounds, a single designation tying his claim of the human agency by which places are made with the mortality that gives animation to human activity (2003: 18–19). The prior ground funds places with energy, a notion of appropriation from Heidegger's aboriginal already there, and anticipates their disappearance to which all markers of death and life point. Determining that Heidegger needs some attachment to historical event, Harrison turns to Vico's civil life of institutional universals that includes burial (2003: 21). Despite Harrison's commitment to historical making of place, the pairing of Heidegger's bones that precede us with Vico's universality eschews appearances of other disappearances or situations of grounds. Harrison refers to ground as literal and non-literal, the literal giving room to Vico's reality of human action, saying that it is in place building that such a distinction takes its validation; in possession and contract the built gives ontological binding to the non-literal ground. However, the distinction wavers. Conditions of loss change grounds, in every sense anthropological, ecological and ontological. How to differentiate one kind of ground loses its agreements becoming less certain, as these architectures contribute to saying.

Memorial grounds

Unprepared for the extent of controversy yet aware that the Vietnam Veterans Memorial design challenges expectations of monumental glory, Lin writes that when a supportive veteran asked how she anticipated people's reactions, she was 'afraid to tell him […] that I knew a returning veteran would cry' (2000: 4:16). The expressiveness that she anticipates comes from a sensibility of suffering in a controversial war that the United States lost. The vulnerability breaks with a history of silences folded into a culture of modern stoic conduct discouraging public and private mention of death. If monuments to figures of victory appear to conclude matters, the Wall indicates receptiveness to the 'experiential and cathartic' (4:16). Initially denied a building permit, given the extent of the criticism, the veteran-funded construction contrasts with other official architecture of the Mall. Abstract in formal upright structure and lack of adornment, the Wall slopes and sinks directly into the ground, indexing rather than representing modern practices, refusing and unable to master conditions of war, change and disorder. What might or might not be possible for a visitor to resolve comes forward as difficult to reconcile instead of answers by completed explanation.

The direct relation to the ground gives horizontal opening for ordinary informal and formal self and socially chosen gestures that leave a mix of the obscure, spare and nostalgic. Not only living veterans but anyone else standing there faces herself or himself reflected in the polished black granite of names in their order of death – the uncanny, destabilizing and certain. Detecting known names among the war dead or missing in action, visitors can make rubbings, as if lifting names from a grave stone. Despite its offer of palpable connections, the Wall's lack of representation resulted in two additional sculptures, the first accepted as part of the compromise of going ahead with Lin's design – agreed to as heroic recognition in Frederick Hart's 1984 figural work portraying three standing soldiers. The Women's Memorial of 1993 shows three women in uniform caring for a collapsed soldier, all bearing strains of war. A Memorial Plaque of 2004 acknowledges those who died later from war causes, such as Agent Orange. The proliferation of architecture further displaces modern propositional clarity of a single agreement and modern reticence towards elaboration as inconsequential and a threat to order.

By predominate modern accounts, death is the key human anxiety. While no longer made conspicuous by traditions of warding off fear with superstition and ritual, death nonetheless persists as the source of fundamental unease that modern societies meet with strategies of denial. Freud's view along these lines is modulated by the First World War. In 'Reflections on War and Death' (1919), he argues that the extreme losses of the war threaten the emotional protection of explanations on which societies have relied. Europeans have minimized the threat of death by containing it as an occurrence of one individual whose end comes with surprise. Confronting large-scale death from the chaos of Continental political failure and new killing technologies in the military, people will now find death less avoidable, he surmises, as human condition meets human conditions.

The First World War anniversary examinations of architectural responses look to battlefield cemeteries and the London Cenotaph, a statement – although in victory – of the unavoidable insistence of large-scale death on attention. In London, how to speak of and to civil life under impressions of a new horror concerned the official state organization implementing plans to name and bury soldiers of all ranks on or near battlefields away from home. Disagreement over depictions of consolation displays the capacity of architecture to say things that make a difference. Conflict emerged between Herbert Baker's proposed cemetery design of comfort, relying on the familiar English church garden with recognizable Christian symbols, and Lutyens's dispassionate geometric lines of rows and stone inviting but not commanding solace; Lutyens largely prevailed (Geurst 2010). For the Cenotaph, the request for a public design went to Lutyens. At first a temporary plywood form for Armistice Day 1919, it became a permanent structure by popular demand. In homage to the dead of a war won, Lutyens blurs monumental convictions of the vertical stone with the disorientation of the shock of loss that he senses himself and among the public. An upright monolith, the Cenotaph sits on a low pedestal of three steps, inscribed only 'To the Glorious Dead'. Calling it 'monumental classicism' Carden-Coyne follows Greek intimations in the curving technique of sculpting for visual straightness and in replacing violence with idealized abstraction (2009: 127).

In its unfamiliarity, the design sparked strong architectural debate along with disagreement from clergy, but the idea offered a presumption for which the public seems to have been prepared. In effect, Lutyens proposes the visual abstraction idea that the awareness of unfamiliar violence wants to encounter the unfamiliar. Rather than represent, the architecture presents the war as incomprehensible. The abstraction further proposes the possibility of something indirectly universalist, not exactly shared yet referenced obliquely among notions of universal in religions, a suggestion in stone that depends on recognizing without symbolizing (Geurst 2010: 8, 22). While separated from cemeteries, the Cenotaph belongs to their declaration of imperial possession and modern sacrifice in reclaiming the capital city from overwhelming experiences of loss and in rectangles of grave rows across Europe reclaiming British dead and landscape wreckage from battles, the analytic frame for Geurst's (2010) close study of Lutyens's cemetery architecture. Carden-Coyne describes the Cenotaph as 'architectural limb', the weak with restored strength, as if a fragment floating and returned to full form (2009: 133). One could add by implication that it is able to retrain senses of memory.

As Jay Winter (1995) observes, Lin studies monuments of the First World War, with their lists of names and lack of symbolic display. She is especially drawn to Lutyens's work at Thiepval (Lin 2000: 4:12). In his study of First World War burial and memorial struggles regarding the dead nearer and farther from home, Winter identifies distressed voices of parents, townspeople, commanders, civil officials and relief organizers contesting authority over bodies, gravesites and commemoration. Examining their disputes, he argues that traditional rather than modern outlooks guide numerous debates and decisions of how to care for and honour the dead. More broadly, Winter (1995) characterizes their exchange as the perpetual contestation between civil and state in the back and forth of local and superintending offices. But this move reduces dense, discursive plurality to a modern binary. With the argument that the Cenotaph and the Wall both turn around trauma, Jenny Edkins (2003) emphasizes their capacities to make undisclosed feelings accessible by locating senses of collective suffering. Rather than a record of endless civil-state tension that she sees in Winter, Edkins discerns the scattered power of places of the 'solidarity of the inexpressible' (64); these memorials express the limits of language in experiences of trauma. Though official, they point to limits of governmental structure in the face of social and societal affect and occurrence, showing institutions of civil-state themselves to be at stake rather than steady assumptions in societal discourse. Still, Edkins retains Western notions of self and society, leaving in place modern institutions of memory and cognition without considering alteration of their figure and ground when trauma casts the performance of authority in doubt.

Alteration to agreed-upon structuring of civil and state, self and society belong to the doubts expressed in building the Vietnam Veterans Wall. Once Lin's submission was ranked first in the competition, it provoked more detailed dissention, emphasizing the breach the war underscored between military and those not serving. Controversy intensified among monument committee members and their publics, particularly military concerns that all reference to valour was lost. Suspicious of Lin's (2000) ethnic heritage, detractors examined her design for signs of Asian disloyalty to the United States. The stone for the Wall was brought from India, after veterans rejected granite from Sweden or Canada, countries that housed those refusing the draft and who stood, by veterans' terms, apart from loyalty, risk and sacrifice. Decisions of colour and thickness engaged veterans' scepticism about how seriously the wall could convey the existential extremity of the dead. Yet, for Lin, awareness of loss by death was crucial to the design, its grounding in an exigency 'to be honest about death' and to be personal in this honesty, distinguishing but not separating death from deaths (4:10).

The London Cenotaph and Vietnam Memorial Wall attest to attenuation of warrior-heroic-sacrificial configurations and their mediations of violence and consolation; their enmeshed theological, legal and political loyalties are evident in the objects and texts of symbolic order and rule, as Agamben (2011) well demonstrates. If reluctantly, the two architectural forms live with this schema in nationally inflected participation. Continuing to ratify governing power, the Cenotaph's empty tomb annually locates the Armistice with Remembrance Day (BBC One 2018) alongside modern and postmodern groundlessness. The Wall inhabits and releases the authority of its governing space, differently incomplete, including that names continue to be added as remains are located, involving the cooperation of the Vietnamese. For the memorial's thirty-fifth anniversary, Lin (2017) spoke of healing at the Veterans Day Ceremony. Worried about the idolatry of any landscape as a possessive act, Harrison comes to architecture 'only half-facetiously' as what will save us with its provision of habitation (2003: 35). In acknowledging the institutional character of human burial, Harrison finds the import of anthropology. It is the Vietnam Wall's encounter with absolute finitude which he sees as its achievement (136); the absence of traditional narrative or figure puts the architecture directly into prior ground, to the agreement that the earth takes back the human. But anthropology does not only sit on top of ground to be evaded by terms of seamlessness or separation. Other architectures intervene differently with less secured grounds.

Identifying grounds

Events of violence and loss may be arguable but are not tentative. Their more tentative memorials include frail mediums, unprotected locations, nearby conflicts, secreted connections and refusals of identification that grounds introduce. Wittgenstein says it is not in knowing itself but recognizing our experience of a kind of circumstances that stands behind knowing how to go on (2009: #154); Blau (2002) speaks of trained improvisation. Whatever the improvisation underway, memorials may take place as circumstances people know how to perform, as Ochs (1993) analyses in Greco-Roman public funereal commemoration and consolation. But memorials may involve circumstances for which no announced way appears or appears to be appropriate. Their architectures trace seizure in urban streets or mass graves thinly covered in fields; both words and silences differ. Mirjana Ristic (2018) holds that the Sarajevo Roses constitutes an architectural decision for silence instead of for political position contesting other positions.

After the 1995 Dayton Accords ended the Bosnian War, the Siege of Sarajevo ceased at the end of February 1996. Describing Sarajevo's 'silent' commemoration, Ristic (2013) reviews decisions in the design proposal awarded to architecture professor Nedzad Kurto. Kurto followed siege social practices: patterns people saw in explosives that shattered places on the pavement evoking flower shapes; between attacks, people left flowers at the shelling sites of those killed and, if possible, wrote their names on nearby walls. In acknowledgement, indentations of killing shots were filled with red resin, and thus, the Sarajevo Roses. To withdraw from 'too much of a monument' (Ristic 2018: 179), Kurto looks to the ground because that is where the violence took place, reminding pedestrians by recollecting the 'bloody roses' where those seeking protection by running across or lying on the ground were hit (Ristic 2013: 114). The unassuageable is not fittingly a monolith to a single unspeakable-unknowable. Equally, people's absences shadow attempts at going on with life while trying to hide, traverse areas for bread or water, attend prayers or play with other children. For lack of funds, only about one hundred were made, mostly in the city centre but otherwise without any overarching scheme. With their colour alone to call attention, Kurto's intent is to remember the collective suffering of ordinary routes rather than distinguish and isolate individuals and places (2018: 181).

In a dispersed notion of silence, Ristic (2013) contrasts the Roses with rhetoric. They give no name and so no ethnicity, for some showing innocence and for others heroic actions of resisting. Plural in allusion, they invite layered mediations of past and present in contrast with other nearby memorials. In particular, Ristic compares them to 'rhetorical' observances, writing on small upright plaques, often stuck in the ground, that convey some views of city history, distinguishing identity groups of those killed and naming the killers as 'evil Serbians', accusation as if documentary fact (Ristic 2013: 120). Their messages of confrontation and generalized guilt lead Ristic to see their depiction of past and present as traumatic. As agitated sites, they suggest injury that would resist or resent healing or consensus. Like the Vietnam Veterans Memorial, Ristic argues, the Roses offer no single authority over interpretation but leave interpretation open, though she considers their attempt at non-traumatic silence to potentially convey the meaninglessness of war and nationalism (2013: 122). More work lies ahead, apparent in friction about a proposed memorial for blameless Serbians who died (Ristic 2018). Increasingly obscure, the Roses wear from ground traffic and cover of new pavement though some have been re-covered by painting (Korchnak 2014), while plaques and proposals indicate common life in grounds of political discord. On different grounds, the Wall carries other discord as shifts in war assessment produce their frictions and as Vietnamese register the absence of recognition of their civilian casualties at the hands of US agencies.

In Cambodia unfinished transactions among legal, government and religious authorities have characterized difficult years following the mass killings. Often focused on the status of skulls and other bones, offices have collided over socially antithetical purposes: in-spirited materials deemed crucial to legal verification of killings and to proper ritual recognition of ancestral death and relations with the living. Since the Khmer Rouge (1975–79), memorial anxieties have mirrored the brutal upheaval of the regime. The death estimate of about one-fifth of the population, around 1.7 million, relies on extensive research into the forced removal of populations into the countryside and the suffering due to work abuse, torture, starvation and execution (Guillou 2014: 151). With the use of evidence by the UN-sponsored tribunal, rulings that began in 2012 eventually led to the sentencing of three leaders for crimes against humanity that directly caused horrible deaths. In November 2018 the decision of genocide was announced, a judgement based on their attempts to cleanse Cambodia of Cham and Vietnamese minorities (Beech 2018: n.pag.). The lack of precedent for international court authority has compounded political and spiritual confusion about preserving bones required to establish age – whether baby, child or adult – and how the killing took place, profiling violations to assess criminal intent and act; during laboratory analysis, forensics may discover someone's name (Fleischman 2016). Even with evidence, disagreement among judges has stalled the actual process of trial (Nachemson 2020).

Most known among these memorials, 'The Killing Fields' references the mass grave at Choeung Ek with the Buddhist stupa outside Phnom Penh. Buddhist ceremonies that normally assist in securing passage and guiding spirits towards ease had been forestalled. Amid ritual confusion, official interventions encouraging proper preservation of bones retained for judicial procedures, including those set apart at memorial sites, only partially allayed public concerns. Those whose lives end by malevolent means induce deepened foreboding, for their spirits are considered to seek revenge, which is particularly dangerous. While tourists visit the Killing Fields Memorial, often so casually that they walk carelessly on remnants of clothing or skeleton, many Cambodians stay away, finding them grounds of further distress. By Buddhist practice, a requirement stipulated that only family could initiate the cremation process. Later allowance of general rituals granted that circumstances of non-identification warrant shifting practices (Guillou 2014: 153); gradually, rules exceed rules in revised assumptions. More recently, bones housed in memorial stupas have received Buddhist ritual protection after being removed for forensic study and later restored to freshly prepared cases at their site (Fleischman 2016: 124). As in Sarajevo, though with other cultural paths, historically noted sites across Cambodia precipitate concord and antagonism, not clear divisions between victims and perpetrators but perplexing moments of reconstructing histories and selves (Manning 2015).

Under different conditions of violence, researchers approach disappearance by seeking networks of affiliation or specific addresses. Remains may or may not have been hidden in a place that can be located, the abduction known. In Buenos Aires, dissidents and those attributed with their association would suddenly vanish; especially between 1976 and 1983, state-organized assassination and torture were recurrent (Hite 2012: 96). To disquiet their injustice Argentinians have developed sidewalk architecture to post information and inquire further about a particular person last seen at a place. Walking becomes treading on public political grounds, outlining dictatorship (O'Higgins 2017). Memory tiles for the Disappeared are laid throughout the city. Each receives its own ceremony, a scene of witnessing the disappearance, gathering with it and drawing lines of terror as part of implementing justice. El Parque de la Memoria includes sculptural pieces that accompany walls inscribed with names of civilian losses, not soldiers, but in a manner recalling the Vietnam Wall (Jessel 2017). As with Vietnam, marchers preceded walls; Mothers of the Disappeared have continued to march in protest and memory, sometimes in political factions. Defiance and redress combine in citizens asserting political authority to account for death and reinstate membership to those removed. Accordingly, architectural gesture observes and directs public agency that had been dismissed or punished, risked or given up, now more recoverable with the appearance of long undisclosed records of dictatorial power (Hite 2012: 98). Securing a name may support a case for human rights transgressions but not offer comfort, as workers have found in Argentina as well as Cambodia. To incorporate someone with the disappeared can seem preferable to knowing that and how this particular person has been murdered (Fleischman 2016: 125).

The commitment to make memorial places for those who can be named is visible in the 'Stolpersteine' or Stumbling Blocks originated by Berlin artist Guenther Demnig who in 1990 began installing stones, some flat and others raised, in walkways where people were forcibly taken from their homes or last seen under their own volition (Harjes 2005). Throughout city neighbourhoods, information of their name, address and date if murdered is engraved on brass plates affixed to the stones. Using informal discussion and the web, Demnig solicits assistance in probing residential records to give proximity to disappearances during the years of National Socialism. Rather than the architectural abstraction of the Berlin Holocaust Memorial, the block embeds the immediate act of abduction and implicates the refusal, fear and studied helplessness of bystanders. Stumbling Blocks are sometimes stolen in casual vandalism or anti-Semitism. Neighbours may participate while some protest the scrutiny directed to their streets or houses, as they too become part of mapping the region. A California family travelled to install stones for a grandfather and an aunt (Shattner 2013). For Demnig localizing the Stumbling Blocks rejects purposes of ritual memory and national representation in the hope of instruction and thinking (Harjes 2005). Different in their respective histories and each disturbing in investigation, the tiles of Buenos Aires and stones of Berlin develop street architectures with silences and notices that are partial yet definite, not filling a space but interrupting a walk to inform it. As with other grounds, the stones are no less serious for making use of routine places, pieces of a story, research by non-experts and modest, small building materials. In Sarajevo, Kurto hopes to avoid the 'noise' of a monument and in Berlin, Demnig its empty state ownership. Not only about resistance, sidesteps of creative resistance take place in all these modes, including those who persisted with the honour of bones in Cambodia and eventually brought forensic experts into their cause. In architectural sensibilities, these experiences of a kind of experience stand close behind their thoughts.

Performing grounds

Reconsidering her earlier concerns with the voyeurism of suffering, Susan Sontag (2003) later sees worry about trivializing, often associated with uses of technologies, now tied to arguable modern suspicions that dismiss sincerity, action and specified attention. In her fresh assessment, the tasks of acknowledgement and protest that circumstances can require are paired with obligations of attention towards injury. Joining specific attention with the contextual and active orientations of the performative, two architectural structures amplify attention and obligation in expanding dimensions of unsettling, one towards African American deaths written out of records as forgettable and the other towards environmental death whose warnings we have ignored. A consequence of the Equal Justice Initiative (2018), the National Memorial for Peace and Justice in Montgomery is dedicated to victims of all forms of racial terror. As the project grew from the initial partnership of the architect Michael Murphy and Bryan Stevenson (the lead lawyer and lead in the organization), other artists joined the collaboration (Bernstein 2018). In a design of terror and injustice, eight hundred rusted steel columns hang in tribute to the thousands of African Americans who were lynched. Often lynching was performed before crowds, some incited under duress to attend. While white pursuit of the systematic death conditions of lynching attests to the public threat to African Americans of being hunted down at every turn of daily life, much about the identifications of lynching continues to be hidden. As with other memorial attempts to identify, the architecture takes up the phenomenology of place. Marked with the county of the lynching by specific site where possible, the columns are inscribed with names of those murdered individuals or more often with name 'unknown'. Labelled by name, location and date, jars contain soil from lynching grounds collected by family or community members. Any county with lynching grounds that shows good-faith efforts towards correcting wrongs of racial injustice can be sent a replicating beam as its own memorial. To further situate within regional environments, the museum houses research sources of photography, maps and a document repository, another materializing aspect of wanting troubled acknowledgement instead of consolation or resignation. Museum staff, mostly lawyers, have further investigated local injustice in racialized law and incarceration making visible the punishment history of the United States (Campbell 2018).

Using a digital architectural forum, Lin (2009) displays 'What Is Missing?', her memorial to the earth that first opened in 2009. A number of other sites around the world link to this project which confronts the loss of species. Charting native habitats, weather patterns, land and water histories, the forum can reproduce earlier place conditions that then experience destruction, damage and attempts at repair. The design highlights the radical precariousness of the earth, intimating but not targeting major agencies of environmental harm. Asking visitors to contribute with points of inquiry and connecting information, the site promotes fluid agency possibilities. With no one single path of entry, the architecture is meant to invite, trouble and engage. Like the Wall, the construction advocates no messages or viewpoints and tries to minimize guiding directions other than efforts to make more obvious paths through the dense overlays without losing subtlety. Sustained through others and Lin, the memorial continues to combine experimental, scientific and personal qualities in tracing endangered life. In a video Lin made in 2010, people around the world recall what is missing in the place where they live, the dark of the night sky or butterflies that once gathered over puddles (n.pag.).

Critical points of exchange belong in the potential elaboration of what cannot be ignored when the two architectures meet regarding power, threat and responsibility. For instance, the land-human burdens of enslaved people bought for unrelieved plantation planting and then of sharecroppers, the same crops in the same soil year after year under the force of the owner of the labour and the ground. Or waterways that concealed decomposing bodies of murdered African Americans thrown into a river to ensure no respectful burial, no grave as evidence. Related to Lin's 1989 Civil Rights Memorial in Montgomery, the expansive architectures cross-reference kinds of circumstances, their senses of conditions far from justice seeking reflective thinking that does not want to end in despair. Viewed online each site relays architectural urgency with a worried beauty and deliberation, uncertain it will find address. Like the other memorializing places of extremity, both locate their interventions as grounds questioning grounds.

My purpose has not been architectural history, criticism or romanticism but to notice sites immersed in historical horror that have more to say about death and deaths with architectural expressions. Architectures inscribe places, change places and incorporate discursive gestures of building and place, including what appears to be architecturally set, yet is not. Lutyens's King's Way built for the British Raj in New Delhi furnishes part of Gandhi's funeral procession, giving route to paradoxes of this moment in Indian national myth (Misra 2007: 258). The decision to bury Parnell in the nationally associated Glasnevin Cemetery in Dublin with his name cut into a plain boulder transported from his home county Wicklow re-inscribes both places in the history of modern Ireland (Dublin Cemeteries Committee 2000). Architecture can be rejected with developing public conscience, thus, removals of Confederate Commander Robert E. Lee statues from venerated positions in the United States. Circumstances may harbour expressive reticence; only recently have memorials appeared to those who died in the 1918 pandemic (Segal 2020).

Public memorial performance regards encounters of events and people, whether a momentarily unified public, a jostling assemblage or individuals and groups in calm or tense coexistence or separation. Rather than segmented and mute, under conditions of loss architectural, ceremonial, civil or sacred reflexively enter negotiation, or fail to enter. These sites are each distinct in experiences of violence, shock, political arguments and silences, relations of everyday and uncanny existential reckoning. What modern thinkers might posit as a premodern agreement of human and ground bears the modern reading of conflict with death (Freud) and separation of the ground space of death (Harrison), wary of illusion or slightness in anthropological effects; as a consequence, evading matters of ground. However interventions of and with architectures may be understood, they present energies of our time with insistence on their own entanglement and the seriousness of their historically unsettled constructions. In that respect they particularly speak to one of the three rhetorical tasks traditionally assigned memorial oration (to instruct), and they give more proximate complication than is often considered to the other two (to remember and to recognize). If the grounds of death are like no other, it is still the case that deaths in their architectures permeate and interrogate agreements of ground leaving no place already set apart.

REFERENCES

Agamben, Giorgio (2011), *The Kingdom and the Glory*, trans. L. Chiesa and M. Mandarini, Stanford, CA: Stanford University Press.

BBC One (2018), 'Remembrance Sunday: The cenotaph', https://www.bbc.co.uk/programmes/b0brgkgt. Accessed 1 June 2020.

Beech, Hannah (2018), 'Khmer Rouge's slaughter in Cambodia is ruled a genocide', *New York Times*, 15 November, https://www.nytimes.com/2018/11/15/world/asia/khmer-rouge-cambodia-genocide.html. Accessed 15 November 2018.

Bernstein, Fred A. (2018), 'Step inside the new national museum for peace and justice', *Architectural Digest*, 25 April, https://www.architecturaldigest.com/story/national-memorial-for-peace-and-justice. Accessed 20 November 2018.

Blair, Carole and Michel, Neil (2007), 'The AIDS memorial quilt and the contemporary culture of public commemoration', *Rhetoric and Public Affairs*, 10:4, pp. 595–626.

Blau, Herbert (2002), *Dubious Spectacle: Extremities of Theater, 1976–2000*, Minneapolis: University of Minnesota Press.

Campbell, Robertson (2018), 'A lynching museum is opening: The country has never seen anything like it', *New York Times*, 25 April, https://www.nytimes.com/2018/04/25/us/lynching-memorial. Accessed 26 April 2018.

Carden-Coyne, Ana (2009), *Reconstruction of the Body: Classicism, Modernism, and the First World War*, Oxford: Oxford University Press.

Detloff, Madelyn (2007), ' "'Tis not in my nature to join in hating, but in loving": Toward survivable public mourning', in P. Rae (ed.), *Modernism and Mourning*, Lewisburg , PA: Bucknell University Press, pp. 51–68.

Dublin Cemeteries Committee (2000), *Death and Design in Victorian Glasnevin*, Dublin: Glasnevin Heritage Project.

Edkins, Jenny (2003), *Trauma and the Memory of Politics*, Cambridge: Cambridge University Press.

Equal Justice Initiative, Montgomery Alabama (2018), https://museumandmemorial.eji.org/. Accessed 2 June 2020.

Fleischman, Julie (2016), 'Working with the remains in Cambodia: Skeletal analysis and human rights after atrocity', *Genocide Study and Prevention*, 10:2, pp. 121– 30, https://scholarcommons.usf.edu/gsp/vol10/iss2/10. Accessed 19 January 2017.

Freud, Sigmund (1919), 'Reflections on war and death', Sophia Project: Philosophy Archives, https://pdfs.semanticscholar.org. Accessed 22 November 2018.

Geurst, Jeroen (2010), *Cemeteries of the Great War by Sir Edward Lutyens*, Rotterdam: 010 Publishers.

Guillou, Anne Yvonne (2014), 'From bones as evidence to tutelary spirits: The status of bodies in the aftermath of the Khmer Rouge genocide', in J.-M. Dreyfus and E. Anstett (eds), *Human Remains and Mass Violence*, Manchester: Manchester University Press, pp. 146–60.

Harjes, Kirsten (2005), 'Stumbling stones: Holocaust memorials, national identity, and democratic inclusion in Berlin', *German Politics and Society*, 23:1 (74), pp. 38–151, https://www.researchgate.net/publication/233697222_Stumbling_Stones_Holocaust_Memorials_. Accessed 25 August 2018.

Harrison, Robert Pogue (2003), *The Dominion of the Dead*, Chicago, IL: University of Chicago Press.

Hite, Katharine (2012), *Politics and the Art of Commemoration: Memorials to Struggle in Latin America and Spain*, London: Routledge.

Jessel, Ella (2017), 'Sidewalks full of handmade monuments to Buenos Aires's disappeared', *CityLab*, 19 April, https://www.citylab.com/equity/2017/04/memory-tiles-sidewalks-buenos-aires/523602/. Accessed 25 August 2018.

Korchnak, Peter (2014), 'Roses of Sarajevo', *Compass Cultura*, 14 December, https://compasscultura.com/roses-of-sarajevo/. Accessed 1 June 2020.

Lin, Maya (2000), *Boundaries*, New York: Simon and Schuster.

Lin, Maya (2009), 'The last memorial: What is missing?', https://whatismissing.net/. Accessed 22 November 2018.

Lin, Maya (2010), 'Maya Lin's memorial to vanishing nature', interviewed by D. Toomey, *YaleEnvironment360*, https://e360.yale.edu/features/maya_lin_a_memorial_to_a_vanishing_natural_world. Accessed 22 November 2018.

Lin, Maya (2017), 'Veterans Day ceremony at the Vietnam Veterans Memorial', 11 November, https://www.c-span.org/video/?436708-1/veterans-day-ceremony-vietnam-veterans-memorial&playEvent. Accessed 2 June 2020.

Lincoln, Bruce (1989), *Discourse and the Construction of Society*, New York: Oxford University Press.

Manning, Peter (2015), 'Reconciliation and perpetrator memorials in Cambodia', *International Journal of Transitional Justice*, 9:3, pp. 386–406, https://www.academia.edu/15199044/Reconciliation_and_Perpetrator_Memories_in_Cambodia. Accessed 30 January 2017.

Misra, Maria (2007), *Vishnu's Crowded Temple: India since the Great Rebellion*, New Haven, CT: Yale University Press.

Mitchell, W. J. T. (2005), *What Do Pictures Want?*, Chicago, IL: University of Chicago.

Nachemson, Andrew (2020), 'Will the last of the Khmer Rouge ever face justice in Cambodian mass killings?', *Los Angeles Times*, 26 February, https://www.latimes.com/world-nation/story/2020-02-26/17-years-300-million-3-convictions-was-cambodias-genocide-tribunal-worth-it. Accessed 2 June 2020.

Ochs, Donovan J. (1993), *Consolatory Rhetoric: Grief, Symbol, and Ritual in the Greco-Roman Era*, Columbia: University of South Carolina.

O'Higgins, Sorcha (2017), '7 places to follow the dictatorship footsteps in Buenos Aires', *Culture Trip*, 18 August, https://theculturetrip.com/south-america/argentina/articles/7-places-to-follow-the-dictatorship-footsteps-in-buenos-aires/. Accessed 1 June 2020.

Ristic, Mirjana (2013), 'Silent vs. rhetorical memorials, Sarajevo memorials and commemorative plaques', in A. Brown and A. Leach (eds), *Proceedings of the Society of Architectural Historians, Australia and New Zealand: 30, Open*, vol. I, Gold Coast, Qld: SAHANZ, pp. 111–22. https://www.sahanz.nct/wp content/uploads/S03_03_Ristic_Silent-vs-Rhetorical.pdf. Accessed 20 January 2017.

Ristic, Mirjana (2018), *Architecture, Urban Space and War: The Destruction and Reconstruction of Sarajevo*, Cham: Palgrave Macmillan.

Segal, David (2020), 'Why are there almost no memorials to the flu of 1918?', *New York Times*, 14 May, https://www.nytimes.com/2020/05/14/business/1918-flu-memorials.html. Accessed 15 May 2020.

Shattner, Howard (2013), 'Stumbling stones (Stolpersteine) for my family', https://www.youtube.com/watch?v=FeQOuQvAi8E. Accessed 1 June 2020.

Sontag, Susan (2003), *Regarding the Pain of Others*, New York: Farrar, Straus and Giroux.

Winter, Jay (1995), *Sites of Memory, Sites of Mourning*, Cambridge: Cambridge University Press.

Wittgenstein, Ludwig (1969), *On Certainty*, ed. G. E. M. Anscombe and G. H. von Wright, trans. D. Paul and G. E. M. Anscombe, New York: Harper and Row.

Wittgenstein, Ludwig (1993), *Philosophical Occasions: 1912–1951*, ed. J. C. Klagge and A. Nordmann, Indianapolis, IN: Hackett Publishing Company.

Wittgenstein, Ludwig (2009), *Philosophical Investigations*, trans. G. E. M. Anscombe, P. M. S. Hacker and J. Schulte, Chichester: Wiley-Blackwell.

9

Sacred Space and Occupation as Protest: Jonathan Z. Smith and Occupy Wall Street

Joshua Edelman

While contemporary movements of political activism and protest often make use of technology and digital culture to both organize their actions and spread word about their cause (via viral videos, Facebook groups, memes and the like), there is a prominent exception. One of the most visible and effective techniques of contemporary protest is the collective occupation of public space. Even without an explicitly coherent agenda or political message, actions that appropriate public space have a particular political and social salience that deserves attention.

These actions, especially those coalescing around the 2011 Occupy Wall Street movement and its cousins around the world, have provoked considerable public and scholarly attention (see, for instance, Shiffman et al. 2012). Many scholars have linked the efficacy of these protests with theories of the politics and performativities of public assembly (e.g. Butler 2015). While not wishing to cast aspersions on the utility of these approaches, I would like to add to them. Part of the reason the occupation of certain spaces is compelling to us, I argue, is a sense of sacred space that we retain in our post-secular culture in Europe and North America. I would suggest that some understanding of this sense of sacred space would be useful to scholars of the arts, performance and public action in conceptualizing the ways in which artists interact with their environments and their communities. In my own work, I have found the academic discipline of the study of religion to be a particularly helpful and under-used dialogue partner for scholars of performance and the arts. A full analysis of the potential of such a dialogue would be valuable but is more than I can offer in this chapter. Here, I will only be able to suggest that dialogue's utility through an engagement with a theorist of place in the contemporary study of religion: Jonathan Z. Smith.

Smith is a historian of religions and places himself in a tradition of the anthropology of religion of Emile Durkheim, Claude Levi-Strauss, Mircea Eliade and Victor Turner. While he specializes in classical Jewish literature from around the sixth century BCE to the fourth century CE, his knowledge of the wider field of religious studies is encyclopaedic. His is a model of the study of religion that relies on comparison. Anthropology, in this tradition, is the study of human beings as such. The desire to explore the cultures most distant historically and geographically from our own, then, is not an exotic fascination but rather to use the sharp contrast this provides as a clarifying lens. If we accept that 'their' experience is as human as 'ours', then we have broadened our understanding of the human experience in general. This is a goal that anthropologists share with philosophers.

Smith's anthropological project, then, is ontological, not touristic. This is why he refers to Durkheim's *Elementary Forms of the Religious Life* as a book that only seems to be a description of Australian aboriginal religion, but is, in fact, through its footnotes, a debate with Kant (Smith 1987: 39). And yet, he has a certain scepticism towards theoretical constructions which makes him far from a conventional Kantian. He is sharply critical of those who are too quick to posit universal patterns that the data do not bear out, such as Mircea Eliade's (1959) theory of the hierophany, but he does not think such patterns are necessarily impossible. The playful plasticity of his ideas has led at least one scholar to call the *homo ludens* of the academic study of religion (Gill 1998).

Place is Smith's central emergent pattern in understanding the workings of the sacred, more so than some of his critics might wish to see. Ronald Grimes, for instance, argues that this focus on place reduces ritual to emplacement, which makes for an overly intellectual understanding of what ritual is and does not make enough space for the multidimensionality of ritual activity (2006: 108–12). Ritual, for Smith, is what makes space sacred, and sacred space is the social and architectural framing that gives ritual its efficacy. But this makes space (and ritual, as a consequence) into formal, not substantial, categories. Ritual action and sacred spaces are a means of providing emphasis, like italics in language. It does not say anything itself, but it marks out as meaningful whatever is being said. As Smith writes:

Ritual is, first and foremost [...] a mode of paying attention. [...] Within the temple, the ordinary (which to any outside eye or ear remains wholly ordinary) becomes significant, becomes 'sacred', simply by being there. A ritual object or action becomes sacred by having attention focus on it in a highly marked way. From such a point of view, there is nothing that is inherently sacred or profane. These are not substantive categories, but rather situational ones. Sacrality is, above all, a category of emplacement.

(1987: 103–04)

Different scholars have tried to specify what that notion of 'highly marked' means, and the lists overlap: traditionalism, formality, invariance, hierarchy and so on. But equally worth noting is the overlap between Smith's concept of sacred emplacement and the performance studies concept of aesthetic emplacement – an act, or an object, becomes artistic simply because of its presence in the museum or theatre, or because we attend to it in a highly marked way. (In a slightly different context, I have, with my colleagues from the Project on European Theatre Systems, discussed this question of marking-out and artistic emplacement by a look at Pierre Bourdieu's notion of the fields of art. See Edelman et al. [2016].)

Smith's view, drawing on Kant, is that we understand sacred space as an extension of our body into the world, and thus as a kind of built home: a location in which we, our memories, our values and our collective senses of identity can dwell. Such a concept of space is not geographic, but architectural: it describes not the features of the landscape, but the ways in which it has been marked up and ordered by human labour (Smith 1987: 27). Significant events, too, can be housed in this way, and like our homes, these structures can travel, moving with the act of remembrance that they mark. Smith's examples here are not only pilgrimages and holy relics, but the spiritual exercises of Ignatius of Loyola, which ask its followers to make a 'mental representation of the place' of Jerusalem when conducting their exercises, but sees no need to ask them to actually travel there.

This view of sacred place, then, is often an architectural one, understood on the model of a human structure. These buildings and the uses they afford are often read by Smith as a structural elaboration of that society's highest values. Because of his intellectual background, Smith's central reference point is the biblical Temple in Jerusalem, though he sees parallels in many other urban cultures. Because Smith sees sacred space as a formal concept, not a substantial one, his interest in sacred buildings is in the principles they use to mark out space, rather than the buildings themselves. His interest is architectural, rather than archaeological. This means that he is equally interested in sacred buildings that were, in fact, built as he is in those which exist only in unrealized plans, such as the heavenly image of the restored temple in Ezekiel 40–48. It also means that these plans are 'transportable', not tied to any particular place, and available for invocation by anyone (politicians, artists, activists) whenever it suits their needs.

Smith notes a pattern in many of these buildings, in which a clear differentiation is made between the authority of kings and the authority of priests. To make sense of this, Smith cites Louis Dumont, who differentiates between hierarchies of power and those of status (1987: 54–55, citing Dumont 1980: 356). While power is what we ordinarily think of political authority – a legal system that constrains and legitimizes the use of force, with the king at its head – status is a hierarchical system based on the notion of purity with the priest at its head. This idea of purity as an alternative to political power may seem foreign to the concerns of contemporary protest movements, but I would argue that it provides a helpful model for contemporary political critique. This distinction fairly neatly matches that sketched out by Giorgio Agamben between the authorities of what he calls 'economy' and 'glory': the first, 'government and effective management', and the second, 'ceremonial and liturgical regality' (2011: xii). This is the distinction between a prime minister and a monarch, or more broadly, between ordinary political action and its justifying authority. The architecture of sacred space traditionally demonstrates the 'submission' of political authority to this other force (the priests in the Temple; Agamben's 'glory'), though the nature of this other force is a question of substance and thus something sacred space can house but not define. Glory can be whatever sacred space is able to house and place above political power. Contemporary artists and activists, then, assert their own idea of what that 'glory' is and make use of variations of this formal relationship in re-creating and reclaiming sacred space.

I argue here that this dynamic can help us better understand the workings of contemporary protest movements whose work is grounded in the occupation of space, rather than the articulation of specific demands. A relatively simple case might be the 2016–17 protest against an oil pipeline that ran through a (disputed) burial ground, the Standing Rock Indian reservation in South Dakota. By living on the land and asserting a claim to it as a sacred space, the protestors defined the pipeline not merely as an environmental hazard but an assault on the correct ordering of space, without thereby needing to define precisely that 'correct order' which the pipeline assaulted.[1] For more on the pipeline protests, see Whyte (2017).

The central example I will concern myself with here – the Occupy Wall Street (OWS) movement in Zuccotti Park, New York – did not use the overtly religious language of the pipeline protestors (signs reading 'Water Is Sacred', for example). I will still argue, however, that it made use of Smith's notion of insubstantial, transportable sacred space that marks out and challenges an architecture of power in order to do its unusual and unsettling political work.

The form of Occupy made it quite particular for both its supporters and critics. Rather than using its members' physical presence to articulate and reinforce political demands, as is the case in most demonstrations (including Standing Rock), for the Occupy movement, the physical presence *was* the closest thing the movement had to a clearly articulated demand. The protest did not make *use* of the occupation of public space: it *was* the occupation of that space. Though there was an initial effort to compose a traditional and clear manifesto of demands in the very beginning of the occupation, this was soon abandoned. This is not to say that the movement did not have clear values that it wished to support with its actions, but that those values were asserted not through the (generally verbal) arguments and demands of political demonstration but through the use and division of space.

Unlike Standing Rock, the space that housed Occupy Wall Street did not come pre-marked as sacred. Instead, it was a small concrete square in the dense, corporate urban environments of Lower Manhattan in which public space is rare and precious. The ordinary public uses of those spaces, however, are fleeting; a few people on a brief stroll, a stop for lunch or, most often, a look out of the office window or on the way to work. By fully inhabiting those spaces – by living there permanently and occupying the space in the gaze of the city – these protests frame the mundane acts of daily life, draw attention to them and force us to consider them. Certainly, artists use aesthetic framing to do this – think of Marina Abramovic's *The House with the Ocean View* (2004) or other pieces that involve living in galleries – but there is something more powerful about doing it outside of the pre-approved aesthetic grounds of a museum or theatre. Because urban parks are part of corporate architecture – they make office buildings more attractive to work in, humanize the urban environment and give local workers a sense of space – their occupation challenges power structures in a way that would not be present in the authorized space of a gallery. One of Smith's conceptions of sacred space is as extensions of the body and the home. The idea that public space is first and foremost to be physically lived in, not to serve abstract commercial and financial interests, is in fact controversial in locations such as lower Manhattan. The space may be public, but this does not necessarily mean that the public has the right to inhabit it.

The (vociferous) public opposition to the Occupy movement did object to its lack of articulated demands, yes, but it more directly attacked this claim to the inhabitance of space. The Occupiers were not living in Zuccotti Park, said their critics: they were despoiling it. A number of scholarly observers have pointed out the degree to which Occupy's critics emphasized the uncleanliness of the movement as a means of critiquing it (Bolton et al. 2016). Many have connected this criticism to Mary Douglas's anthropological understanding of the idea of dirt as 'matter out of place' ([1966] 2003: 44). Douglas's argument is not simply about bits of material soil or dust, but a conceptual one. Ideas, substances, objects and people which do not find a place within the intellectual and cultural system which organizes a society are seen as dirty and therefore dangerous and infectious and are thus necessarily avoided and shunned. Examples of this may include bodily discharges, lepers, newly dead bodies and certain kinds of foods which are not clearly categorizable (such as shellfish, which are un-fish-like fish).[2] While there may be considerable overlaps between the subjects of these traditional pollution taboos and those identified as dangerous by modern germ theory, Douglas emphasizes that the nature of pollution she is describing is spiritual before it is medical. As she writes with respect to traditional Jewish prohibitions on foods that might contain parasites,

'Even if some of Moses's dietary rules were hygienically beneficial it is a pity to treat him as an enlightened public health administrator, rather than as a spiritual leader' ([1966] 2003: 30).

So the apparent despoiling of public space by the Occupy protests was not simply a public health hazard (of which there are many in New York), but it was a violation of the correct ordering of how space ought to be used. Parks are for wandering and lunching; apartments are for sleeping. That this was expressed in concerns about dirt and cleanliness, as Bolton et al. (2016) describe, is what we should expect if our secular notions of public sociality still follow (some of) the patterns of their religious forbearers.

Ultimately, however, I think this is an inadequate reading of Occupy. It rests on the idea that the spatial work of the movement was a 'dismantling' of (implicit but) accepted power dynamics. Yes, the movement used its occupation of space to disrupt the economic and political architecture of the global megacity. But it did more than that: hesitantly but demonstrably, it built an architecture of its own as well. Smith can help us understand the constructive spatial work that the movement did, not just its disruptions of established norms.

Matthew Bolton et al. (2013) have done the most important analysis of Occupy Wall Street's engagement with architecture and urban planning. They trace out the geographic logic of 'enclosure' – the piecemeal privatization of the commons which led to fencing and segmentation of the American plains into ranches and square, even Jeffersonian townships and states – through the Manhattan grid planned in 1811 and its twentieth-century cleaning and modernization through the work of New York's master planner, Robert Moses. This systematic organization of space, at first, seems to be reflective of the contemporary hyperglobalized capitalism that Wall Street is known for. But of course, there are gaps and lacunae within that system. Public parks, like Zuccotti, are examples of such authorized gaps which can, in theory, operate as the very sort of commons that the rest of the system excludes. These spaces may provide a release valve for the stressors of capitalist organization – the lunchtime walk, the breath of fresh air – but they necessarily do so in highly circumscribed, limited ways. This function closely resembles the arts' autonomy within society, which, while necessarily limited, allows them to operate outside of dominant social values and conventions (see Edelman et al. 2016). The cost of that autonomy, however, is often irrelevance; the political work done by the arts, for instance, is necessarily limited by the fact that the artistic field is designated as non-political.

In these terms, Bolton et al. describe the way in which the space that Occupy Wall Street chose both worked with the privatized system of Manhattan and offered something of a freedom from that system: what they call an 'open enclosure' (2013: 142). Zuccotti Park, like many New York parks, was an odd hybrid of public and private space; a privately owned and managed space that was designated as public as part of a zoning deal that allowed the U.S. Steel Corporation to build a larger skyscraper nearby (now called One Liberty Plaza). It was a largely concrete-paved space, with few trees or other human comforts. While the park did 'suggest openness and a potential for mixing and play' (Bolton et al. 2013: 144), the architects' description of it is one that suggests a resistance to the creation of structures as such:

> The smooth, hard granite surface communicates cleanliness and sanitation through a suggested impermeability. Inclined on a slope, the design repels matter: accumulated debris could simply be sprayed off and drain out into the street in the same way that the functional architectural design resists sustained human activity or inhabitation.
>
> (Bolton et al. 2013: 143)

This suggests that any 'sustained human activity' in this space which does not make affordances for such would, indeed, be seen as dirt in the Douglasian sense: this was a place designed for a certain sort of temporary leisure, like the regulated, limited freedom of the theatre, and anything that remained of that after hours should be cleaned away by the nightly power wash that cleaned the park.

And indeed, at first, this seemed to be a legitimate reading of Occupy Wall Street. The occupation had no tents or other permanent structures; it was a congregation of people who refused to disperse. But in time, and in negotiation with the vigilant New York Police Department, structures emerged and developed an organizational system of their own. Bolton et al. see in this the encroachment of the techniques of the dominant patterns of capitalist urbanism into the Occupy movement, writing that OWS 'enlisted techniques and practices that echoed the very systems of urban planning that constrain the city's commons: noise regulation, mapping, zoning, gridding, even gentrification' (2013: 138). I do not wholly disagree, but would argue that we can also see a new pattern emerging in the spatial choices of Occupy, ones that can be understood within a Smithian understanding of the formation and definition of sacred space. We can see the movement using its spatial development to assert a supra-political authority.

Though clearly a secular movement, it is notable that the first structure that OWS erected was, in fact, religious. At the beginning of the occupation, the police were enforcing certain rules that prevented any serious structures: any combustible fuel, suspended tarp or permanent structure was not permitted. One of the first 'beachheads of expeditionary architecture' built during the Occupation was an explicitly religious structure: the group Occupy Judaism built a sukkah in the park to mark the Jewish holiday of Sukkot (Bolton et al. 2013: 145). A sukkah is an open-air temporary structure that gives this holiday its name. It echoes the light shelters that farmers would build in their fields at harvest, but also the temporary and mobile tabernacles that the Israelites used in their journey through the desert after Egypt. A sukkah, then, is an ideal structure for a community looking to create a temporary cornucopia. The timing of the festival during the occupation may have been serendipity, but the structure's religious nature may also have led the authorities to give it permission to stay up in a way a secular building may not have. According to Bolton et al., 'When intervening police learned its [the sukkah's] meaning, they decided to leave it unharassed: "We're not messing with that", an officer reportedly said, backing away' (2013: 145).[3] The next structure that was allowed to stand was a medical tent. While the sukkah overtly appealed to an authority above the state that it was bound to respect, the medical tent did the same implicitly. Here, though, it was not organized religion but human life itself – and its continuity and preservation – that served as a higher authority over the ordinary political rules of the city.[4]

These first two structures, then, served as a precedent and opened the door for a wide variety of other structures that spatially marked out the central (if implicit) claim of the Occupy movement: the priority of human life and its development over the capitalist system of governance. In the following weeks, a wide range of new tents and temporary structures began to appear: housing, libraries, sanitation, food and so on. But the organization of this space was not random or haphazard: they were the project of a number of formal working groups of the General Assembly of Occupy Wall Street with responsibility for such topics as sanitation, security, architecture and town planning. Bolton et al. state that these groups explicitly thought of their work as a 'communicative project' and as a means of 'imagining alternative social structures' (2013: 147).

It is instructive to compare the maps that these working groups made of the Occupy site with Smith's maps of Ezekiel's heavenly temple. Both are idealized images of a social structure, but the two are quite different. Ezekiel's temple (in Smith's rendition) represents a perfectly ordered and hierarchical cosmos, in which clear boundaries are set that define the precise relationships between the priests, the king and the people. The original Occupy map is much looser. It marks the general areas in which each kind of activity takes place, but offers no clear dividing lines between them. It is more suggestive than definitive, requires its users to engage with it playfully and tries to capture the ad hoc, flexible structure of the Occupy movement itself. In contrast to the rest of Manhattan, Bolton and colleagues describe it as an 'anti-grid' (2013: 147). They connect it specifically to the broad, cartoonish maps of outdoor music festivals.

Unlike the temple map, the first OWS map, known as the 'festival' map, lacks a clear hierarchical organization. It represents what Bjarke Skærlund Risager calls the 'horizontalist ideas' of the movement (2017: 724). But this is not to say that it does express certain values. The first of those is the preservation and mainten-ance of life itself: central spaces is given to facilities to eat, sleep, wash and receive medical attention. Spaces for art and reading are also given far more prominence than one might expect: indeed, they are the only two 'leisure activities' present on the map, and in a situation in which space was at a premium, this is notable.

But the largest single space was assigned to the general assembly, the daily meeting that oversaw and operated the occupation as a whole. It is a commonplace that the space authorized for making authoritative decisions on behalf of the col-lective is given a central location in that collective's spatial layout. But here, that space is not a palace, castle or capital; it is not even a tent, but rather a broad open plaza with essentially no differentiation within it. I think it is more useful to see the centrality of this open space as a particular sort of (horizontalist) 'structure', one tailored for the use of the particular decision-making practices and technolo-gies of the Occupy movement (the human microphone, the use of hand signals, a lack of authorized leaders, consensus decision-making and so on) rather than (only) the ripping down of structure or the absence of it.

As Smith describes as well, however, the hyper-coherent geography of sacred spaces does not remain pure for long, certainly not for actually existing and inhabited structures (unlike Ezekiel's temple). Smith often describes the way in which the geographies of sacred spaces are complicated and rewritten through cir-cumstance and the development of new social power dynamics (Smith 1982: 53).[5] In the case of Occupy Wall Street, these changes came through the internal ten-sions that necessarily grew as the Occupy movement grew larger and more varied and a need for more systematic regulation of space for the sake of access, health and neighbourliness became necessary. Bolton and colleagues even discuss this in terms of the gentrification of the Zuccotti Park site, with a tension between the whiter, more middle-class and intellectual occupiers congregating in the eastern part of the park, near the library, and the more diverse and more 'hippie' elements (typified by a 24-hour drum circle that others found annoying) in the western part (2013: 149). The OWS Town Planning working group took up this challenge and conduced a formal survey of the park and, with the help of the park's original plans and computer-aided design (CAD) software, created a much more detailed and exact plan of the occupation, the sort of formal architectural drawing one would expect from urban planners. (One version of this plan is reprinted in Bolton et al. [2013: 148]. Another version, dated 10 October 2011 and credited to Jake Deg, is included in Massey and Snyder [2012a]. For details, see the same authors' sidebar to that article [Massey and Snyder 2012b].) The structure this second map pro-vides is not substantially different than that of the first 'festival' map. The differ-ence is in the level of precise detail this second map provides. That detail reflected a much more aggressive practice of governing space, not just a cartography: as

Bolton and colleagues report, the mapping exercise led to town planners 'tap[ing] out zones in the park, making out a diagonal Broadway-esque access route and other "streets", denoting them with "uniform signage" [and] negotiat[ing] and polic[ing] with their zoning regulations' (2013: 150). This also led to other forms of policing of bodies and spaces, including a designated 'Security Team' with responsibilities for quality of life issues and even turning over some 'undesirable' people within the occupation to the police.

Some occupiers thought of these limitations on personal freedom as a betrayal of the complete horizontal equality that ought to characterize the Occupy movement. Bolton and colleagues have sympathy with this argument, but also note that, at some level, such organization was simply necessary. If the goal of OWS was to put the sustenance and development of life at the centre of its geography so that it could be seen, attended to and held up as the reigning force to which capitalist activity should simply minister, then efforts to support and facilitate that living are not betrayals of that horizontalism, but systems designed to serve it. As they argue, 'Dissent cannot be dematerialized, it requires physical ground, and often urban planning – a counter-geography – to sustain the bodies and voices of those who protest' (Bolton et al. 2013: 154). This counter-geography served as a clarifying foil to the capitalist, gridded geography of the Manhattan geography that surrounded it. But it was also a geography of its own, with all of the internal tensions and contradictions that can entail.

I have tried to make the case here that we can better understand that structure through the lens of a Smithian notion of sacred space. But a note of caution is in order. Unlike the Standing Rock protests, the Occupy movement was explicitly secular. Its claim to the centrality of human life may have been implicitly following religious models, as I suggest here, but officially it rejected them. In the later, formal architectural drawing of the Zuccotti Park occupation, there is a small circle in the northwest corner (surrounding a tree with a sculpture of a seated businessman next to it) labelled as 'sacred space'. Possibly the vestige of the (annoying) drum circle which was 'gentrified' to the edge of the camp proper, James Massey and Brett Snyder (2012a) describe it as a 'space for solitary meditation and prayer'. But this space seems to have played little role in the central political and social work of the movement. Indeed, there were a great many ways in which explicitly religious institutions and individuals supported and participated in the movement: from the sukkah of Occupy Judaism, as discussed earlier, to the practical support in terms of meeting spaces, electricity, bathrooms, blankets and pastoral care that churches around Manhattan provided to the occupiers. Clergy of many different faiths (including a group of so-called protest chaplains from Harvard Divinity School) worked with the occupiers, providing spaces and moments for religious ritual, and used the performative power of their offices to, for instance, place themselves between the police and the occupiers to help manage a non-violent confrontation (Cloke et al. 2016: 511).

Paul Cloke et al. argue that this religious participation was more than just practical support; it influenced the occupiers to think in broader terms about the goals of their movement. Religious voices within Occupy insist that it was not just a material life that needs to be reclaimed from the neoliberal paradigm, but affective psychospiritual life as well (Cloke et al. 2016: 518). This is to argue that Occupy was a post-secular movement, taking inspiration from, incorporating elements of, and taking up a position that, historically, has been associated with religion. While this is undoubtedly true, it would be a mistake to think that this post-secularism was associated by many of the occupiers with religion as such. Yes, the pattern of sacred space was there, and that pattern had certain effects. The use of state violence to oppose the occupation, for instance, was particularly shocking in the context of a sacred-analogous space, even without a common concept of the sacred on which all can agree.

But the main relationship that the Occupy movement had to organized religion was as a landlord. In New York, the neighbouring Trinity Church – one of lower Manhattan's largest landowners – initially supported OWS, but tensions began to erupt when elements within the church sought to evict the occupiers from church-owned land. In London, police prevented Occupy protestors from occupying Paternoster Square, in front of the London Stock Exchange, and so they turned to the neighbouring churchyard of the imposing St Paul's Cathedral. At first, this led to a dialogue between the occupiers and leaders of the Church of England, and a level of overt religiosity that was less present in New York (such as the interfaith service known as the Sermon on the Steps). But in time, the church authorities moved to evict the occupiers, leading the dean of St Paul's, Graham Knowles, to resign in protest. The Occupy movement proved a prophetic challenge for large institutionalized churches, which, through their history and wealth, had developed close and comfortable links with the capitalist establishment. That challenge cast the churches as social institutions which needed to be resisted; it did not treat those churches themselves as a site of the sacred.

In her article on the Occupy movement, Margaret Kohn (2013) describes two theories of publicness that, she argues, were contested in the legal fights around the eviction of the Occupy protestors.[6] One theory she calls the 'sovereigntist' theory and connects with (German readings of) Hobbes, in which the democratically elected state is the legitimate manifestation of the public; attempts by non-state actors to appropriate state-controlled space for their own purposes are thus attempts at privatization. The alternative is the 'populist' theory, which she derives from her fascinating reading of Machiavelli; here, the 'public' denotes not the state but the hoi polloi who stand in opposition to the grandees and functionaries with government authority. Occasionally, the public may rise up in anger at assaults to their liberty, even by means that may be 'extra-legal and almost bestial' (quoted in Kohn 2013: 102) and thus force politicians to give in to their (not necessarily articulate) demands. This model does not accept the logic of property and engage in rational debate over its use within the legal or political process; instead, it sets up an alternative force ('the public') that simply asserts an alternative authority apart from the negotiations and reasonings of law and politics with which the political and legal world must contend.

Clearly, I see a connection between Kohn's Machiavellian populist theories of public space and the tradition of sacred space, which can assert a (non-discursive) authority which demands a certain respect. But the fact that this 'public' which makes such an assertion no longer self-evidently exists but must be hailed into being, and the lack of a demand that can actually be accepted or rejected leads me to the idea that these protests are better understood as social than political (or, at best, as meta-political). The Occupy movement's question was fundamentally not about the assertion of power, but the structure of it – does living legitimate capitalism, or does capitalism legitimate life? The Occupy Wall Street protestors in Zuccotti Park were criticized for not articulating a clear political demand. But if we think of their work in terms of ritual, especially the sort of creation of new rituals that Ronald Grimes (2000) calls 'ritology', we can talk about this work not as issue-based politics, but as an attempt to build a new architecture of power as an alternative to the capitalism that surrounded it. The practical issues that took up much of the activists' time – hygiene, housing, safety, food and the rest – were not distractions from the protest's purpose, but aspects of the very life that the protestors sought to assert as an anti-capitalist authority. The focus and attention offered by a space built along the analogy to a temple – a dwelling place of glory – means that these mundane activities are not mundane. They are the very bricks from which a new architecture of power might be built, and we may better notice this with the focus that such a space provides.

Of course, I do not intend the readings I have offered in this chapter of Occupy to be definitive. Scholars from a range of disciplines have investigated them, and scholars of performance and the arts have brought their own disciplinary techniques and views to bear on protests like these productively. But, through my reading of Smith, I do intend here to contribute an added dimension to these analyses. More broadly, I hope that this particular example will demonstrate the broader possibilities of engagement with the academic study of religion for scholars of performance and the arts. Smith's rigorous yet ludic work, dancing between overlaying and developing patterns, engaging with history to make space for innovation, represents some of the most helpful of that scholarly tradition.

While I hope that this chapter has offered insight on the cases it has considered, I hope even more that it has whet readers' appetites for a richer and more complex intellectual dialogue between the arts and religion.

NOTES

1. The ill-defined sacred value that the protesters claimed above that of American petrocapitalism could be seen as a respect for the history of the American continent, Sioux tribal religion and sovereignty, anti-capitalism, an Earth-based spirituality that sees transcendent value in the natural world or any combination of these. Particularly relevant is the historical tendency in US political thought to ground American sovereignty (i.e. glory) in some kind of legitimating handover of authority from Native American ancestors to the (mostly white settler) state that took power from them. Needless to say, no such occidental analogue of the Donation of Constantine exists, but the desire for this has fascinating consequences for the performance of American political power.

2. Arts scholars more familiar with Victor Turner's work may see a link between Douglas's notion of dirt as the socially placeless and Turner's concept of liminality. While the two do overlap in describing cultural taboos around those people and objects which slip between the cracks of cultural categories, the key difference is that liminality, per Turner, is part of a transitional process. A person (or thing) moves 'through' it from one recognized state into another. Douglasian dirt, on the other hand, is not necessarily a transitional state; dirty objects (or people) are not necessarily on their way to becoming clean ones. In that, Douglas's concept has more in common with Giorgio Agamben's notion of the *homo sacer* than the Turnerian liminal.

3. Whether or not this is an accurate quotation (and no overt source is provided), the sukkah was allowed to stay up at a time when other structures were not permitted.

4. Though there was an effort by the city authorities to remove the medical tent, a mass protest surrounding it led the police to back down. More theoretically, I would argue that my term 'life' here can be properly replaced with Agamben's notion of 'bare life'. The claims to democracy and justice that the Occupy movement made greatly exceed Agamben's conception of bare life, though it is the case that the physical fact of life was central to the specific justification for the medical tent.

5. Smith's metaphor for this comes from Kafka's famous parable of the leopards in the temple (from his *Parables and Paradoxes*): 'Leopards break into the temple and drink the sacrificial chalices dry; this occurs repeatedly, again and again: finally it can be reckoned on beforehand and becomes a part of the ceremony.' The actual activities that take place in the space designated as sacred in turn shape the understanding of sacredness being described there.

6. Kohn's discussion primarily refers to Occupy Toronto, but the questions of legal and political theory, as she notes, apply much more broadly.

REFERENCES

Abramovic, Marina (2004), *The House with the Ocean View*, New York: Charta and Sean Kelly Gallery.

Agamben, Giorgio (2011), *The Kingdom and the Glory: For a Theological Genealogy of Ecology and Government*, Stanford, CA: Stanford University Press.

Bolton, Matthew, Froese, Stephen and Jeffrey, Alex (2013), 'This space is occupied! The politics of occupy Wall Street's expeditionary architecture and de-gentrifying urbanism', in E. Welty, M. Bolton, M. Nayak and C. Malone (eds), *Occupying Political Science*, New York: Palgrave, pp. 135–62.

Bolton, Matthew, Froese, Stephen and Jeffrey, Alex (2016), ' "Go get a job right after you take a bath": Occupy Wall Street as matter out of place', *Antipode*, 48:4, pp. 857–76.

Butler, Judith (2015), *Notes toward a Performative Theory of Assembly*, Cambridge, MA: Harvard University Press.

Cloke, Paul, Sutherland, Callum and Williams, Andrew (2016), 'Postsecularity, political resistance, and protest in the Occupy movement', *Antipode*, 48:3, pp. 497–523.

Deloria, Philip (1999), *Playing Indian*, New Haven, CT: Yale University Press.

Douglas, Mary ([1966] 2003), *Purity and Danger: An Analysis of Concepts of Pollution and Taboo*, London: Routledge.

Dumont, Louis (1980), *Homo Hiererchicus: The Caste System and Its Implications*, 2nd ed., Chicago, IL: University of Chicago Press.

Edelman, Joshua, Hansen, Louise and van der Hoogen, Quirijn (2016), *The Problem of Theatrical Autonomy*, Amsterdam: Amsterdam University Press.

Eliade, Mircea (1959), *The Sacred and the Profane: The Nature of Religion*, Orlando, FL: Harcourt.

Gill, Sam (1998), 'No place to stand: Jonathan Z. Smith as *Homo Ludens*, the academic study of religion *Sub Specie Ludi*', *Journal of the American Academy of Religion*, 66:2, pp. 283–312.

Grimes, Ronald (2000), *Deeply into the Bone: Re-inventing Rites of Passage*, Berkeley: University of California Press.

Grimes, Ronald (2006), *Rite Out of Place: Ritual, Media and the Arts*, Oxford: Oxford University Press.

Kohn, Margaret (2013), 'Privatization and protest: Occupy Wall Street, occupy Toronto, and the occupation of public space in a democracy', *Perspectives on Politics*, 11:1, pp. 99–110.

Massey, Jonathan and Snyder, Brett (2012a), 'Occupying Wall Street: Places and spaces of political action', *Places Journal*, September, https://placesjournal.org/article/occupying-wall-street-places-and-spaces-of-political-action/. Accessed 25 October 2019.

Massey, Jonathan and Snyder, Brett (2012b), 'Mapping liberty plaza', *Places Journal*, September, https://placesjournal.org/article/mapping-liberty-plaza/. Accessed 25 October 2019.

Rappaport, Roy (1999), *Ritual and Religion in the Making of Humanity*, Cambridge: Cambridge University Press.

Risager, Bjarke Skærlund (2017), 'The evental places of occupy Wall Street and Tarir Square: Cosmopolitan imagination and social movements', *Globalizations*, 14:5, pp. 714–29.

Shiffman, Ron, Bell, Rick, Brown, Lance J. and Elizabeth, Lynne (eds) (2012), *Beyond Zuccotti Park: Freedom of Assembly and the Occupation of Public Space*, Oakland, CA: New Village Press.

Smith, Jonathan Z. (1982), *Imagining Religion: From Babylon to Jonestown*, Chicago, IL: University of Chicago Press

Smith, Jonathan Z. (1987), *To Take Place: Towards Theory in Ritual*, Chicago, IL: University of Chicago Press.

Whyte, Kyle (2017), 'The Dakota access pipeline, environmental injustice and U.S. colonialism', *Red Ink: An International Journal of Indigenous Literature, Arts & Humanities*, 19:1, pp. 154–69.

Contributors

ANNALAURA ALIFUOCO (AL) is a researcher and artist working and living in Liverpool, United Kingdom. In 2014, AL completed an AHRC-funded Ph.D. at the University of Roehampton on performance and/as affective archive. Since 2015, she/they have held a lecturer post in drama and performance studies at Liverpool Hope University. Her/their practice is promiscuous and eclectic in the flirtation with performance, liveness and experimentation. The work explores performance as a frame for queer collaborations between (so-called) human and non-human forms, agencies and environments. The methods rely on sensuous and affective modes of communication. The creative process is invested in exploring 'aesthetic atmospheres' – the sensory fields that thrust things into relations. It follows how bodies, objects, gestures and metaphors fall into each other. It wonders how they make poetic sense of politics. It relays intimate and impersonal desires. It wonders about the possibilities of healing with resistance. It hopes to be assisted and attended by other visions, actions, intuitions, medi(t)ations. It aims to give and receive in measures that can support the urgent and necessary work called art-making.

* * * * *

SILVIA BATTISTA is senior lecturer at Liverpool Hope University; an interdisciplinary artist and researcher who works across drawing, writing, performance and sound. She started combining storytelling with ethnography to engage with social and political issues, the outcomes of which have been presented internationally. She realized a two-year project, in collaboration with Jeffery Doughtie, in the death row of the maximum security prison in Huntsville, Texas (United States); a one-year ethnographic research/performance project in Prague, Czech Republic, on the city's changing landscape from communism to capitalism; and a two-year project on the theme of falling/failing through the myth of Icarus. In London she worked for *The Independent* newspaper and assisted the Turner Prize winner Wolfgang Tillmans. Meanwhile Battista continued to practice and research meditative, contemplative and ecstatic technologies and languages leading her exploration towards posthuman discourses, ecology and performance. This informed her monograph *Posthuman Spiritualities in Contemporary Performance: Politics, Ecologies and Perception*, which was published in 2018. At present, she is researching on animistic- and 'shamanic'-informed environmental practices and symbolisms in European contexts; the nature of visceral, non-human voices; subtle energies; interspecies transmissions; deep listening, active imagination and 'polyphonic' methodologies.

* * * * *

KRIS DARBY is a senior lecturer in drama and performance at Liverpool Hope. He is the author of numerous articles on drama, theatre and performance. His research concerns walking as an aesthetic practice with a specific focus on imaginative travel. He has explored the significance of walking on the stage and has recently developed this research into studies of the symbolic walking of labyrinths and mazes as well as digital ambulation within walking simulator video games. As a sound artist, Darby's work engages with the merging of self with place, exemplified by his ongoing project *If Walls Could Hear* (2014), which captures the listening of places through binaural recording.

* * * * *

JOSHUA EDELMAN is senior lecturer at the Manchester School of Theatre, Manchester Metropolitan University, England. His research looks at both theatre and religion as fields of social performance, especially in the contemporary West. He is the editor of the journal *Performance, Religion and Spirituality* and a member of the Project on European Theatre Systems (STEP). His books include *Performing Religion in Public* (co-edited with Claire Chambers and Simon du Toit, 2013) and *The Problem of Theatrical Autonomy: Analysing Theatre as a Social Practice* (co-authored with Quirijn van den Hoogen and Louise Hansen, 2016). Edelman's articles have appeared in journals, including *Performance Research, Amfiteater, Nordic Theatre Studies, Ecumenica* and *Liturgy*.

* * * * *

LISA LEWIS is professor of theatre and performance at the Faculty of Creative Industries at the University of South Wales, and co-director of the University's Centre for Media and Culture in Small Nations. Between 2015 and 2019 she was lead investigator on 'Welsh and Khasi Cultural Dialogues: An Interdisciplinary Arts and

Performance Project', funded by the Leverhulme Trust, which used creative practice to investigate the historic cultural exchange between Welsh missionaries and the Khasi people of Northeast India. Her work in the Centre for Small Nations involves researching the performance of minority cultures and minor transnationalisms. More generally, Lisa's practice and research examines the relationships between place, memory and performance in Welsh language and culture – relationships that are investigated in her monograph *Performing Wales: People, Memory and Place* (2018).

* * * * *

SIMON PIASECKI has enjoyed a connective career as an academic as well as a researcher, artist, performer and writer. His Ph.D. considered cartography, Self and Other in performance, examining identity and place. Research interests developed around the politics of human travel, belonging and landscape, most recently evolving with an interest in endured travel and the relative impacts on mind and body, drawing his focus naturally towards notions of pilgrimage. He has exhibited, directed and performed in international contexts for 30 years as a painter and performer, making short films, photographs and installations and transporting audiences over mountains at night with performance and music. Piasecki is also an illustrator, currently producing a set of tarot cards dedicated to the nomadic. His recent theatre show, an adaptation of St-Exupery's Flight to Arras, directed by Shelley Piasecka, considered the plight of refugees and was performed internationally, including at the Memorial Programme to the Armenian Genocide at Highfest in Yerevan, Armenia. He was invited to address the European Parliament regarding the work at World Refugee Day in 2018. He is a scout leader, a trained Lowland leader and currently professor and head of subject for creative writing and drama at Liverpool John Moores University.

* * * * *

ILARIA SALONNA is currently a Ph.D. student in cultural studies at the Faculty of 'Artes Liberales', University of Warsaw (Poland). She holds a master's degree in philosophy with a specialization in aesthetics from the University of Milan (Italy) and a diploma as actor from the Accademia dei Filodrammatici di Milano. Salonna worked as actor from 2003 to 2014 and trained with Anatoli Vassiliev in his theatre laboratory at the Grotowski Institute in Wroclaw (Poland) between 2011 and 2013. Her field of interest lies in between aesthetics and anthropology of theatre, with a particular focus on the relation between performance practice and philosophy. She is a member of the working group 'Performance, Religion and Spirituality' within the International Federation of Theatre Research. Her doctoral thesis is about the notion of atmosphere in aesthetics and in the history of acting techniques.

* * * * *

RUTH L. SMITH has taught philosophy, religious studies and rhetorical theory at Worcester Polytechnic Institute in Worcester, MA, United States, and she has also advised at European sites for interdisciplinary student projects in technology and society. She is recently professor emeritus. Additionally, in Worcester, she has taught philosophy at the Bard College Clemente Program (National Humanities Award 2014) for adults who have not had access to study of the liberal arts. Her research interests address modern–postmodern constructions of social-moral life, with particular concern for grammatical questions of agreement. Smith's publications emphasize theoretical inflections amidst historical, literary and anthropological documentation, including articles in *Signs: Journal of Women in Culture and Society, Cultural Critique, Journal of Religious Ethics* and *Rhetoric Society Quarterly*. While advising student environmental projects at the University of Worcester, United Kingdom, in 2017, she was appreciative of thoughtful presentation discussions at the *Liverpool Hope Conference on Sacred Place and Performance* and on religion and politics at the *Oxford Religious Studies Symposium*.

* * * * *

LOUISE ANN WILSON is an artist, scenographer and researcher who creates site-specific walking-performances in rural landscapes that give a voice to 'missing' or marginal life-events – with transformative and therapeutic outcomes. Her work has addressed terminal illness, bereavement, in/fertility and involuntary childlessness, the effects of ageing and the impact of change. Each project is transdisciplinary and developed in close collaboration with people with knowledge of the chosen landscape, scientists and experts in the field of the life-event in question *and* those experiencing it. These have included: geologists, botanists and shepherds; neurologists, embryologists and palliative care nurses; women experiencing involuntary childlessness, care-home residents and fishermen. This methodology is underpinned by seven 'scenographic' principles inspired by Dorothy Wordsworth and her female contemporaries' approaches to landscape and theoretical concepts relating to the feminine 'material' sublime and therapeutic landscapes. Recent works include: *Women's Walks to Remember: 'With Memory I Was There'* (2018–19) and Dorothy's *Rydal Journals, Mulliontide* (2016), *Warnscale: A Land Mark Walk Reflecting on in/Fertility and Childlessness* (2015), *The Gathering/ Yr Helfa* (2014) and *Fissure* (2011). In 2017 Louise was awarded a Ph.D. from Lancaster Institute of the Contemporary Arts, Lancaster University. https://www.louiseannwilson.com.

Index

Note: italic indicates an illustration and n refers to an endnote (with its numeral) that contains additional information.